Collins

AQA

SCIENCE

FOR AQA GCSE
BIOLOGY
CHEMISTRY
PHYSICS

WAVE ENERGY TESTING

HEIGHT 6 METRES
SPEED 20 M/S

Ken Gadd SERIES EDITOR
Charles Golabek
Aleks Jedrosz
Mary Jones
Emma Poole
Louise Petheram
Kathryn Senior
Edmund Walsh

William Collins' dream of knowledge for all began with the publication of his first book in 1819. A self-educated mill worker, he not only enriched millions of lives, but also founded a flourishing publishing house. Today, staying true to this spirit, Collins books are packed with inspiration, innovation and a practical expertise. They place you at the centre of a world of possibility and give you exactly what you need to explore it.

Collins. Freedom to teach.

Published by Collins
An imprint of HarperCollinsPublishers
77–85 Fulham Palace Road
Hammersmith
London
W6 8JB

Browse the complete Collins catalogue at
www.collinseducation.com

© HarperCollinsPublishers Limited 2006
10 9 8 7 6 5 4 3 2 1
ISBN-13 978-0-00-722582-8
ISBN-10 0-00-722582-2
The authors assert their moral right to be identified as the authors of this work.

British Library Cataloguing in Publication Data. A Catalogue record for this publication is available from the British Library.

Commissioned by Cassandra Birmingham; Publishing Manager: Melanie Hoffman; Project Editor: Penny Fowler; Page make-up and picture research by Hart McLeod, Cambridge; Page make-up by eMC Design; Edited by: Ruth Burns; Proof reader: Camilla Behrens; Internal design by JPD; Cover design by John Fordham; Cover artwork by Bob Lea; Exam questions written by John Marrill, Lesley Owen and Karen Nicola Thomas; Glossary written by Gareth Price; Illustrations by Peters and Zabransky, John Dillow, Laszlo Veres, Mark Turner, Peters & Zabransky, Peter Cornwell and Rory Walker; Production by Natasha Buckland; Printed and bound in Hong Kong by Printing Express Ltd.

Acknowledgements

The authors and publishers are grateful to the following for permission to reproduce photographs. Whilst every effort has been made to trace the copyright holders, in cases where this has been unsuccessful or if any have been inadvertently overlooked, the Publishers will be pleased to make the necessary arrangement at the first opportunity.

Contents page t-b ©Frans Lanting/Corbis, ©David Aubrey/SPL, ©Kevin Foy/Alamy, ©Rave/istockphoto.com, ©Adam Woolfitt/Corbis; p.6 tl ©Dr Jeremy Burgess/SPL, tr ©Sheila Terry/SPL, bl ©Philippe Plailly/Eurelios/SPL, br ©Kenneth Eward/Biografx/SPL; p.7 tl ©John Durham/SPL, tr ©Science Pictures Ltd/SPL, bl ©Steve Gschmeissner/SPL, br ©TEK Images/SPL; p.8 tl ©Lorena Martinez,istockphotos.com, tr & bl ©Jupiterimages corporation/photos.com, br ©Perttu Sironen/istockphotos.com; p.9 tr ©Radu Razvan/istockphotos.com, tl ©Kenny Chi/istockphotos.com, bl ©Slawomir Fajer/istockphotos.com, br ©Alexei Zaycev/istockphotos.com; p.10 tr ©Jupiterimages corporation/photos.com, bl ©David Rose/istockphotos.com, br ©Adam Hart-Davis/SPL; p.11 tr ©Thomas Mounsey/istockphotos.com, bl ©Jupiterimages corporation/photos.com, br ©Cristian Matei/istockphotos.com; p12/13 ©Andrew Syred/SPL; p.14 1 ©CNRI/SPL; p.16 1 ©Eye of Science/SPL; p.17 3 ©Biophoto Associates/SPL, 5 ©Jerry Mason/SPL; p.18 1 ©1999 Butch Weaver <mailto:butch@irupe.com> , used with kind permission, 2 both ©Dr Jeremy Burgess/SPL, 3 ©Andrew Syred/SPL; p.20 top ©Christian Darkin/SPL, 2 ©CNRI/SPL; p.21 3 ©Frans Lanting/Corbis; p.22 1 ©Pat & Tom Leeson/SPL, 2 tl ©BSIP AMAR/SPL, tr ©Steve Gschmeissner/SPL, bl ©St Bartholomew's Hospital/SPL, br ©David Mack/SPL; p.23 6 ©Michael Donne/SPL; p.28 1

©Mango Productions/Corbis; p.29 3 ©Dimitri Iundt/Corbis; p.30 1 ©Dr P. Marazzi/SPL, 2 ©SIU/SPL; p.32 1 ©Sovereign, ISM/SPL; p.33 3 ©Brad Nelson/Custom Medical Stock Photo/SPL, 4 ©Victor De Schwanberg/SPL; p.34 t ©Sebastian Kaulitzki/istockphotos.com, b ©Jupiterimages corporation/photos.com; p.35 ©NASA/SPL; p.38/39 ©Science Pictures Ltd/SPL; p.40 1 ©Microfield Scientific Ltd/SPL, 3 ©Karl Weatherly/Corbis; p.41 4 ©David Lyons/Alamy, 5 ©Owaki-Kulla/Corbis, 6 ©Charles O'Rear/Corbis, 7 ©Alan King; p.42 1 ©Becky Luigart-Stayner/Corbis, 2 ©SCIMAT/SPL, 3 ©Bob Krist/Corbis; p.43 4 ©Helene Rogers/Alamy, 5 ©Brian Bell/SPL, 6 ©Jean Pierre Fizet/Sygma/Corbis; p.44 1 ©David Aubrey/SPL, 2 ©Biodisc/Visuals Unlimited/Getty Images; p.45 3 ©Science Photo Library, 4 ©Custom Medical Stock Photo/SPL, 5 ©Charles O'Rear/Corbis, 6 ©Lynette Cook/SPL; p.46/47 ©Foodpix/photolibrary.com, inset http://www.carolinawinesupply.com, used with kind permission; p.48 1 ©Dr Jeremy Burgess/SPL; p.49 4 ©Gusto/SPL, 5 ©Cordelia Molloy/SPL; p.50 1 ©Ashden Awards, used with kind permission, 3 ©Prof. David Hall/SPL, 4 ©Tommaso Guicciardini/SPL; p.51 5 ©Greenenergy, used with kind permission, 6 ©Sotiris Zafeiris/SPL; p.53 5 ©Daniel Morel/Reuters/Corbis, 6 ©Tek Image/SPL; p.54 t ©Andrei Tchernov/istockphotos.com, b ©istockphotos.com; p.55 ©Science Photo Library; p.58/59 ©Andrew Lambert Photography/SPL; p.60 l – r ©Science Photo Library, ©Hulton Archive/Getty Images, ©Science Photo Library; p.64 1 ©Charles D. Winters/SPL; p.65 2 ©Cordelia Molloy/SPL; p.66 1 ©Bettmann/Corbis, 2 ©Andrew Lambert Photography/SPL; p.70 1 l ©Kevin Foy/Alamy, r ©Dorothy Burrows/Travel Ink/Alamy; p.71 3 ©Andrew Lambert Photography/SPL; p.72 1 ©Arlindo Silva/istockphotos.com; p.74 1 ©Science Photo Library; p.75 2 ©Science Photo Library, 3 ©Andrew Lambert Photography/SPL, 4 ©Lawrence Berkely National Laboratory/SPL; p.76 t ©istockphotos.com, b ©Andrew Lambert Photography/SPL; p.77 ©Jupiterimages corporation/photos.com; p.80/81 ©Booth/GarionSPL; p.82 1 ©Kenneth Libbrecht/SPL, 2 ©Rave/istockphoto.com, 3 ©Priyendu Subashchandran/istockphoto.com; p.83 6 ©Kateryna Govorushchenko/istockphoto.com; p.84 1 ©Karen Roach/istockphoto.com, 2 ©Djordje Korovljeviic/istockphoto.com, 3 ©Joey Nelson/istockphoto.com; p.86 1 ©istockphotos.com; p.87 5 ©Christopher O Driscoll/istockphoto.com, 6 ©Richard Gunion/istockphoto.com; p.88 1 ©Charles D. Winters/SPL; p.90/91 ©Steve Sands/New York Newswire/Corbis; p.92 1 ©Graca Victoria/istockphoto.com; 2 ©Edyta Pawtowska/istockphoto.com; p.93 5 ©Dennis MacDonald/Alamy; p.94 1 ©Monica Wilde 2005, Faerie Flames. www.faerieflames.com, used with kind permission; p.95 5 ©Klinge Foods Limited, used with kind permission; p.96 1 Geoff Tompkinson/SPL; p.98 1;©Jaimie D. Travis/istockphoto.com, 2 ©Martyn F. Chillmaid/SPL; p.99 2 ©Jim Parkin/istockphoto.com; p.100 1 ©George Argyropoulos/istockphotos.com; p.101 2 ©Geoff Tompkinson/SPL; p.102 t ©Nathawat Wongrat/istockphotos.com, c ©Rebecca Ellis/istockphotos.com, b ©David Taylor/SPL; p.103 ©Julie de Leseleuc/istockphotos.com; p.106/107 ©Chris Butler/SPL; p.108 1 ©istockphoto; p.111 7 ©Reuters/Corbis; p.112 1 ©Adam Woolfitt/Corbis; p.114 1 ©NASA/SPL, 2 ©George Argyropoulos/istockphoto; p.115 3 ©NASA/SPL; P.116 1 ©Mark Evans/istockphoto; p.118/119 ©Martin Bond/SPL, ©NASA/SPL; p.121 5 l ©Royalty-Free/Corbis, r ©Cordelia Molloy/SPL; p.124 3 © Cydney Conger/Corbis; p.126 1 ©NASA/SPL; p.128 1 ©Oxford Scientific; p.129 5 ©Saturn Stills/SPL; p.130 tr & c ©Jupiterimages corporation/photos.com, b ©Kenneth C. Zirkel/SPL; p.134/135 ©Lynette Cook/SPL; p.136 1 t-b ©Istockphoto, ©Greg Boiarsky/Istockphoto, ©Andrew Lambert Photography/SPL, ©Ryan KC Wong/stockphoto; p.138 1 main ©Maximilian Stock Ltd/SPL, inset ©Carmen Martínez Banús/istockphoto; p.140 1 both ©First Hydro, used with kind permission; p.142/143 ©Science Photo Library; p.144 1 ©Leslie Garland Picture Library/Alamy; p.145 4 ©David R. Frazier/SPL; p.146 1 t ©Roger Harris/SPL, b ©NASA/SPL; p.147 4 ©Mark Garlick/SPL; p.148 1 ©Celestial Image Co./SPL, 3 ©Mark Garlick/SPL; p.149 4 ©NASA/ESA/Stsci/ SPL, 5 ©Mark Garlick/SPL, 6 ©Chris Butler/SPL, 7 ©Mark Garlick/SPL, p.150 t ©David Weintraub/SPL, b ©Brandon Alms/istockphotos.com; p.155 ©Jaimie D. Travis/istockphotos.com; p.159 ©Jonathan Ling/istockphotos.com; glossary p.161 &165 ©George Ranalli/SPL; p.162 &166 ©Dr Jeremy Burgess/SPL; p.163 & 167 ©Dr Jeremy Burgess/SPL; p.163 &167 ©Dr Kari Lounatmaa/SPL; all others Collins Education

Contents

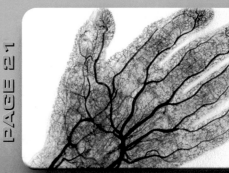

PAGE 21

Biology gets under your skin!

PAGE 44

Why are these called barnacle geese?

PAGE 70

That's one shiny bean!

PAGE 82

You've seen sunrise – now here's Earthrise!

PAGE 112

Physics in full swing!

Welcome to Collins GCSE Science!

This book aims to give you a fascinating insight into contemporary science that is relevant and useful to you, right now today. We have written it to convey the excitement of Biology, Chemistry and Physics, and hope it will help you to carry a knowledge and understanding of science and scientific thinking with you throughout life.

USING THIS BOOK

What you should know

Think back to what you have already learnt for GCSE Science. You need to remember and understand this work as your teacher will now develop it, explaining things in more detail. We've summarised what you should know for each main section: biology, chemistry and physics.

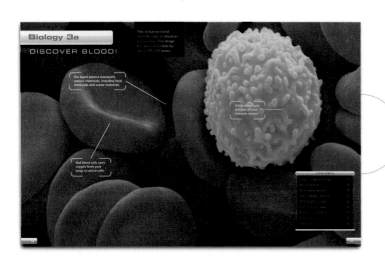

Unit opener

There are six units: two biology, two chemistry and two physics. Each begins with an image showing just some of the exciting science you will learn about. Also listed on this page are the spreads you will work through in the unit.

Main content

Each of the six units is made up of between 6 and 10 double page spreads. These tell you all you need to know. As you read through a spread you will start with some basic ideas and be guided to a more detailed understanding of the science. There are also questions for you to check your progress.

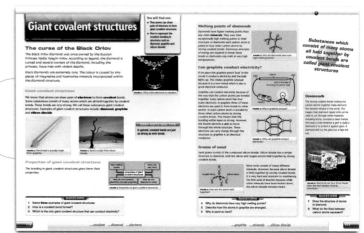

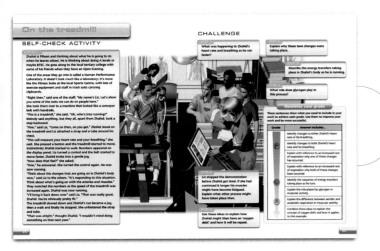

Mid-unit assessment

These give you opportunities to see how you are getting on. There are assessments for you to learn from. Each gives you a mini-case study to read, think about and then answer some questions on.

Unit summary

Key facts and ideas, and the links between them, are summarised in spider diagrams. A really useful way of revising is to make your own concept maps. The diagrams are a good starting point for doing this. There is a quiz for you to try and an activity as well.

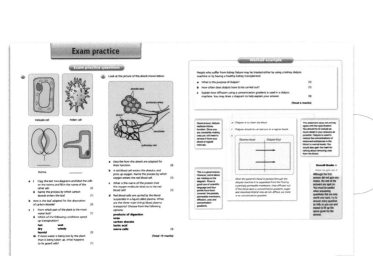

Exam practice

Once you've learned the science you have to show in an exam what you know and can do. Exam technique helps. It's important to be clear about what the examiner is looking for. It's also important to give your answer as clearly as possible. So we've provided you with some practice questions.

How Science Works

Scientists make observations and measurements. They try to make sense of these data and use them to develop scientific ideas. They design and carry out investigations. This section gives you some activities and questions to help you explore how science works further.

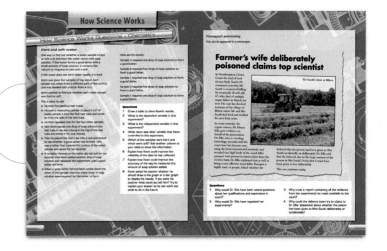

How useful things are absorbed

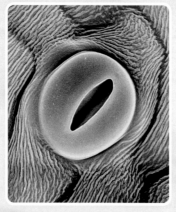

Humans eat in order to supply their bodies with the substances they need. Once it has been broken down and made soluble, digested food is absorbed into the blood system.

Plants need carbon dioxide from the air and water from the soil to be able to photosynthesise. Root hairs help them absorb water and minerals from the soil. Diffusion and osmosis are two important processes in getting substances into and out of the cells of living things.

1 Name **two** gases that diffuse through stomata like this one, in a plant's leaf.
2 Where do plants get water from?

Blood and circulation

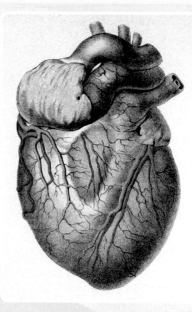

Once food has been digested and absorbed into the bloodstream, it is transported throughout the body by the blood. Oxygen is also moved by the blood from the lungs to where it is needed. As the heart beats it pushes the blood around the body.

3 Where does the blood transport digested food to?
4 Where does the blood transport oxygen to?

Exercising your body

Aerobic respiration happens when food (glucose) and oxygen react together to release energy. Carbon dioxide and water are made as by-products and are waste. The equation for aerobic respiration is:

glucose + oxygen $\longrightarrow$ carbon dioxide + water + energy (J)

When you exercise, your brain makes your heart beat rate (pulse) increase. It also makes you breathe more deeply and faster to get rid of more carbon dioxide.

5 Which gas is produced as the result of aerobic respiration?
6 Aerobic respiration releases energy. What is this used for?

Kidneys and what can go wrong

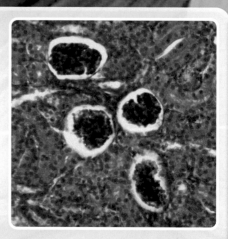

Your kidneys contain millions of tiny tubes called nephrons. These are constantly filtering your blood. They remove poisonous waste from your body and control its water balance. Urine is about 95% water and it contains various chemicals in solution. These chemicals include salt and urea.

7 Your kidneys remove poisonous waste from your blood. How can you tell they are working properly?
8 What do think would happen if they stopped working?

Cells

All living things are made of cells. Some organisms are made of just one single cell. This cell has to carry out all the activities that would be done by many specialised cells in a multicellular organism like a human or a plant.

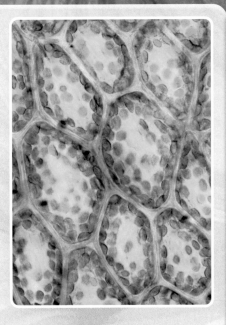

9 Are the cells in the photograph animal cells or plant cells? How can you tell?
10 Make a list of **seven** characteristics of all living things.

Respiration

All living things obtain energy from nutrients such as glucose. The glucose is broken down and the energy released is used by living cells. Sometimes this is

done by combining the glucose with oxygen, and this is called aerobic respiration. Carbon dioxide is produced as a waste product. For example, when yeast grows in a liquid containing sugars, it releases carbon dioxide which forms bubbles and froth.

11 Write down the word equation for aerobic respiration.
12 Which cells in your body respire?
13 The photograph shows the top of some beer that is brewing in a huge vat. Why is it frothy?

Microbes

This photograph shows bacteria growing inside someone's nose. Bacteria are microbes – organisms that are too small for us to see with the naked eye. Yeast is another kind of microbe. A few microbes cause diseases,

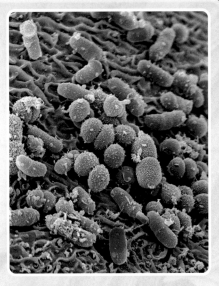

but many others are not harmful at all. We use microbes to make foods like yoghurt, cheese and bread, as well as alcohol for drinks and for fuel.

14 How does yeast help to make bread?
15 Name **one** disease that is caused by microbes.

Growing microbes

We can grow microbes if we give them something to live on, called a medium, which contains food for them. Agar jelly makes a

good medium. We usually put the agar jelly into a Petri dish. It is important to keep everything really clean, so that we do not add microbes from our bodies or dirty equipment to the ones we want to grow. We also have to take great care not to let any microbes from the dish get onto our bodies.

16 Why are the people working in this laboratory wearing white coats?
17 What other precautions are they taking?

Acids and bases

Acids and bases have particular chemical properties and there are plenty of examples of common acids and bases: lemon juice and vinegar are acids, soap powder and indigestion tablets are bases.

Indicators can show whether a solution is acidic, alkaline or neutral. Common indicators include litmus and universal indicator.

Acids are at the bottom of the pH scale – the most concentrated and strongest acids are pH 1. Neutral solutions are pH 7. Bases have pH values up to 14.

Acids and bases react together and neutralise each other.

1 Name **two** acids and **two** bases that are used in a school laboratory.
2 If a solution is pH 5, is it acidic or alkaline?

Atoms and elements

An element is a substance that cannot be broken down by chemical reaction into anything else. It contains one type of atom only. Atoms from different elements can react with each other and form a huge range of different compounds.

The number of elements that exist on Earth is quite small. Elements are classified as metals or non-metals. These can exist in the three states of matter: solids, liquids and gases.

Elements have their own characteristic physical and chemical properties. There are families of elements that behave in very similar ways.

3 Is gold a reactive element? Explain your answer.
4 If an element is a gas at room temperature, does it have a high or a low boiling point?

Atomic structure and symbols

Atoms have a small central nucleus around which orbit electrons.

Atoms of each element are represented by a chemical symbol. Gold is Au, oxygen is O and chlorine is Cl.

When a reaction occurs between different elements, their atoms join with other atoms to form compounds. The formula of a compound shows the number and type of atoms that are present.

No atoms are lost or made during a chemical reaction, so the mass of the products equals the mass of the reactants and it is possible to write balanced equations showing the atoms involved.

5 Write down the chemical symbols for sodium and chlorine. What compound do they form when they react together?
6 What elements does sulfuric acid (H_2SO_4) contain?

Atomic theory

Elements are classified into the periodic table according to the number of protons in atoms. This is called the atomic number of an element.

The electrons which orbit the nucleus of an atom are arranged in different energy levels or shells. It is the electrons in the outer shell that become involved in reactions with other atoms. Electrons can be donated or gained – the bond formed here is ionic. In some compounds, electrons are shared – the bond formed in this case is covalent.

Elements in the same group in the periodic table have the same number of electrons in the highest energy levels (their outer shell).

7 What is the difference between an ionic bond and a covalent bond?
8 According to what property are elements in the periodic table arranged?

Solutions

Some solids dissolve in liquids to form mixtures called solutions. If a substance dissolves we say that it is soluble; one that does not dissolve is insoluble.

Temperature can affect how soluble a substance is. Salt can dissolve in water to form a solution. Distillation can be used to get a sample of pure water from a solution of salty water.

9 What is made when a solid dissolves in a liquid?

10 How can we get a sample of pure water from salty water?

Rocks

Rocks at the Earth's surface are continually being worn away by weathering. Rainwater is slightly acidic and dissolves rocks. Some rocks like limestone are weathered much faster than other rocks, such as

granite. Limestone rocks contain a lot of calcium carbonate. When the rainwater dissolves rocks like limestone, it forms a solution that contains calcium ions.

11 Name a type of rock that is weathered quite quickly.

12 What is the name of the chemical found in limestone rocks?

Food

We get our energy from the food that we eat. Foods contain a mixture of proteins, carbohydrates, fats, minerals, vitamins, fibre and water. Fats and carbohydrates

are particularly good sources of energy. We should make sure that we eat a balanced diet that contains the right amount of energy to keep us healthy.

13 Where do we get our energy from?

14 What types of food provide us with most of our energy?

Types of reaction

Fuels often contain carbon and hydrogen atoms. When fuels are burnt they release heat energy. Different fuels release different amounts of energy.

Most reactions release heat energy and we see a temperature rise, but a few reactions take in heat energy and we see a fall in temperature.

15 What elements are found in most fuels?

16 What is released when fuels are burnt?

Forces and moments

You already know that sometimes forces make things turn, rather than just move in a straight line. The picture shows a force being used to make a lever work. The force of the person on the crowbar is called the effort, the weight of the paving slab they are trying to move is the load, and the point that the lever rotates about is called the pivot. Do you remember that the lever can be used to overcome a bigger load if the load is close to the pivot and the effort is further from the pivot?

1 Name **one** thing, other than the distances, that would make the lever able to overcome a bigger load.

2 Describe **one** other example where we use a lever. Say where the load, the pivot and the effort are.

Gravity and space

You know that mass and weight are not the same thing. The astronaut's mass stays the same wherever he is, but his weight is much less on the Moon than it is on Earth. That is because the gravitational force is less on the Moon, because the mass of the Moon is much less than the mass of the Earth. Gravity acts between all objects that have mass. So it not only holds the astronaut on the surface of the Moon or the Earth, it also holds the Moon in orbit around Earth and the Earth in orbit around the Sun.

3 Why is weight different on the Moon and on Earth?

4 Describe how the gravitational force affects the Moon and the Earth.

Mirrors

In the photograph, the flat surface of the water is acting as a plane mirror. You see two 'pictures' of the seagull: one where the rays of light have come straight from the seagull to your eyes (this is the object), and a second where the rays of light have been reflected from the surface of the water, then come to your eyes. This is the image or the reflection. The image is virtual, or imaginary – it is not really there. It only looks like this because our brain always thinks light has travelled in straight lines.

5 Draw a ray diagram for what you see when you look at the seagull and its reflection.

6 What can you say about the sizes of the seagull and its reflection?

Refraction

You have probably seen examples of refraction, like this ruler dipping into water. Refraction also makes water look shallower than it really is, and makes a ray of light change direction when it goes through a glass block. It happens because the light changes direction when it passes from water or glass into air, or when light passes from air into water or glass. The light bends towards the normal going into glass or water, and away from the normal coming out again.

7 Which way does a ray of light bend when it goes from water into air?

8 If the light bent the other way, what effect would this have on how deep the water looked?

Sound

Sounds are caused by things vibrating. We hear sounds because the vibrations have been transmitted through the air, by vibrating air particles, to our ears. Our eardrum inside our ear vibrates, and eventually the signal is passed to our brain. Sound cannot travel through a vacuum because there are no air particles in a vacuum to transmit the vibrations. If the vibrations are larger, we hear a louder sound.

9 Give **three** examples of things that make sounds. For each example, say what is vibrating.
10 Explain in your own words why sound cannot travel through a vacuum.

Magnetic fields

A magnet has an invisible field around it. Inside the field is an area where there are lines of force which run from North to South. Other magnets and certain metals will experience a force when they enter the region of a magnetic field. The closer together the field lines, the stronger the magnetic field and the stronger the acting force.

When two magnets are brought close together, the two magnetic fields exert a force on each other. Like magnetic poles will repel each other and unlike poles will attract.

When a piece of soft iron enters a magnetic field it also experiences a force, but only one of attraction. Iron, nickel and cobalt are the only materials which experience the magnetic force of attraction.

11 What is it that surrounds a magnet?
12 What happens when an object enters a magnetic field?

Electromagnets

When a current flows through a coil, it produces a magnetic field similar to that of a permanent bar magnet. The coil has a North and South Pole and field lines flow from North to South.

The strength of the magnetic field can be intensified by increasing the number of coils, increasing the current and using a soft-iron core.

The electromagnet has one major advantage over the permanent magnet: it can be switched on and off.

Electromagnets are used on cranes to lift and drop heavy metal objects. They are used in hospitals to remove iron splinters from the eye. Other common uses are: the electric bell, the relay, radio earphones and loudspeakers.

13 What effect do you get when an electric current flows through a wire coil?
14 How can you strengthen this effect?

The Earth and beyond

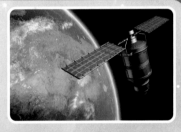

The solar system consists of the Sun plus eight planets. The inner four are called the rock planets and the outer four are the gas giants.

The planets move in flat anti-clockwise orbits. It is the force of gravity between them and the huge Sun that keeps them from flying off into space. The orbits are elliptical.

The planets closer to the Sun, travel faster and have shorter years than those further away.

Only the Sun is a luminous object. Planets do not give out their own light, but you can see them because they reflect the Sun's light.

15 Make a sketch of our solar system and name the **eight** planets.
16 Describe how the planets move around the Sun.

Biology 3a

DISCOVER BLOOD!

This is human blood seen through an electron microscope. The image has been magnified by about 20 000 times.

The liquid plasma transports various chemicals, including food molecules and waste materials.

Red blood cells carry oxygen from your lungs to active cells.

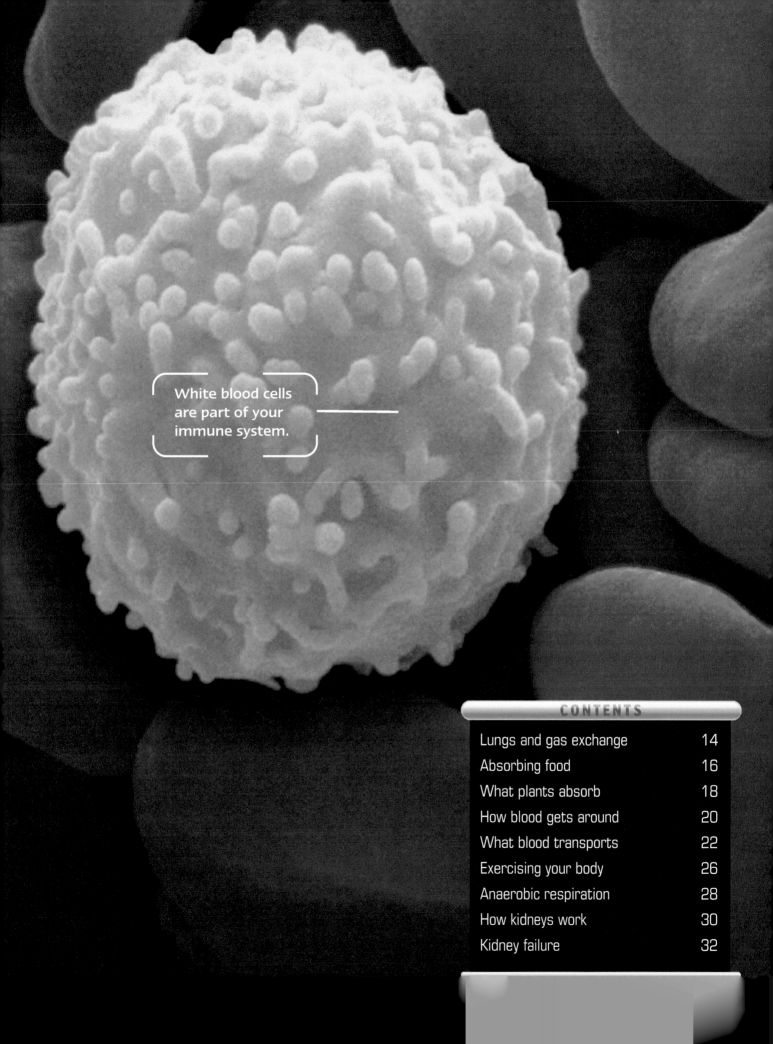

White blood cells
are part of your
immune system.

CONTENTS

Lungs and gas exchange

You will find out:
- Where the lungs are in the body and how they are protected
- How the lungs work
- How the lungs are adapted for gas exchange
- How you breathe

Air spaces in your body

Figure 1 shows a cross-section of a piece of human lung. It's mostly air spaces (the white gaps). The pink lines are the walls of the air sacs. The air sacs provide your lungs with an incredibly large surface area – about the size of a tennis court. This is just one of the **adaptations** your body has for gas exchange.

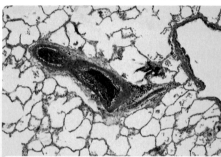

FIGURE 1: A cross-section of human lung – it's mostly air spaces!

Location, location, location

Your two **lungs** are in the upper part of your body, called the **thorax** (chest). They are very delicate and so are protected by the **rib cage**. The thorax is separated from the lower part of the body (abdomen) by a sheet of muscle called the **diaphragm**.

When you breathe in, oxygen is absorbed from the air. When you breathe out, carbon dioxide is removed from your body. Oxygen and carbon dioxide are called **respiratory gases**. The overall process is called **gas exchange**.

You have to breathe!

To stay alive, you have to respire:

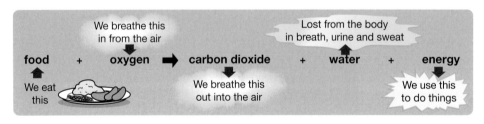

| food | + | oxygen | ➡ | carbon dioxide | + | water | + | energy |

We eat this / We breathe this in from the air / We breathe this out into the air / Lost from the body in breath, urine and sweat / We use this to do things

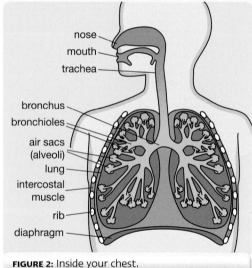

FIGURE 2: Inside your chest.

nose, mouth, trachea, bronchus, bronchioles, air sacs (alveoli), lung, intercostal muscle, rib, diaphragm

Adaptations for gas exchange

The lungs are adapted (specialised) for gas exchange in a number of ways.

- They have millions of tiny air sacs, called **alveoli** (singular, **alveolus**), giving them a very large surface area.
- The alveoli are moist; they are lined with a thin layer of water.
- They have a very rich blood supply; millions of capillaries bring blood to the lungs.
- The walls of the alveoli are only one cell thick, so the respiratory gases do not have to diffuse very far.

QUESTIONS

1 What is gas exchange?
2 Why do you need oxygen?
3 Explain how the lungs are adapted for gas exchange.

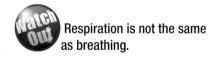

Respiration is not the same as breathing.

...adaptation ...alveolus (pl. alveoli) ...diaphragm ...concentration gradient ...expiration

Oxygen in, carbon dioxide out

For gas exchange to happen there has to be a **concentration gradient**. Diffusion is the movement of molecules, or particles, from an area of high concentration to an area of low concentration. Look at the gas concentrations in Table 1.

Oxygen diffuses from breathed in air in the alveoli down a concentration gradient into the red blood cells. As this is happening, carbon dioxide diffuses in the opposite direction, from the blood plasma into the alveoli.

Gas	Approximate % in the air we breathe OUT	Approximate % in the air we breathe IN
Oxygen	21	16
Carbon dioxide	0.04	4
Nitrogen	79	79
Water vapour	variable	high

TABLE 1: Percentages of gases in inhaled and exhaled air.

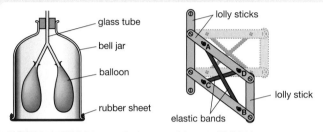

FIGURE 3: How do these models relate to your body?

Breathing in and out

By constantly breathing in and out, your body is able to maintain a concentration gradient for the respiratory gases. Breathing in is called **inspiration** and breathing out is called **expiration**. Both are brought about by muscles – the diaphragm and two sets of intercostal muscles (found between the ribs).

If you sit quietly you will feel your chest go up and down. The movement up is breathing in and the movement going down is breathing out.

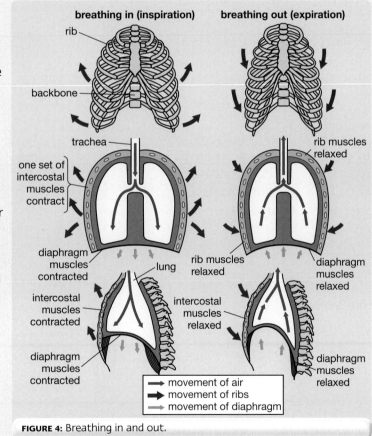

FIGURE 4: Breathing in and out.

Breathing rates and risk assessment

When using chemicals assessing risk is very important. Some chemicals are harmless and others are very dangerous. The risk from breathing in a potentially dangerous chemical depends on how much of it is inhaled.

Imagine this scenario: Some hamsters breathe in a chemical and become ill. A scientist uses this information (data) and calculates a predicted risk for humans. Hamsters take about 100 breaths per minute. Are they likely to inhale the toxic chemical faster than humans who only breathe 12–20 times per minute?

QUESTIONS

8　Why is it important to assess the risk of using different chemicals?

9　Is it reasonable to use animals for risk assessment? Explain your answer.

10　If a laboratory animal, e.g. a hamster, becomes ill as the result of being exposed to a chemical, is it valid to conclude that the chemical will make humans become ill too? Explain your answer.

QUESTIONS

4　What is diffusion? Explain what a concentration gradient is.

5　Why is a concentration gradient needed for gas exchange in your lungs?

6　When you sit quietly, your chest goes up and down. How will these movements change when you do vigorous activity?

7　Figure 3 shows models of how you breathe. Explain what each part of the models represents. (Hint: use figure 4.)

Absorbing food

You will find out:
- How the small intestine is adapted to absorb digested food
- About the roles of diffusion and active transport in the absorption of food

In your small intestine

Your small intestine is full of bacteria. Don't worry, most of them are harmless. In fact many are positively healthy – they aid the processes that go on in the gut. Mostly they just help themselves to the food in your gut. You eat it, they use it! Luckily you can spare it.

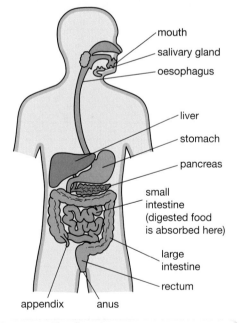

FIGURE 1: Inside the small intestines – the lining of the intestinal wall, magnified about 50 times.

Products of digestion (H)

You eat millions of food molecules every day. Most of them are too big to be absorbed into the blood, so they have to be digested. **Digestion** is the process of breaking down large, insoluble food molecules into smaller, soluble ones. This happens in the stomach and small intestine. The products of digestion are absorbed in the small intestines.

carbohydrates —(broken down by carbohydrase enzymes)→ glucose

proteins —(broken down by protease enzymes)→ amino acids

fats —(broken down by lipase enzymes)→ glycerol and fatty acids

Some products of digestion are absorbed by **diffusion** in the direction of the concentration gradient. This is a **passive** process and does not use energy. Others are absorbed *against* a concentration gradient. As this uses energy (from respiration), the process is called **active transport**. It enables cells to absorb ions from very dilute solutions.

What is absorbed?

glucose —(diffusion and active transport)→ absorbed into the blood

amino acids —(diffusion and active transport)→ absorbed into the blood

glycerol and fatty acids —(diffusion)→ cells lining the small intestine —(active transport)→ fats are reformed and pass into the lymphatic system

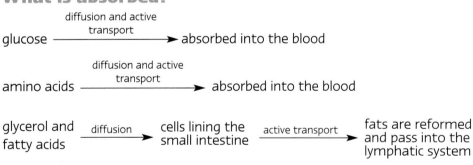

FIGURE 2: The digestive system.

mouth
salivary gland
oesophagus
liver
stomach
pancreas
small intestine (digested food is absorbed here)
large intestine
rectum
appendix
anus

The **lymphatic system** returns fluids, which have leaked out of the blood capillaries, back to the blood system.

QUESTIONS

1 Why does your body need to digest the food you eat?
2 What is the difference between diffusion and active transport?
3 Which food molecules are absorbed by diffusion?
4 Which foods molecules are absorbed by active transport?

...active transport ...diffusion ...digestion ...essential amino acids

Adaptations for absorption

When food is absorbed, it is removed from the gut. It passes through the gut walls and into the body's transport systems. The digested food is first taken to the liver where some of it is stored. The rest is taken to active cells of your body where it is used for growth, repair or respiration.

The small intestine is adapted to absorb digested food:

- It is long – about 3 metres long!
- There are millions of finger-like projections on its inner surface called **villi** (singular, **villus**) – these vastly increase the **surface area** of the small intestine.
- Each villus has a very rich blood capillary system for transporting absorbed glucose and amino acids.
- Each villus also has a branch of the lymphatic system for transporting absorbed fats.

A vast surface area

As well as having villi to increase the surface area of the small intestines, there are also microvilli. These are found on the cells that cover the villi on the lining of the small intestine. The microvilli increase still further the surface area of the ileum (the last section of the small intestine) which means that digested soluble food is absorbed more efficiently.

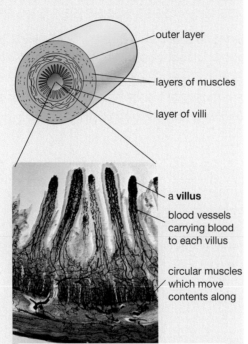

outer layer

layers of muscles

layer of villi

a **villus**

blood vessels carrying blood to each villus

circular muscles which move contents along

FIGURE 3: Photomicrograph of villi on the inner surface of the small intestine. The diagram above shows a cross-section of the small intestine.

blood capillary

blood arrives at the villus to pick up soluble food

lymph coming to villus

glucose and amino acids are absorbed into the blood system

fats are absorbed into the lymphatic system

blood system takes food molecules to the rest of the body

lymphatic system transports fats

lymphatic system

blood capillary

villus wall

microvilli

glucose

fats

amino acids

FIGURE 4: Absorption in a villus.

Diets are a way of life

People go on special diets for different reasons – fat-free, lo-carb, nut-free, to gain weight, to lose weight – the list is almost endless.

We need proteins for growth and repair. Proteins are made up of amino acids. **Essential amino acids** are those that we have to include in our diet (the food you eat), as they either cannot be made by our bodies or they are made too slowly to meet our needs. Eight of the 20 amino acids are essential. Foods rich in these essential amino acids include animal protein, dairy products, meat, fish and eggs. Soya, a plant product, is also a good source of essential amino acids.

FIGURE 5: Is this 'organic junk food' healthy?

QUESTIONS

8 Think of **three** further reasons for going on a special diet.

9 A 12-year-old friend wants to become a vegetarian. What advice would you give him?

QUESTIONS

5 Why is the small intestine adapted to absorb food?

6 How is the small intestine adapted to absorb food?

7 Write a short paragraph to describe how the products of digestion are absorbed.

What plants absorb

You will find out:
- How leaves are adapted for gas exchange
- How roots are adapted to absorb water and minerals
- About transpiration, what it is and what environmental factors affect it.

Floating leaves

Plant leaves come in all sorts of shapes and sizes. This *Victoria* plant lives in the Amazon basin in South America. Discovered in the middle of the 19th century, it was named after Queen Victoria. Its leaves can grow up to three metres in diameter and could support a baby. The edges of the floating leaves are turned up so that the leaves do not sink.

FIGURE 1: Most plants' leaves are not quite as impressive as these.

Roots and leaves

Plants have two main parts for absorbing the things they need from their surroundings – **roots** and **leaves**. As well as anchoring the plant to the ground, the roots absorb lots of **water** and **mineral ions** from the soil. Every plant has millions of tiny **root hairs**, which are specially adapted cells that vastly increase the surface area of the roots so that they can absorb all they need.

When the stomata are open a lot of water is lost

When the stomata are closed very little water is lost

Leaves and water loss

Plants lose water, as water vapour, from the surfaces of their leaves. This loss is called **transpiration**. Most transpiration happens when the weather is hot, dry and windy. Wet clothes on a washing line dry most quickly in these conditions too.

Plants have to absorb lots of water through their roots to replace the water they lose through their leaves. If a plant loses more water by transpiration than is replaced through its roots it will **wilt** and eventually die.

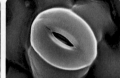

FIGURE 2: An open and closed stoma on the underside of a leaf.

Stomata can open and close

On the undersides of leaves there are tiny pores, called **stomata** (singular, **stoma**). Most transpiration happens through the stomata. Each stoma is surrounded by two **guard cells**. These can open and close to control the size of the stoma. The stomata close to reduce water loss and prevent wilting.

When the stomata are open, **carbon dioxide** diffuses into the leaf from the air. Plants need carbon dioxide to make food through photosynthesis.

Air spaces

Upper epidermis

Palisade layer – most photosynthesis happens here

Spongy layer – lots of air spaces between the cells for gas exchange

Lower epidermis

Carbon dioxide enters the leaf by diffusion

Guard cells surround the stoma

FIGURE 3: Cross section of a leaf – cells and air spaces.

▫▫ QUESTIONS ▫▫

1. What do roots do?
2. How are roots adapted to carry out their jobs?
3. What is transpiration?
4. Why are stomata important in transpiration?

...*carbon dioxide* ...*concentration gradient* ...*guard cell* ...*leaf* ...*mineral ions*

Absorbing water from the soil

The root hairs are special cells that grow just behind the root tips. They absorb water from the soil.

Follow the stages of water absorption in figure 4:

1 Soil water is a weak solution of mineral ions.

2 Inside the root hair cell is a more concentrated solution.

3 Water is absorbed into the cell by **osmosis**; mineral ions are also absorbed.

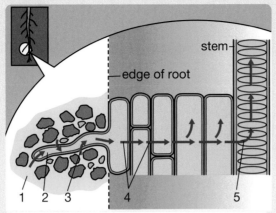

FIGURE 4: How water is absorbed and transported in a plant.

4 Water and the ions pass from one cell to another until they reach the xylem vessels.

5 Xylem vessels are found in the plant's veins; they transport water and ions up the plant.

Factors affecting transpiration

Most transpiration happens during daylight hours, not at night. This is because the stomata are open during the daytime and closed when it is dark.

Diffusion is a very important process in transpiration. For transpiration to occur, a **concentration gradient** has to be maintained.

Other factors that affect the rate of transpiration are:

■ wind (moving air)

■ humidity (how damp the air is)

■ warmth (the temperature of the air).

When environmental conditions are optimum, plants transpire at a high rate. This means that they lose a lot of water.

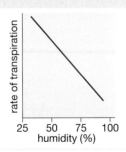
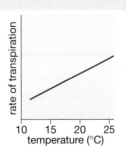

FIGURE 5: The effect of wind, humidity and temperature on the rate of transpiration.

━━━━ QUESTIONS ━━━━

5 Describe how root hair cells absorb water and mineral ions.

6 When the weather is very humid, the rate of transpiration is low. Use the idea of diffusion to explain why.

7 Explain why wind increases the rate of transpiration.

8 Why do oak trees have very high rates of transpiration in spring and summer?

Measuring the rate of water uptake

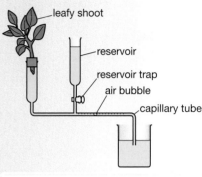

FIGURE 6: A potometer.

A potometer is used to measure the rate of water uptake by a leafy shoot. If you know the internal diameter of the capillary tube, you can work out the volume of water the shoot has lost in a given period of time. The apparatus can be reset by opening the reservoir tap.

The following results were obtained using the potometer shown in figure 6.

Time of day	Water taken up (cm³/hour)	Time of day	Water taken up (cm³/hour)
4:00	3	16:00	39
6:00	3	18:00	16
8:00	4	20:00	7
10:00	18	22:00	3
12:00	47	24:00	3
14:00	53	2:00	3

━━━━ QUESTIONS ━━━━

9 Present the data in a graph.

10 Do the data show a pattern? If yes, what is it?

11 Why is it more accurate to say that the data show *water uptake* rather than *transpiration*?

12 Suggest how the data would differ if the conditions around the potometer were:
a cold, humid and still;
b warm, dry and windy.

How blood gets around

You will find out:
- About the structure of the blood system
- About the three different types of blood vessel
- How the heart and blood system work

Have a heart!

Blue whales are very big. They are the largest animal in the world. They can grow up to 30 metres long – that makes them larger than any known dinosaur. Their heart is the size of a family car. It pumps 10 tonnes of blood. Its main artery, the aorta, is large enough for you to crawl through.

The need for a transport system

You need to move food, oxygen, carbon dioxide and waste substances around your body quickly and efficiently:
- food: from intestines to active cells
- oxygen: from lungs to active cells
- carbon dioxide: from active cells to lungs
- other waste substances: from active cells to where they are removed from the body

Your body's transport system consists of:
- the **heart** ■ **blood vessels** ■ **blood**.

These three parts together are referred to as the **circulation system**.

The heart and blood vessels

Your heart pumps blood through blood vessels around your body. It starts beating before you are born and it never stops until you die. It is made of special muscle called cardiac muscle.

You have three different types of blood vessel. **Arteries** take blood away from your heart to the organs. They have thick walls to be able to withstand the pressure of the heartbeat. You can feel the heartbeat through their walls. This is your **pulse**.

In the organs, blood flows through **capillaries** – many different substances can pass through their thin walls. They are found in your tissues and they connect arteries to **veins**. Veins bring blood back to the heart from the tissues and organs of your body.

Compare your right hand with that in figure 3. You will be able to see the big blood vessels through your skin, but the capillaries are so narrow they are 'invisible'.

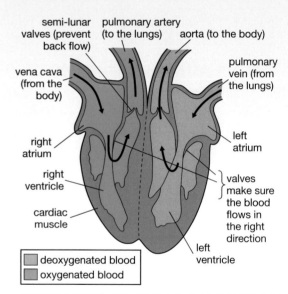

FIGURE 1: Inside the heart – can you see the four chambers and four blood vessels?

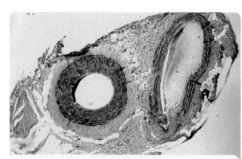

FIGURE 2: Cross section of an artery (left) and a vein (right). What do you notice about the thickness of their walls?

QUESTIONS

1 Why does your body need a transport system?
2 What waste substances need moving around our bodies?
3 What is your pulse?

...arteries ...blood ...blood vessels ...capillaries ...circulation system

How the heart and blood vessels work together

The circulation system consists of two separate loops. It is called **double circulation**. One loop goes from the heart to the lungs and then back to the heart. The second loop goes from the heart to all the other organs of the body and back to the heart.

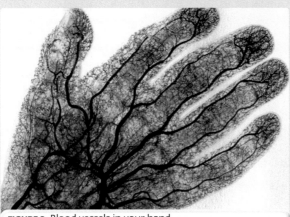

FIGURE 3: Blood vessels in your hand.

Differences between veins, arteries and capillaries

	Arteries	Capillaries	Veins
Take blood:	away from the heart	between arteries and veins	to the heart
Valves?	no valves	no valves	valves to prevent backflow of blood
Wall thickness	many cells thick	one cell thick	many cells thick
Pulse?	present (due to pressure surges from heartbeat)	no pulse	no pulse
Blood flow	quick	slowing down	slow
Oxygenated blood?	oxygenated blood (except the pulmonary artery)	mixed oxygenated and deoxygenated blood	deoxygenated blood (except the pulmonary vein)
Lumen (space for blood)	small	very small – red blood cells can only get through one at a time	large
Structure	Lining: one layer of cells / Elastic fibres and muscle / Tough non-elastic fibres		Layer of cells / Elastic fibres and muscle / Non-elastic fibres

TABLE 1: Differences between arteries, capillaries and veins.

Advantage of double circulation

As blood passes through the blood vessels it loses pressure. The blood gradually slows down. Double circulation means that the blood passes through the heart twice each time it goes through the body. Check this by tracing the path of blood in figure 4 with your finger. As the blood passes through the heart, the pressure gets a boost to keep the blood moving.

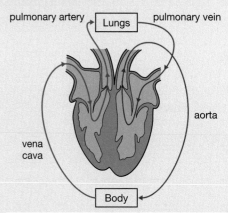

FIGURE 4: Double circulation – one heart, two loops.

Capillaries – exchange of substances

As capillary walls are just one cell thick, the fluid from the blood can ooze out of them into the body's tissues. This means that your body cells can get the oxygen and food they need for respiration. Some waste substances are removed through another set of vessels which are part of the lymphatic system.

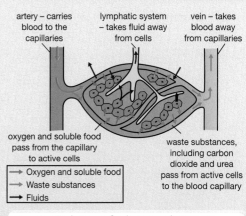

FIGURE 5: Exchange of substances between capillaries and body tissues.

▥▥▥ QUESTIONS ▥▥▥

4 What are the **three** components of the circulation system?

5 Describe **three** differences between arteries, veins and capillaries.

6 Explain what double circulation is.

7 Explain how double circulation stops blood pressure from falling.

8 Why are capillaries necessary for efficient exchange of substances between tissues and the blood system?

What blood transports

You will find out:
- That blood consists of red blood cells, white blood cells, plasma and platelets
- What plasma transports
- What red blood cells transport

All that blood!

The pigmy shrew, the smallest British mammal, only has a few cm^3 of blood. We each have about 5 500 cm^3 of blood.

An elephant has an awful lot. From the tip of its trunk to the end of its tail, **blood** transports various substances to and from active cells. All mammals have blood that transports substances around their bodies.

FIGURE 1: How much blood do you think this African elephant has?

Blood

Your blood does two important jobs: it **transports** things around your body and it **defends** it.

Blood consists of four parts:
- Transporters: **red blood cells** (**RBCs**) and **plasma**
- Defenders: **platelets** and **white blood cells** (**WBCs**).

Red blood cells

Red blood cells (RBCs) contain a very special chemical, the iron-containing red pigment called **haemoglobin**. It picks up **oxygen** when blood passes through the lungs and becomes **oxyhaemoglobin**:

haemoglobin + oxygen → oxyhaemoglobin

The oxygenated blood is then pumped to the tissues and organs of the body. The oxygen is released to the cells for respiration and the oxyhaemoglobin becomes haemoglobin again:

oxyhaemoglobin → haemoglobin + oxygen

Plasma

Plasma is about 90% water. The other 10% is dissolved chemicals which are being transported to different parts of the body:

Blood

Transporters

Defenders

Platelets
clot the blood at the site of a cut

Plasma
is a yellow liquid which transports CO_2, soluble food and waste materials

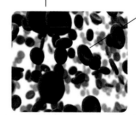

white blood cells
some surround and digest bacteria, others make antibodies to destroy bacteria

Red blood cells
– no nucleus but lots of iron containing haemoglobin to transport oxygen

FIGURE 2: The components and functions of blood.

- **carbon dioxide** is taken from respiring cells in tissues and organs to the lungs
- **soluble food** absorbed from the small intestine is transported to cells and tissues
- **urea** from the breakdown of proteins is moved from the liver to the kidneys to be excreted.

QUESTIONS

1. What are the **two** main jobs of blood in the body?
2. Describe how red blood cells transport oxygen.
3. What is plasma?
4. List **three** chemicals that are transported by plasma. Explain where each chemical is taken from and where it is taken to.

...blood ...carbon dioxide ...defend ...haemoglobin ...oxygen ...oxyhaemoglobin ...plasma

Transport of respiratory gases – oxygen and carbon dioxide

Oxygen is absorbed from the air in the lungs. It diffuses into the blood capillaries from the alveoli down an oxygen concentration gradient. It then combines with haemoglobin in the red blood cells. At the same time, carbon dioxide diffuses down its own concentration gradient from the blood plasma into the alveoli. (See figure 3.)

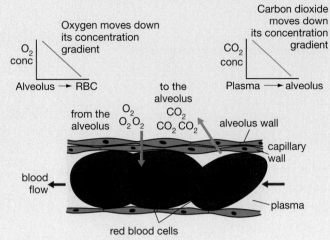

Oxygen moves down its concentration gradient

O_2 conc

Alveolus → RBC

Carbon dioxide moves down its concentration gradient

CO_2 conc

Plasma → alveolus

from the alveolus O_2 O_2 O_2

to the alveolus CO_2 CO_2 CO_2

alveolus wall

capillary wall

blood flow

plasma

red blood cells

FIGURE 3: The transport of respiratory gases.

Transport of urea

Excess amino acids and proteins are converted to urea by the liver. The urea is then transported in solution in the plasma to the kidneys. (See figure 4.)

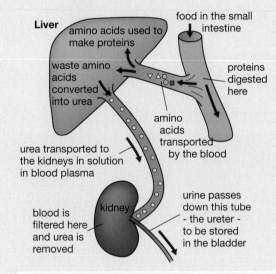

Liver

amino acids used to make proteins

food in the small intestine

waste amino acids converted into urea

proteins digested here

amino acids transported by the blood

urea transported to the kidneys in solution in blood plasma

kidney

blood is filtered here and urea is removed

urine passes down this tube - the ureter - to be stored in the bladder

FIGURE 4: How your body removes urea.

Transport of food

Once food has been digested, the soluble products are absorbed from the villi of the small intestine into the blood system.

Foods that are absorbed into the blood system are glucose, amino acids and other water-soluble substances. These molecules are transported in solution in the plasma to organs and tissues where they are needed.

Fats (which do not dissolve in water) are transported by the lymphatic system. (See figure 4 on page 17.)

QUESTIONS

5 Why are concentration gradients needed for gas exchange to happen?
6 How does urea get to the kidneys?
7 Why does food have to be digested?
8 What happens to the products of digestion?

Be a blood donor

When you donate blood, you attend a donor session. (You have to be at least 17-years-old.) A tube is inserted into a vein in your arm and usually 475 cm³ of blood is taken and collected in a bag. Small samples are also taken for screening for diseases, including hepatitis and HIV, as well as testing to see which blood group you belong to. There are several different blood groups and some are very rare. Donated blood is given to patients in transfusions to replace blood lost in accidents or during surgery. In Britain, blood donations are voluntary, but in some countries people can sell their blood to hospitals.

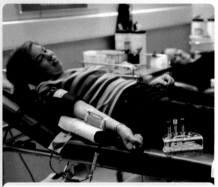

FIGURE 5: Being a blood donor can save lives!

QUESTIONS

9 What does 'screening' mean?
10 It takes about 30 minutes for your body to replace the volume of fluid after you donate blood, but blood donors are encouraged to give blood only about every 4–5 months. Suggest why they should not donate blood more frequently.
11 Do you think blood donations should be voluntary or should donors be paid for their blood? Explain your answer.

On the treadmill

SELF-CHECK ACTIVITY

CONTEXT

Zhahid is fifteen and thinking about what he is going to do when he leaves school. He is thinking about doing A levels or maybe BTEC. He goes along to the local tertiary college with some of his friends when they have an Open Evening.

One of the areas they go into is called a Human Performance Laboratory. It doesn't look much like a laboratory; it's more like the Fitness Suite at the local Sports Centre, with lots of exercise equipment and staff in track suits carrying clipboards.

"Right then," said one of the staff, "My name's Liz. Let's show you some of the tests we can do on people here."
She took them over to a machine that looked like a conveyor belt with handrails.
"This is a treadmill," she said, "OK, who's into running?"
Nobody said anything, but they all, apart from Zhahid, took a step backward.
"Fine," said Liz, "Come on then, on you get." Zhahid stood on the treadmill and Liz attached a strap and a tube around his chest.
"This will measure your heart rate and your breathing," she said. She pressed a button and the treadmill started to move. Instinctively Zhahid started to walk. Numbers appeared on the display panel. Liz turned a control and the belt started to move faster. Zhahid broke into a gentle jog.
"How does that feel?" she asked.
"Fine," he answered. She turned the control again. He was now running.
"Think about the changes that are going on in Zhahid's body now," said Liz to the others. "It's responding to this situation. Think about what's going on with the arteries and muscles."
They watched the numbers as the speed of the treadmill was increased again. Zhahid was now running.
"I'll bring it back down now" said Liz, "That was really good, Zhahid. You're obviously pretty fit."
The treadmill slowed down and Zhahid's run became a jog, then a walk and finally he stopped. She unfastened the strap and tube.
"That was alright," thought Zhahid. "I wouldn't mind doing something on that next year."

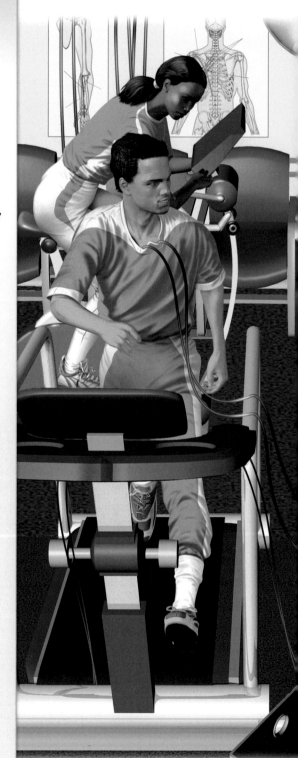

CHALLENGE

STEP 1

What was happening to Zhahid's heart rate and breathing as he ran faster?

STEP 2

Explain why these **two** changes were taking place.

STEP 3

Describe the energy transfers taking place in Zhahid's body as he is running.

STEP 4

What role does glycogen play in this process?

Maximise your grade

These sentences show what you need to include in your work to achieve each grade. Use them to improve your work and be more successful.

Grade	Answer includes...
F	Identify changes to either Zhahid's heart rate or his breathing.
	Identify changes to both Zhahid's heart rate and his breathing.
	Explain with reference to an increased rate of respiration why one of these changes has occurred.
	Explain with reference to an increased rate of respiration why both of these changes have occurred.
C	Identify the sequence of energy transfers taking place as he runs.
	Explain the role played by glycogen in muscular activity.
A	Explain the difference between aerobic and anaerobic respiration in muscular activity.
	Combine these ideas to explain the concept of oxygen debt and how it applies to this example.

STEP 5

Liz stopped the demonstration before Zhahid got tired. If she had continued it longer his muscles might have become fatigued. Explain what other process might have taken place then.

STEP 6

Use these ideas to explain how Zhahid might then have an 'oxygen debt' and how it will be repaid.

Exercising your body

You will find out:
- About the changes that happen in your body during exercise
- How muscles obtain the materials they need during exercise
- What happens after long periods of exercise

Exercise for health

Exercise has many benefits. In the short term, it improves your posture and coordination as well as reducing stress levels. It also makes you feel better about yourself. In the long term, it improves your cardio-respiratory system, increases your strength and flexibility, and reduces the risk of injury. Whatever your race, age or sex, exercise is the way to a healthy life!

Short-term effects of exercise

Exercise is any physical activity you do to improve your health and fitness. When you exercise, changes occur in your body:

- your **heartbeat rate** increases
- your **breathing rate** increases
- **arteries** supplying your **muscles dilate**
- **glycogen** reserves in your muscles are used up (glycogen is converted into sugar for respiration).

Heart rate increases

When you exercise, your muscles use up more **oxygen** and **sugars** and produce more **carbon dioxide**. These are all transported by the blood. Your heart beats faster – your heart rate increases – to remove the carbon dioxide from the muscles and to supply them with sufficient oxygen and sugars. Your normal (resting) heart rate is about 70–80 beats per minute. During exercise this can increase to 220 beats per minute. When you stop exercising, your heartbeat returns to normal.

FIGURE 1: How your body changes with exercise.

Breathing rate increases

You get oxygen from the air as you breathe. At the same time, you get rid of carbon dioxide. Because you use up more oxygen and produce more carbon dioxide during exercise, your breathing rate will increase. Normally you breathe between 10 and 18 times a minute. After exercise, that can increase to over 30 breaths per minute.

Arteries dilate

The smaller arteries (called **arterioles**) dilate. This means they get wider. This has the effect of increasing **blood flow** to active muscles. This is why you look red, or darker, when you are exercising. More sugar and oxygen can be supplied to the muscles and the waste carbon dioxide is removed. When you stop exercising, your arterioles gradually return to their normal state and your skin returns to its usual colour.

All of these changes are quite natural and happen spontaneously – you do not have to think about them: they just happen!

QUESTIONS

1. Why do people exercise?
2. What happens to your heart beat rate when you play a hockey match?
3. What happens to your breathing rate when you run 100 metres to catch a bus?
4. Why do your glycogen reserves go down when you exercise?

WOW FACTOR!

During an average life a heart beats over 2 500 000 000 times and pumps 340 million litres of blood.

...artery   ...arterioles   ...blood flow   ...breathing rate   ...carbon dioxide   ...dilate

Long-term effects of exercise

If exercising is a regular part of your lifestyle then your body will experience more permanent changes.

In your circulatory system:

■ your body will make more red blood cells for transporting oxygen from your lungs to active muscles

■ your arteries will become larger and more stretchy – this keeps your blood pressure down

■ more blood capillaries will develop in your muscles and around your alveoli – this means there can be a more efficient exchange of substances between the lungs, the blood and active cells

■ your heart will become bigger – this will enable it to pump blood more efficiently. It also means that your heart will be able to beat more slowly and still pump the same amount of blood

■ blood will be redirected to your muscles and away from internal organs such as the stomach and intestines.

Fewer capillaries   More capillaries

FIGURE 2: A richer blood supply to well-exercised muscles.

In your respiratory system:

■ your intercostal muscles and diaphragm become stronger – this means your thorax/chest will become larger

■ because your chest is larger you will be able to breathe in more air

■ as you have more capillaries around your alveoli, gas exchange is quicker – this means you can exercise longer before becoming tired.

The energy that is released during respiration is used to make muscles contract.

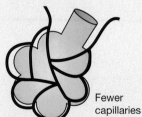

Fewer capillaries   More capillaries

FIGURE 3: A richer blood supply to the alveoli of well-exercised lungs.

QUESTIONS

5 Why do your arteries dilate during exercise?

6 What are the long-term effects of exercise on your heart?

7 Explain what the advantage is of having more capillaries around your alveoli and in your muscles.

So you think you're fit?

Compare these two people:

John	Mussa
Eats lots of 'junk food', loves deep-fried chicken	Eats a well-balanced diet, lots of fresh fruit and vegetables
Watches lots of TV and plays lots of computer games	Takes his dog for a 5 km walk every day; plays lots of sport
Takes the bus to school, even though it's only two stops	Cycles to school, even though it's all up hill (but down hill on the way home!)
Is 15 kilograms overweight	Is not overweight

The boys were monitored and the following data were electronically recorded during a football game:

Time (mins)	0	5	10	15	20	25	30	35	40
Person A: breaths/min	10	12	17	25	26	25	18	12	10
Heart beats/min	72	73	86	90	92	87	79	74	72
Person B: breaths/min	15	19	28	33	36	39	30	25	20
Heart beats/min	73	81	99	135	162	169	154	149	137

QUESTIONS

8 Draw graphs to represent the data.

9 Which person, **A** or **B**, is Mussa? Explain your answer.

10 When did the game start and when did it finish? How can you tell?

11 What advice would you give Mussa and John about their lifestyles?

Anaerobic respiration

You will find out:
● What anaerobic respiration is
● How anaerobic respiration can lead to oxygen debt

Are they fast enough?

Feet, in running shoes, are carefully placed into starting blocks. Fingers are meticulously positioned just behind the starting line. Senses are straining for the signal to start. Mind and body are totally focused on the race. BANG! Many months of training are now put to the test. Will there be enough energy available in the body to get it over the finish line in first place?

FIGURE 1: Will there be enough energy to win the race?

Aerobic vs anaerobic respiration (H)

Respiration happens in all living cells. It releases energy by breaking down glucose. When **oxygen** is used to release energy from glucose, the process is called **aerobic** respiration.

glucose + oxygen → carbon dioxide + water + energy

Sometimes, when your muscles work very hard, they use a lot of oxygen. When insufficient oxygen gets to the muscles respiration continues, but it is **anaerobic** respiration.

glucose → lactic acid + a little energy

Anaerobic respiration releases far less energy than aerobic respiration (see Table 1).

Anaerobic respiration produces **lactic acid**. Lactic acid is a mild poison. It makes muscles feel tired and can cause cramps. Muscles cannot work properly when lactic acid builds up in them. They stop contracting efficiently.

Lactic acid is produced because of the incomplete breakdown of glucose when there is not enough oxygen. This shortage of oxygen is called the **oxygen debt**. When you stop exercising you continue to breathe heavily. This takes in the extra oxygen you need to pay off the oxygen debt.

	Energy released (kJ/g of glucose)
Aerobic respiration	16.1
Anaerobic respiration	0.8

TABLE 1: Comparison of energy released by aerobic and anaerobic respiration.

QUESTIONS

1. What is the difference between aerobic respiration and anaerobic respiration?
2. Why does anaerobic respiration release less energy than aerobic respiration?
3. What effect does lactic acid have on your muscles?

...aerobic ...anaerobic ...fatigue ...lactic acid

Oxygen debt   (H)

When you take strenuous exercise, for example, running a 1500 m race, the amount of oxygen you absorb in your lungs quickly increases. Unfortunately, this increase is not usually enough to meet your aerobic respiration needs, so glucose is not completely broken down to carbon dioxide and water. Anaerobic respiration starts and lactic acid is produced. As the level of lactic acid increases, your muscles gradually stop contracting efficiently. This is called **fatigue**. It hurts! You gradually build up an oxygen debt.

When you stop exercising, you don't stop breathing! In fact you continue to breathe more quickly and deeply than you usually do when you are at rest. Oxygen continues to be absorbed at a higher rate than normal to pay back the oxygen debt. This carries on until the levels of lactic acid fall back to normal. The lactic acid is converted to carbon dioxide and water:

lactic acid + oxygen → carbon dioxide + water + some energy

Energy that is released is used to replace the chemical energy that has been used up in muscle cells.

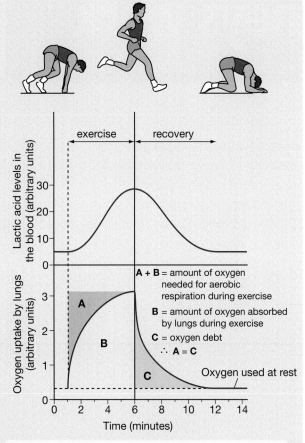

FIGURE 2: Lactic acid and the oxygen debt.

A + B = amount of oxygen needed for aerobic respiration during exercise

B = amount of oxygen absorbed by lungs during exercise

C = oxygen debt

∴ A = C

Oxygen used at rest

The point of training

When athletes train they:

■ increase the rate at which they absorb oxygen from the air

■ develop a tolerance to the discomfort that lactic acid causes.

FIGURE 3: Number 990 wins! Might this have anything to do with lactic acid tolerance?

QUESTIONS

4   Why does anaerobic respiration start during strenuous activity?

5   Why do you continue to breathe deeply after strenuous exercise has stopped?

6   What eventually happens to the lactic acid?

7   Explain the relationships between areas **A**, **B** and **C** in figure 2.

Maximum oxygen   (H) uptake

When you exercise, your muscles use more oxygen. To obtain this extra oxygen you breathe more deeply and more quickly. Your heart beats faster so that oxygenated blood is pumped to your active muscles more quickly. The maximum volume of oxygen your body uses per minute is called **VO₂ max**. The fitter you are, the higher the value of your VO_2 max. The graph in figure 4 compares VO_2 max values for athletes specialising in different sports.

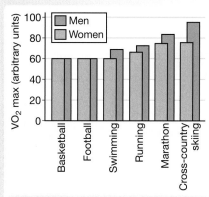

FIGURE 4: VO_2 max values for different sportspeople.

QUESTIONS

8   Athletes playing which sport show the lowest and the highest VO_2 max values?

9   Where would you place netball and tennis in the graph? Explain why.

10 Which athletes do you think would be able to pay off an oxygen debt quickest? Explain why.

11 How could an athlete develop a higher VO_2 max?

How kidneys work

You will find out:
- Where the kidneys are in your body
- The structure of the kidneys
- What the kidneys do
- How the kidneys work

Kidney stones

The X-ray in figure 1 does not show the **kidney**, but it does show some kidney stones. Kidney stones are made from some of the mineral salts and ions that are filtered in the kidney. Small stones have no effect. Larger ones can cause severe pain, especially if they start to move down the urinary tract.

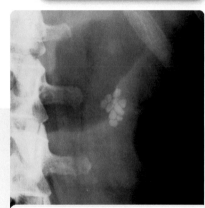

FIGURE 1: X-ray of kidney stones (The patient's spine runs down the far left of the image).

Where are your kidneys and what do they do?

Your kidneys are in your abdomen. You (most probably) have two, one on either side of your spine.

The kidneys have two very important jobs:

- **osmoregulation** – controlling the water and ion content of your body
- **excretion** – removing waste substances from your blood.

Kidneys do this by producing **urine**. A normal, healthy kidney produces urine by **filtering** the blood. Blood is pumped to the kidneys by the heart through the renal arteries. As the blood passes through the kidney it is filtered. Useful substances, such as **sugars** and **amino acids** are filtered out, as well as waste substances. The useful substances are **reabsorbed** back into the blood. Waste substances, such as **urea** (made from excess amino acids by the liver) and **ions** stay in the urine.

All this happens in millions of microscopic tubes in the kidney called **kidney tubules** (also known as **nephrons**).

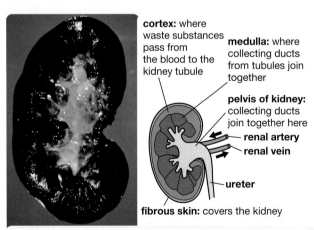

cortex: where waste substances pass from the blood to the kidney tubule

medulla: where collecting ducts from tubules join together

pelvis of kidney: collecting ducts join together here

renal artery

renal vein

ureter

fibrous skin: covers the kidney

FIGURE 2: Inside a kidney – compare the diagram with the photograph of the real thing.

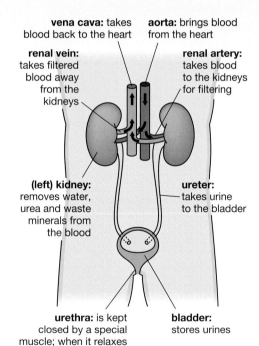

vena cava: takes blood back to the heart

aorta: brings blood from the heart

renal vein: takes filtered blood away from the kidneys

renal artery: takes blood to the kidneys for filtering

(left) kidney: removes water, urea and waste minerals from the blood

ureter: takes urine to the bladder

urethra: is kept closed by a special muscle; when it relaxes urine leaves the body

bladder: stores urines

FIGURE 3: Kidneys in your body.

QUESTIONS

1. Where are your kidneys?
2. What are the **two** important jobs that your kidneys do?
3. What is urine?
4. Why are there no amino acids or sugar in the urine of a healthy person?

...amino acids   ...excretion   ...filter   ...ion   ...kidney   ...kidney tubule   ...nephron

How kidney tubules work   (H)

Three things happen in the kidney tubules:

- blood is filtered
- useful materials are reabsorbed back into the blood
- the waste forms urine and passes to the bladder.

Follow what happens in figure 4.

1 Branch of the renal artery: wider on the way in, therefore there is an increase in pressure here.

2 Knot of capillaries called the glomerulus – fluids leak out, under pressure.

3 Bowman's capsule acts like a sieve.

4 Pressure builds up here and causes liquid plasma to be filtered out: blood cells stay in the capillaries; water, glucose, amino acids, ions and urea pass out of the blood.

5 Glucose and amino acids and ions needed by the body are reabsorbed back into the blood, together with some water.

6 Loop of Henle – some more water is reabsorbed here.

7 Urine is made up of urea, excess ions and water.

8 Urine passes down the ureter to the bladder.

9 Blood flows back to the heart.

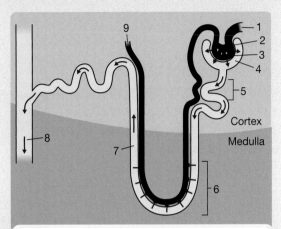

FIGURE 4: How urine is made in the kidney tubule.

Substance	Approximate % in blood plasma entering the kidneys	Approximate % in urine
Water	90	96
Sugar (glucose)	0.1	0
Ions (salts)	1	1.6
Urea	0.03	2
Amino acids and proteins	8	0

TABLE 1: Substances in the blood entering the kidneys and in urine.

As urine passes down along the kidney tubule, more and more of the sugars and ions are reabsorbed back into the blood. Eventually there will be a higher concentration of these in the blood than in the urine. The rest have to be actively absorbed against a concentration gradient. This means energy from respiration has to be used.

QUESTIONS

5 What **three** processes happen in kidney tubules?

6 Explain what each of the following parts of the kidney does: knot of capillaries (glomerulus), Bowman's capsule, loop of Henle.

7 Explain why energy is needed to absorb the last of the sugars from the urine as it passes down the kidney tubule to the ureter.

Keeping a balance

Every day your body gains and loses water. We gain it from the food and drink we consume and we lose it through urine, sweat, breathing out and in faeces. If you lose too much water you will suffer from dehydration and this can be very dangerous. The kidneys are clearly very important in keeping the balance.

A scientist wanted to investigate whether there was a correlation between how we lose water from our bodies and environmental temperature. She collected the following results from some volunteers:

Outside temp (°C)	Volume of urine produced (cm³/h)	Volume of sweat produced (cm³/h)
0	100	5
5	91	6
10	79	10
15	68	19
20	58	37
25	45	62
30	30	112
35	19	210
40	10	265

TABLE 2: Water loss from the body in relation to outside temperature.

QUESTIONS

8 Draw line graphs of the data. Draw both curves on the same pair of axes.

9 What are the trends in water lost as sweat and urine in relation to outside temperature?

10 What is happening in the kidneys as the temperature increases?

Kidney failure

You will find out:
● What kidney failure is
● How kidney failure can be treated

Kidney cancer

The CT scan in figure 1 shows a section through the abdomen of a patient suffering from cancer. The **kidneys** can be seen on either side of the spine (white lower centre). The purple patch shows that the right kidney is cancerous. The left kidney (red and yellow) looks quite healthy. Even though the diseased kidney almost certainly no longer works properly, the patient can survive with just one healthy kidney.

What happens if your kidneys fail?

Normal, healthy kidneys remove excess water, ions and urea from your blood. If your kidneys fail to work properly, these substances build up. Waste substances prevent your body from working properly and your blood pressure may rise. When this happens you need medical care.

There are basically two treatments for kidney failure – **dialysis** and kidney **transplantation**.

Dialysis

During dialysis, all the patient's blood is made to flow through a dialysis machine. It filters the blood and restores the concentrations of dissolved substances in the blood to normal levels. Some patients go to hospital for dialysis every few days, others are provided with the equipment they need to dialyse at home.

Kidney transplantation

A person with a diseased kidney can be given a healthy, replacement one – a kidney transplant. If the transplanted kidney comes from a close relative, there will be less chance of **rejection**. This is because it will have a similar **tissue type** to the patient. The new kidney is attached to the renal blood vessels at the front of the abdomen. After a recovery period the patient can lead a normal life and no longer needs dialysis.

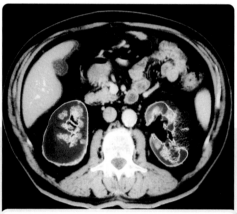

FIGURE 1: A CT scan showing a cancerous kidney.

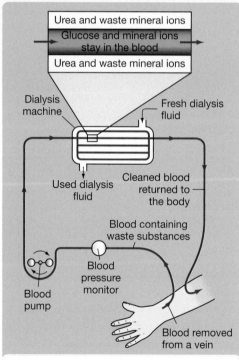

FIGURE 2: How a kidney dialysis machine works.

▣ QUESTIONS ▣

1   What jobs do healthy kidneys do?
2   What can waste substances do to your body if they are not removed?
3   What is kidney failure?
4   How can kidney failure be treated?

...*dialysis*   ...*donor*   ...*immune system*   ...*kidney*

What's best – transplant or dialysis?

Different people respond differently to circumstances. What is acceptable for one person might be difficult for another to accept. Table 1 below summarises some of the advantages and disadvantages of the different possible treatments for kidney failure.

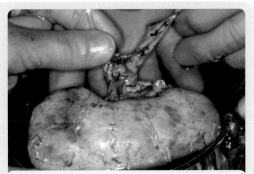

FIGURE 3: A human kidney being prepared for a transplantation.

TABLE 1: Pros (+) and cons (−) of treatments for kidney failure.

	Hospital-based dialysis	Home-based dialysis	Transplantation
Advantages	+ facilities are widely available + hospital staff are trained professionals + you get to know others with the same condition	+ you can dialyse at times that suit you (as often as doctors tell you) + no travel involved	+ after transplantation, your new kidney will work like a normal kidney + fewer dietary restrictions + you do not have to spend up to 18 hours per week dialysing + some people see transplants as a cure
Disadvantages	− hospital sessions are set and it is generally not possible to change them − you have to get to the hospital − you may have to watch your diet − dialysis is not a cure	− you need a helper − you and your helper need professional training − quite a lot of space is needed to store the dialysis machine and supplies − you may have to watch your diet − dialysis is not a cure	− major surgery is needed − possible long wait to find a suitable donor (in some cases, years) − possible rejection of the transplanted kidney − will need to take anti-rejection drugs for the rest of life

Preventing transplant rejection

It is the body's **immune system** that causes the body to reject a transplant if it recognises it as 'different'. Two things can be done to prevent a transplanted kidney being rejected. The doctors make sure that the **donor** kidney is of a tissue type that is as close as possible to the **recipient's**, and the recipient is given drugs (medicines) that suppress the body's immune system.

QUESTIONS

5 Imagine you are a doctor. Write a letter to a patient whose kidneys have failed outlining the advantages of home dialysis over hospital-based dialysis.

6 Look at the Transplantation column in Table 1. Which is the main advantage? Explain your choice.

7 Now look at the disadvantages of transplantation. Which is the biggest drawback? Explain your choice.

8 What can be done to prevent a patient's body from rejecting a transplanted kidney?

Kidneys for sale

We each have two kidneys but can survive on one. The first kidney transplant was in 1933 in Boston, United States. Sadly the operation was not successful and the patient died. The first successful kidney transplant took place 21 years later, also in the United States. Today kidney transplants are almost a routine procedure in hospitals for patients suffering from kidney failure.

Unfortunately, there is always a shortage of donor organs. Since you can live quite well with one kidney, you could donate one kidney. Some people choose to sell one of their kidneys for transplantation. One man from Brazil recently sold one of his kidneys for about £750. But is this ethical? In most countries such trading of kidneys, and other body organs, is illegal.

FIGURE 4: Should people be allowed to sell their kidney?

QUESTIONS

9 You have been asked to advise the Government on the subject of organ sales for transplants. List as many arguments for and against selling organs as you can think of. Explain each point as fully as you can.

10 Write a letter to the Minister of Health advising them of your conclusions.

Unit summary

Concept map

Lungs are the body's main gas-exchange organs.

Diffusion is important in absorbing oxygen and excreting carbon dioxide.

Absorption

Plants absorb water by osmosis through the root hairs on their roots.

Root hairs absorb mineral ions by diffusion and active transport.

Digested food is absorbed in the intestines. The surface area is vastly increased by villi.

Blood and circulation

The heart pumps blood around the body through arteries, capillaries and veins.

Your body has a double circulatory system.

Plasma transports soluble food and urea. It also takes carbon dioxide from active cells to be excreted in the lungs.

Red blood cells transport oxygen from your lungs to active cells.

Exercise

During exercise your body goes through various changes.

These changes enable your body to do the exercise more efficiently.

During strenuous exercise your body can respire anaerobically.

Anaerobic respiration releases much less energy than aerobic respiration.

Strenuous exercise can lead to an oxygen debt.

These are excretory organs.

Kidneys

Kidney failure can be rectified by dialysis or a kidney transplant.

Unit quiz

1 Name the **two** gases that pass through the walls of the alveoli in the lungs.

2 What must happen to the food you eat before it is absorbed into the blood system?

3 In which part of the digestive system is most food absorbed?

4 What processes allow plants to absorb: **a** water and **b** mineral ions?

5 Which part of the root system is specially adapted for absorption?

6 What is so special about heart muscle?

7 What is your pulse?

8 Which parts of the blood transport: **a** oxygen and **b** carbon dioxide?

9 List **two** things that happen in your body during exercise.

10 What is the difference between aerobic respiration and anaerobic respiration?

11 What **two** important jobs are done by the kidneys?

12 How can kidney failure be treated?

Literacy activity

Surviving in space

A spacecraft must protect its crew from the extremes of space. 7000 km above the Earth's surface, the number of gas molecules is infinitesimally small and the pressure approaches that of a perfect vacuum. A spaceship must, therefore, provide a breathable atmosphere and protection against extremes of pressure. Space is also extremely cold, almost $-270\,°C$, but solar rays heat up objects in their path fast, so spacecraft must have a temperature control system that is able to cope with extremes of heat and cold. Damage from micrometeoroids or space debris is a constant concern. Even a small flake of paint chipped off a satellite and travelling at several thousands of miles an hour can fatally puncture a spacecraft. The windows of the space shuttle are so regularly dented by micrometeorites that they must be renewed every few flights.

QUESTIONS

1 In the second sentence, what does the word 'infinitesimally' mean?

2 What does a 'breathable atmosphere' contain?

3 Which 'extremes of space' are referred to?

4 Explain why space debris is dangerous.

Exam practice questions

1

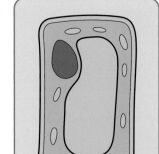

Palisade cell

Pollen cell

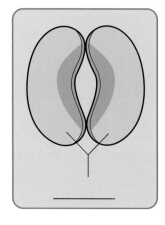

Stoma

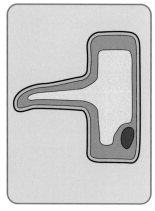

_____

a i Copy the last two diagrams and label the cells on the stoma and fill in the name of the other cell. [2]

ii Name the process by which carbon dioxide enters the leaf. [1]

b How is the leaf adapted for the absorption of carbon dioxide? [3]

c i From which part of the plant is the most water lost? [1]

ii Which of the following conditions speed up transpiration?

hot　　　　**wet**
dry　　　　**windy**
humid [3]

iii If more water is being lost by the plant than is being taken up, what happens to its guard cells? [1]

2 Look at the picture of the alveoli shown below:

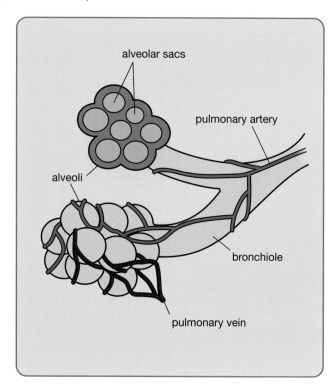

a Describe how the alveoli are adapted for their function. [3]

b A red blood cell enters the alveolus and picks up oxygen. Name the process by which oxygen enters the red blood cell. [1]

c What is the name of the protein that the oxygen molecule binds to in the red blood cell? [1]

d Red blood cells are carried by the blood suspended in a liquid called plasma. What are the three main things blood plasma transports? Choose from the following options:

products of digestion
urea
carbon dioxide
lactic acid
nerve cells [3]

(Total 19 marks)

People who suffer from kidney failure may be treated either by using a kidney dialysis machine or by having a healthy kidney transplanted.

a What is the purpose of dialysis? [1]

b How often does dialysis have to be carried out? [1]

c Explain how diffusion using a concentration gradient is used in a dialysis machine. You may draw a diagram to help explain your answer. [4]

(Total 6 marks)

Good answer, dialysis replaces kidney function. Since you are constantly making urea you will need to remove it from your blood at regular intervals.

ai *Dialysis is to clean the blood.*

ii *Dialysis should be carried out on a regular basis.*

iii

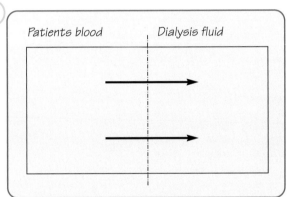

Patients blood   Dialysis fluid

This statement does not entirely agree with the specification. You should try to include as much detail in your answers as possible. Dialysis is used to restore the concentrations of dissolved substances in the blood to normal levels. You would also gain the mark for talking about removing urea from the blood.

This is a good answer. However, some labels are missing on the diagram. There is good use of scientific language and four points have been covered: the partially permeable membrane, diffusion, urea and concentration gradients.

When the patient's blood is passed through the dialysis machine it is separated from the fluid by a partially permeable membrane. Urea diffuses out of the blood down a concentration gradient, sugar and dissolved mineral ions do not diffuse, as there is no concentration gradient.

Overall Grade: A

How to get an A

Although the first answer did not gain any marks, the rest of the answers are spot on. You must be careful when answering questions that are only worth one mark, try to answer every question as fully as you can and expect to fill up the space given for the answer.

DISCOVER MICRO-ORGANISMS!

Micro-organisms are everywhere. This is an imprint of a hand that its owner thought was clean. Each colony grew from a bacterium that was on the hand. How many do you think you have on your whole body? How many might there be on a dirty hand?

Micro-organisms can grow on almost anything. This is agar jelly, made from seaweed – bacteria thrive on it.

An individual bacterium is so tiny you can scarcely see it even with a school microscope. But when you get thousands of them together, they form colonies – each of these little blobs contains millions of them.

CONTENTS

Yeast

You will find out:
- That yeast is a single-celled organism that is used to make bread and alcoholic drinks
- That yeast cells can respire aerobically and anaerobically
- How beer and wine are made

What is yeast used for?

Yeast lives in many different places, for example on the outside of berries and just floating around in the air. People have used yeast for thousands of years. Yeast is used to make wine, beer and bread.

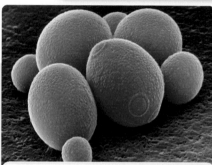

FIGURE 1: These are yeast cells, magnified 1500 times.

Using yeast

Yeast is a fungus. It is a very unusual fungus, because it only has one cell. It is a **single-celled** organism. It reproduces by growing buds out of the cell. You can see two buds in the photograph in figure 1.

The diagram (figure 2) shows the structure of a yeast cell. It has a nucleus, cytoplasm and a cell membrane. It also has a cell wall, but this is not made of cellulose like a plant cell wall.

Yeast cells don't have chloroplasts, so they cannot photosynthesise. Yeast feeds on sugars, for example, glucose. It can use **anaerobic respiration** to get energy for itself from sugars. In this process, the yeast makes **alcohol** and carbon dioxide. The kind of alcohol that yeast makes is called **ethanol**.

$$glucose \rightarrow ethanol + carbon\ dioxide$$

This process is called **fermentation**.

We use yeast to make beer and wine. The yeast feeds on sugars in the barley (for beer) or grapes (for wine). It respires anaerobically, and produces alcohol.

We also use yeast to make bread. When the yeast respires, it produces carbon dioxide that fills the bread dough with bubbles and makes it rise.

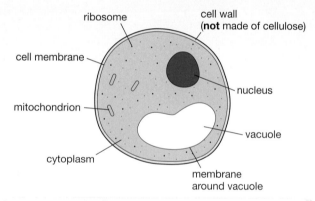

FIGURE 2: A yeast cell.

ribosome
cell wall (**not** made of cellulose)
cell membrane
nucleus
mitochondrion
vacuole
cytoplasm
membrane around vacuole

FIGURE 3: These grapes will be used to make wine.

▌▌ QUESTIONS ▌▌

1 What kind of organism is yeast?
2 What kind of respiration is yeast using when it produces ethanol?
3 What else does yeast produce when it respires in this way?
4 Name **three** products that are made using yeast.

...alcohol ...anaerobic respiration ...distilled ...ethanol

Making beer

Beer is made from the seeds (grain) of barley. The harvested grain is spread out on a big floor, moistened and then left to germinate. The barley grains contain starch. When they start to germinate, they produce enzymes that break down the starch to a sugar called **maltose**. This is called **malting**.

FIGURE 4: Barley grains being spread in readiness for malting.

FIGURE 5: Hops are added to beer to give it its distinctive flavour.

The malted barley is heated with water. The barley sugar, maltose, dissolves in the warm water. The maltose solution is then mixed with yeast in huge vats. Fermentation takes place, in which the yeast respires anaerobically, breaking down the sugar and making alcohol.

Usually, hops are added to the beer to give it flavour. Hops are the fruits of tall vines. They have a bitter flavour that gives the beer a particular taste and aroma.

Making wine

Wine is made in a similar way to beer, but grapes are used instead of malted barley. The grapes are crushed and mixed with water, which releases their natural sugars. Yeast is then added to ferment the mixture, producing alcohol.

FIGURE 6: These huge presses are squeezing juice from grapes to make champagne.

Aerobic respiration in yeast

Although yeast can respire anaerobically, producing alcohol, it doesn't do this all of the time. Anaerobic respiration only provides the yeast with a small amount of energy. To grow and reproduce, yeast needs to respire aerobically (using oxygen).

glucose + oxygen → carbon dioxide + water

▰▰▰ QUESTIONS ▰▰▰

5   How is maltose produced when barley grains germinate?

6   How is this sugar used to make beer?

7   What is the energy source for the yeast when making wine?

8   Why does yeast need to respire aerobically as well as anaerobically?

Alcohol production

Yeast produces alcohol when it respires anaerobically and the alcohol gradually builds up in the fermenting liquid.

Yeast cannot grow when the alcohol concentration is high. For example, the yeast that is used to make champagne stops working when the alcohol makes up about 18% of the liquid (the medium) in which it is growing.

This puts a limit on the alcohol content of wine and beer. To get a higher alcohol content, the wine or beer has to be **distilled**. This is how spirits are made. For example, brandy is made by distilling wine.

FIGURE 7: Do you think distillation was used to get this alcohol content?

▰▰▰ QUESTIONS ▰▰▰

9   A recipe for homemade cherry wine lists these ingredients:
   - cherries
   - sugar
   - water
   - yeast

   a Suggest what you should do with the cherries in order to start making the wine. Why would you do this?

   b What would you do with the sugar and water?

   c Explain how the yeast would help to make the wine.

   d How could cherry wine be made into cherry brandy?

Bacteria and food production

You will find out:
- That bacteria are used for making yoghurt and cheese
- That bacteria ferment the sugars in milk, making lactic acid
- That lactic acid makes milk solidify

Bacteria – they aren't all bad!

Bacteria have a bit of an image problem. We tend to think they are 'bad', because some of them can cause illness. But in fact most bacteria aren't harmful at all, and many of them are helpful. We use bacteria to make several different kinds of food. Have you eaten any bacteria today?

Using bacteria to make food

Yoghurt and **cheese** are made using bacteria. To make yoghurt, some milk is warmed, then a **starter culture** is added. The starter culture contains two kinds of bacteria.

The bacteria ferment the sugar in the milk. The sugar in milk is called **lactose**. The bacteria change the lactose into **lactic acid**.

$$\text{lactose} \xrightarrow{\text{fermentation}} \text{lactic acid}$$

The lactic acid gives yoghurt its sharp taste. It makes the milk clot, which is why yoghurt is thicker and more solid than milk.

Yoghurt recipe

Here is a recipe you can use to make yoghurt at home.

> *You will need:*
> - *250 cm^3 milk*
> - *1 tablespoon of 'live' natural yoghurt*
>
> *You can buy live yoghurt – that is, yoghurt containing live bacteria – from most supermarkets.*
>
> *Heat the milk in a saucepan until it is almost boiling. Cover it and leave it to cool until you can comfortably touch the pan.*
>
> *Sterilise a spoon by holding it in boiling water. Let the spoon cool, then use it to add the live yoghurt to the warm milk. Stir.*
>
> *Cover, and leave in a warm place for several hours or overnight.*

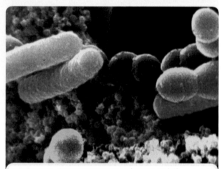

FIGURE 1: Fajitas and yoghurt – say "thank you" to the bacteria!

FIGURE 2: *Streptococcus thermophilus* and *Lactobacillus bulgaricus*, the two bacteria added to milk to make yoghurt.

FIGURE 3: What makes yoghurt thicker than milk?

▪▪ QUESTIONS ▪▪

1. What is in the starter culture that is used to make yoghurt?
2. In the recipe for home-made yoghurt, where does the starter culture come from?
3. Suggest why the milk is heated to a high temperature before using it to make yoghurt.
4. Suggest why the milk is allowed to cool down before the starter culture is added.

...bacteria ...cheese ...curds ...lactic acid ...lactose

Is yoghurt good for you?

There are many different kinds of yoghurt on sale. You can buy low-fat yoghurt or creamy yoghurt, plain yoghurt or fruit yoghurt, thick Greek-style yoghurt or thin yoghurt that you can drink.

Many people choose low-fat yoghurt (made with skimmed milk), because they want to keep their weight down. They may also be trying to keep their blood cholesterol levels down – there is some evidence that a diet rich in animal fats can raise blood cholesterol levels and increase the risk of heart disease.

FIGURE 4: Why might low-fat yoghurt be a healthier choice than full-fat yoghurt?

Milk contains protein and calcium, so these nutrients are also present in yoghurt. Protein is an important part of our diet. Our bodies use the protein we eat to help cells to grow and repair themselves, and to make specialised proteins such as antibodies, haemoglobin and keratin. Calcium helps to keep bones and teeth strong.

So yoghurt can indeed be a good addition to your diet.

Making cheese

Like yoghurt, cheese is made by the action of bacteria on milk. People have been making cheese for thousands of years. It is a good way of preserving milk – some kinds of cheese can last months and even years and still be good to eat.

First, the milk is warmed and a starter culture of bacteria is added. Then an enzyme called **rennet** is added, which makes the milk separate into **curds** (solid lumps containing protein and fat) and **whey** (a liquid). The whey is drained off, and the curds are pressed together to make the cheese.

FIGURE 5: Does this cheese look good to you?

FIGURE 6: The blue patches in blue cheeses are made by a fungus called *Penicillium*.

QUESTIONS

5 Explain why low-fat yoghurt can be a healthier choice than full-fat yoghurt (yoghurt made with full-cream milk).

6 List **two** nutrients present in yoghurt, and explain their role in a balanced diet.

7 What makes the blue 'veins' in blue cheeses?

Choose your bacteria

Using different kinds of bacteria in a starter culture when making cheese can have a big effect on the final product.

For example, for making cheeses like cheddar, a bacterium called *Lactococcus lactis* is used. A bacterium called *Lactobacillus delbreuckii* is used for making Swiss-type cheeses.

When the bacteria ferment the milk sugar (lactose) in the milk, the pH of the milk falls. The cheese manufacturer wants this to happen quickly. However, there are sometimes problems with residues of antibiotics in the milk, which can slow down the activities of the bacteria in the starter culture. Cheesemakers can test the milk they are going to use, to make sure that the concentration of antibiotics in it won't affect the manufacturing process.

QUESTIONS

8 Suggest why the bacteria used for making cheese have been given names beginning with '*Lact-*'.

9 Why does the pH fall when the bacteria ferment the sugars in milk?

10 How might antibiotics get into milk? As well as causing problems for cheesemakers, this could possibly cause difficulties in the treatment of infectious diseases. Can you suggest why?

The first microbiologists

You will find out:
- That biogenesis means the production of living things from non-living things
- About Spallanzani and Pasteur's experiments that disproved the idea that micro-organisms could appear from non-living materials

Birds from shells?

Barnacle geese spend their winters in Britain, but fly north to breed. In the 18th century, people did not know this. All they knew was that the geese disappeared in the spring, and reappeared in the winter. They never saw barnacle goose eggs or goslings. They thought that they must hatch from the grey-white 'eggs' found on rocky seashores. These shells belong to barnacles, and this is why the geese were named 'barnacle geese' and the barnacles 'goose barnacles'.

FIGURE 1: Barnacle geese were thought to hatch from 'eggs' on rocky seashores. What, in fact, were the 'eggs'?

Living from non-living?

What do barnacle geese and barnacles have to do with **micro-organisms**? Until the 18th century, people not only believed that one kind of living thing could appear from another, but also that living things could appear from non-living things.

For example, they thought that maggots just grew out of meat (dead tissue). They did not know that flies lay eggs on meat, which hatch into maggots, which grow into adult flies.

So when microscopes were first invented and people began to see tiny 'animals' swimming around in samples of gravy or sour milk, they decided that these tiny organisms – which they called **microbes** – must just develop out of the liquid.

One name for this idea is **biogenesis**. Biogenesis means the production of living things from non-living things.

Disproving biogenesis

Lazarro **Spallanzani**, an Italian scientist who lived between 1729 and 1799, was one of the first people to do experiments that showed that microbes could only develop from other microbes. In the mid-19th century, the great French scientist, Louis **Pasteur**, carried out similar experiments that went even further to disprove the theory of biogenesis. Now we know that micro-organisms (microbes) can only develop from other living micro-organisms. Living things can only develop from other living things.

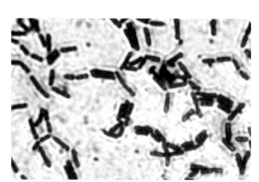

FIGURE 2: Micro-organisms in milk – this kind of bacteria makes milk go sour.

QUESTIONS

1 Why did people once think that barnacle geese grew from barnacles?
2 What does 'biogenesis' mean?
3 Name **two** scientists who helped to disprove the theory of biogenesis.
4 Where do micro-organisms come from?

...biogenesis ...microbes ...micro-organisms

Spallanzani disproves biogenesis

Lazarro Spallanzani was born in Italy in 1729. He did not believe in biogenesis. In those days, no-one really did experiments to find out if their ideas were right or not. But Spallanzani wanted to find out who was right about biogenesis.

Spallanzani took various foods – meat, eggs, vegetables – and boiled them in water. Then he put the water into clean glass flasks and sealed the tops firmly, so nothing could get in. After a while, he looked at the liquids under the microscope. There were no microbes in them. Spallanzani decided that this proved that the microbes must come from tiny living things that dropped into liquids from the air. If you kept microbes out, then no new microbes appeared.

FIGURE 3: Lazarro Spallanzani (standing), carrying out an experiment to investigate how food is digested in a bird's stomach.

Pasteur adds evidence

FIGURE 4: Louis Pasteur (1822–95).

Louis Pasteur was born in France in 1822. He made many discoveries in many different fields of science. One of Pasteur's most famous experiments built on Spallanzani's work. First, he made some special glass flasks, called **swan-necked flasks**.

Pasteur boiled some juice to kill any micro-organisms that might be in it. He put the juice into a sterilised swan-necked flask and sealed the tip. He found that he could leave the juice in there for months, and no micro-organisms grew in it. When he cut the tip off the flask, dust from the air dropped in and settled in the base of the curved 'neck' of the flask. But still no micro-organisms grew in the juice.

Next, Pasteur gently tipped the flask so that the juice came into contact with the dust in the neck. Within a day, there were thousands of micro-organisms growing and multiplying in the juice.

Some of Pasteur's preparations are at the Pasteur Institute, Paris, where they continue to remain sterile after more than 100 years.

FIGURE 5: One of Pasteur's swan-necked flasks.

The origin of life

If life only comes from life, then where did the first living things come from?

We still don't know the answer to this question, although scientists have several different theories. One possibility is that, here on Earth, chemicals such as amino acids were made, just by simple chemical reactions that happened in the atmosphere or in water. When the Earth was young, the composition of the atmosphere was very different from now, and it was more likely that these reactions could take place.

Other theories are that life might have begun in places like volcanic vents deep beneath the oceans. Some think that it may have begun on another planet, and have been carried to Earth on meteors or asteroids.

All the theories have some evidence to support them. But as yet we don't know which if any of them is correct, and it looks as though it will be a long time before we will find out the answer.

FIGURE 6: Did life on Earth begin on another planet?

▦▦▦ QUESTIONS ▦▦▦

5 How did Spallanzani's experiments help to disprove the theory of biogenesis?

6 When Spallanzani carried out his experiments, no-one knew about how to design a good experiment. How would you improve his experiment, so that you could be more certain of the meaning of the results?

7 How did the results of Pasteur's experiment help to disprove the theory of biogenesis?

8 Why was Pasteur's experiment better than Spallanzani's?

▦▦▦ QUESTIONS ▦▦▦

9 List some of the chemicals that you would need in order to make a living organism.

10 One day, it may be possible for people to make living organisms from non-living materials. Do you think this should be allowed to happen?

Richard's home brew

SELF-CHECK ACTIVITY

CONTEXT

Richard works for the local authority in a city in the north of England. He has lived there ever since he was a student and still enjoys the taste of beer. These days he's sometimes disappointed by the flavour of what he calls 'keg beers' – he's actually happier drinking real ale.

For some years now he's brewed his own beer as well and has become something of an expert. Some of his first attempts were pretty grim – they had certainly fermented, but the cloudiness was a bit off-putting, and so was the taste. A bit of experimenting and picking the brains of other people soon got things sorted out.

It's all down to the tiny single-celled organisms known as yeast. Like all organisms, yeast respires in order to release energy for living processes, but yeast has two ways of respiring: anaerobic and aerobic. It is only the first of these that produces alcohol though. Like other respiring organisms, yeast needs a food supply. To make beer, the yeast are fed on malted barely, which is quite sweet.

In the living room of Richard's house are a row of demijohns, the large glass bottles he uses for the brew. At first they make little popping noises; nothing very loud, but quite persistent.

"It's the air lock," he explains. "What you can hear is the gas escaping. As the brew ferments the gas builds up and it has to be let out."

The airlock consists of a tube with two 180° bends in it. Water is put in the 'U'-shaped bend and sits there. Gas can push through it, but nothing can pass through the other way.

It may look a bit odd to have all these demijohns lined up in the living room, but the fermentation works better if they're warm. It takes several weeks and some careful filtering, but Richard swears by the outcome.

"I could win prizes with this," he says. "It's like nectar."

CHALLENGE

STEP 1

What is the gas that is being formed? Write down the word equation that shows its formation.

STEP 2

What are the conditions needed for the fermentation to work effectively? How has Richard set things up to provide these?

STEP 3

Write down the word equation that describes the process of fermentation. What is the function of yeast in this process? How is it being fed? What is it producing?

STEP 5

Explain why it is important that the gas is allowed to escape.
Explain why it is important that air from the outside is not allowed to enter.

Maximise your grade

These sentences show what you need to be including in your work. Use them to improve your work and to be successful.

Grade	Answer includes...
	Describe some of the conditions needed for fermentation.
F	Describe all of the conditions needed for fermentation.
	State the products of fermentation.
	Write down the word equation for fermentation.
C	Write down the word equation for fermentation and explain why air has to be kept out.
	Write down the word equation for fermentation and explain how this applies to this context.
A	Explain fully the role that temperature plays in this process.
	Explain fully the role that temperature plays in this process and why air has to be kept out but the gas allowed to escape.

STEP 4

What determines whether the yeast will respire aerobically or anaerobically? Why does Richard want them to respire anaerobically?

Fermenters

You will find out:
- That a fermenter is a vessel in which micro-organisms are grown to make useful products
- That the mould Penicillium is used to produce the antibiotic penicillin
- That the fungus Fusarium is used to make mycoprotein

Life-saving mould!

The blue mould in figure 1 is a **mould** (**fungus**) called Penicillium. This sample has been grown on some agar jelly with some starch added to it. The very first **antibiotic** ever discovered, **penicillin**, is made by this mould. It is grown (cultured) on a very large scale, making huge quantities of the antibiotic that can be used to cure many different diseases caused by bacteria.

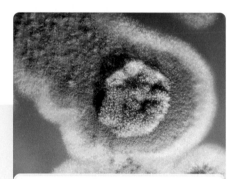

FIGURE 1: *Penicillium chrysogenum* – a mould that can save lives!

Fermenters

The diagram in figure 2 shows a **fermenter**. A fermenter is a large vessel, usually made of metal, in which micro-organisms are grown in great quantities to produce useful substances such as antibiotics.

A small quantity of the mould is put inside the fermenter and mixed into a liquid containing all the nutrients that it needs. These include:

- sugar, to provide energy
- amino acids and proteins, to help the fungus to grow and produce new cells.

The fermenter is designed to provide the mould with everything that it needs. It has:

- an air supply, so that the mould can respire aerobically
- a stirrer, so that the mould doesn't sink to the bottom
- a water-cooled 'jacket', to stop the contents of the fermenter getting too hot
- a thermometer, to monitor the temperature inside the fermenter
- a pH meter, to monitor the level of acidity inside the fermenter.

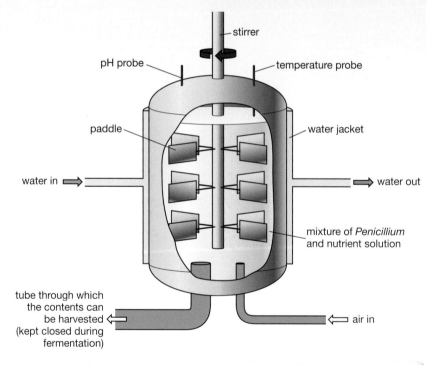

FIGURE 2: This fermenter is being used to grow *Penicillium chrysogenum*.

QUESTIONS

1   What is the difference between *Penicillium* and penicillin?
2   Why do fermenters have an air supply?
3   What might happen if the liquid inside the fermenter gets too hot?

...antibiotic   ...batch culture   ...continuous culture   ...fermenter   ...fungus

Making penicillin

The graph in figure 3 shows the timescale of the production of penicillin in the fermenter. You can see from the graph that the mould doesn't start to make *penicillin* straight away. First, it just grows, gradually using up the sugars and amino acids in the liquid inside the fermenter.

The *Penicillium* doesn't start to make penicillin until it has used up practically all of the nutrients in the fermenter.

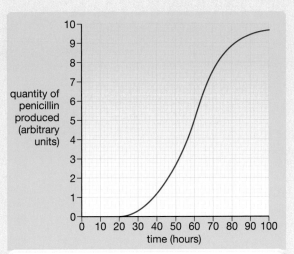

FIGURE 3: Production of penicillin.

Making mycoprotein

A fungus called **Fusarium** *graminearum* is grown in fermenters to produce a food called **mycoprotein**. It was developed as an alternative to meat for use in vegetarian diets.

The fungus is grown in huge vats, containing starch on which it feeds. The starch often comes from waste from the processing of other foods. For example, it might come from the left-overs from processing wheat to make flour. The fungus is given plenty of air, so that it can respire aerobically for maximum growth.

FIGURE 4: Mycoprotein produced by fermentation of *Fusarium* makes an excellent protein-rich food.

Unlike *Penicillium*, *Fusarium* is made up of long, thin threads called **hyphae**. So no stirrer is used – it would just tangle and break the hyphae. When they have grown enough, the threads are harvested, dried and pressed into cakes. They can be flavoured and shaped to make vegetarian 'meat' products.

Batch vs continuous culture

Penicillin is produced by a method called **batch culture**. This means that the fungus and its nutrients are put into the fermenter and no more nutrients are added during the fermentation. When fermentation stops, that batch of penicillin is harvested. The fermenter is cleaned out and a fresh batch is mixed.

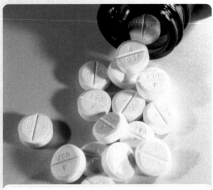

FIGURE 5: Penicillin tablets.

Mycoprotein is produced by **continuous culture**. The fungus and its nutrients are put into the fermenter. As the fungus produces new hyphae, it is steadily harvested from the base of the fermenter. Nutrients are added continuously.

QUESTIONS

Use the graph in figure 3 to answers questions 4, 5 and 6.

4 How long after being put into the fermenter does *Penicillium* start to produce penicillin?

5 During which time period is the rate of production of penicillin greatest?

6 What time do you think would be best to stop the fermentation and extract the penicillin? Explain your answer.

7 Suggest what needs to be done to the contents of the fermenter in order to extract the penicillin.

8 Why does mycoprotein make a good food for vegetarians?

QUESTIONS

9 Explain the difference between batch culture and continuous culture.

10 Suggest the advantages of making a product using continuous culture rather than batch culture.

11 Why can penicillin not be made by continuous culture?

Microbes and fuels

You will find out:
- About fuels that can be made by fermenting biological materials
- What biogas is and how it is made by anaerobic fermentation
- That ethanol can be made by fermenting sugars, and can be used as a fuel

What a waste!

Have you ever thought what a waste it is to flush all that lovely brown stuff down the toilet? In villages in some developing countries, not only cow dung but also human dung is made use of. It is used to produce a gas, called **biogas**, that can be used as fuel for cooking and lighting.

Biogas

Biogas is a fuel made from waste from living organisms. Biogas is made by allowing bacteria to ferment waste material from animals and plants.

Figures 2 and 3 show simple biogas generators. Waste material, such as cattle dung, human urine and faeces, and waste from processing vegetables, is put into the biogas generator. The generator is tightly covered, so that air cannot get in. Inside it, micro-organisms respire anaerobically, using the waste material. They produce a mixture of carbon dioxide and **methane**. This mixture is biogas.

The biogas rises and collects at the top of the closed fermenter. It can flow along pipes to wherever it is needed. People can burn it to keep warm, to cook food or to produce light.

FIGURE 1: A biogas generator in a Nepalese village.

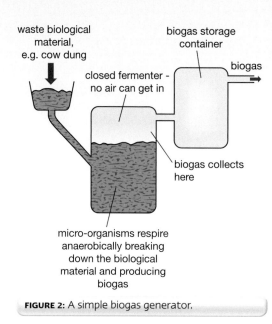

waste biological material, e.g. cow dung

closed fermenter - no air can get in

biogas storage container

biogas

biogas collects here

micro-organisms respire anaerobically breaking down the biological material and producing biogas

FIGURE 2: A simple biogas generator.

FIGURE 3: A biogas generator in India. Can you see where the fuel goes in, and where the lid of the fermenter is?

Many people living in villages in developing countries use biogas generators. But biogas can also be produced on a much larger scale. Figure 4 shows a biogas production plant in Italy. It runs on waste from processing sorghum (a grain). The gas produced in this plant is used as a fuel to generate electricity.

QUESTIONS

1   Suggest why 'biogas' is given this name.
2   Name the **two** gases that make up biogas.
3   Which one of these gases burns?
4   After the biogas has been made, there is still some solid waste material left in the biogas generator. How might people in a village in Nepal or India use this waste?

FIGURE 4: A large-scale biogas plant in Italy.

...anaerobic respiration   ...bioethanol   ...biogas   ...carbohydrase

Bioethanol

When we looked at **fermentation** to produce wine (page 41), we learnt that **yeast** can ferment sugars to produce **ethanol**. This can be done on a very large scale to produce ethanol that can be used as a fuel. It is sometimes called **bioethanol**.

One of the first countries to produce ethanol for fuel was Brazil. A lot of sugar cane is grown in Brazil, and the juices and waste from the sugar cane can be used by yeast in **anaerobic respiration** to produce ethanol.

Now other countries are also producing ethanol for fuel. For example, in the United States, starch from maize is broken down by the enzyme **carbohydrase** to produce the sugar glucose. Yeast is added to ferment the glucose in huge fermenters to produce ethanol.

In the UK, we import bioethanol from Brazil. It is mixed with petrol to make a fuel that we can use in cars. Most cars can run well on a mixture of 90% petrol and 10% ethanol. The fuel can be sold at the usual petrol pumps, and used in exactly the same way as ordinary petrol.

To run cars on pure ethanol requires major modifications to the design of the car engines. This has been done in Brazil, and about 5 million cars there run on ethanol alone. In the UK, we are beginning to produce some of our own bioethanol for fuel, and perhaps soon there will be cars designed to run just on ethanol, rather than petrol or diesel.

FIGURE 5: This rally car is running on bioethanol.

Green energy

Using biogas and bioenergy has several environmental advantages.

- If we use biological waste to make biogas or bioethanol, then we don't need to dispose of it in other ways that might cause pollution.

- Burning biogas or bioethanol doesn't produce sulfur dioxide.

- Using biogas or bioethanol is 'carbon neutral'. This means that the carbon dioxide emitted when the fuel burns is balanced out by the carbon dioxide taken in by the crops being grown to produce the fuels.

- We don't have to worry about the fuel running out. It is renewable.

- It might reduce the quantity of crude oil and petroleum products that are transported around the world, which would reduce the risk of oil pollution in the sea.

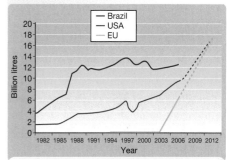

FIGURE 6: Actual and predicted (predicted shown as dotted line) ethanol production in Brazil, the USA and the EU since 1982.

Using microbes safely

You will find out:
- How to grow micro-organisms in a nutrient medium
- How to sterilise equipment used for growing micro-organisms
- How to avoid contamination with unwanted micro-organisms

Take care!

The door into your school laboratory probably doesn't have quite as many safety notices as the one in the photograph. Through this door, people work with dangerous micro-organisms. They have be very careful to take precautions not to infect themselves or anyone else with a serious disease.

In your school laboratory, you won't be growing anything dangerous. All the same, you need to treat the micro-organisms as though they might be nasty, just in case.

FIGURE 1: What do these notices tell you?

How to grow micro-organisms

It is quite easy to grow micro-organisms. Bacteria and fungi need these things to grow:

- carbohydrates, to provide them with energy
- mineral ions.

Sometimes, they also need:

- proteins
- vitamins

although sometimes they can make these for themselves.

We can put these things either into a liquid or a jelly. The micro-organisms can then grow in or on the mixture. The liquid or jelly is called a **nutrient medium**.

Growing micro-organisms in agar

Figures 2 and 3 show you how you can safely grow micro-organisms in jelly in a Petri dish. The jelly is called **agar**.

Hold the metal loop in the flame to kill off any micro-organisms on it.

Then dip the sterile loop into the liquid where you want to get the micro-organisms from.

Hold the base of the Petri dish upside down (so no bacteria falls into it from the air) and gently spread the loop over it.

Then put the lid on quickly. Once again, seal the lid with adhesive tape.

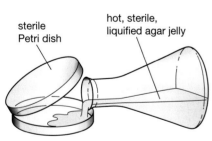

sterile Petri dish

hot, sterile, liquified agar jelly

Only lift the lid just as much as you need to, to pour in the sterile jelly.

Put the lid back on as quickly as possible. Seal the lid with adhesive tape to prevent micro-organisms from the air contaminating the agar. Then leave the jelly to cool and solidify.

FIGURE 2: Preparing a Petri dish of agar jelly.

FIGURE 3: Putting micro-organisms on to the jelly.

QUESTIONS

1. What is meant by a 'nutrient medium'?
2. What should be contained in a nutrient medium?

...agar ...nutrient medium ...pure culture

Avoiding contamination

If we want micro-organisms to make something useful for us, then it is important that we grow only the particular kind of micro-organisms that we want. A culture of just one species of micro-organism is called a **pure culture**.

There are several things we can do to prevent unwanted micro-organisms getting into a culture. These procedures are called **sterile technique**.

Keep the dish upside down, so condensation doesn't drip down onto the agar jelly

Tape the base to the top

FIGURE 4: How to avoid contamination of a loaded Petri dish.

- All equipment should be **sterilised** before we begin. Sterilising means killing all micro-organisms that might be on the equipment. Metal objects, such as a wire loop, can be sterilised by holding them in a flame. Plastic Petri dishes are sterile when we buy them, and are packed inside sterile bags. We can sterilise glass Petri dishes by heating them to a high temperature.

- The nutrient medium should also be sterilised. If it is a liquid, it should be boiled thoroughly and then sealed and allowed to cool. To make agar jelly, agar powder is dissolved in liquid then heated to a high temperature. It is allowed to cool until it is still just runny, then quickly poured into the sterile dish.

- You must not touch the agar jelly with your fingers, because there will be bacteria on them, however clean you think they are! Don't breathe over it, either.

- After putting the micro-organisms on to the agar jelly in the Petri dish, seal the dish with tape so that no-one can accidentally take the top off.

It also helps to keep the cultures at a temperature of about 25 °C. If we kept them at human body temperature, then we might encourage the growth of micro-organisms that live and breed in the body. These might be pathogens.

FIGURE 5: A microbiologist transferring micro-organisms from one culture to another.

Obtaining a pure culture

Imagine you want to find out what bacteria are present in a sample of liquid. You would like to identify some of the species, then grow pure cultures of them so that you can study their characteristics.

A good way to start is to try growing the bacteria on different nutrient media, such as different kinds of nutrient agar. The nutrient media can be made up so that only one or two species of bacteria are able to grow well on each kind. They are called **selective media**.

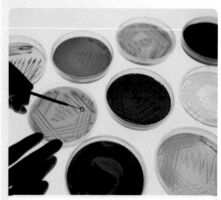
FIGURE 6: Different bacterial strains will have grown on the different nutrient agar jellies.

Each little blob – a bacterial colony – that appears on the agar jelly will have grown from a single bacterium. With luck, you will only have two or three species of bacterium growing on each of the different kinds of agar.

QUESTIONS

3 What does 'sterilised' mean?

4 Suggest **two** reasons why it is important to stop people taking the top off a Petri dish containing a culture.

5 Look at figure 5.
   a Suggest what the flame is for.
   b Suggest why the microbiologist is wearing a lab. coat and gloves.

QUESTIONS

6 Suggest why the colonies of bacteria growing in the dishes in figure 6 are arranged in a squiggly pattern.

7 What would you do next, to obtain a pure culture of just one species of bacterium?

Unit summary

Biogas is made by fermentation of biological waste.

Micro-organisms are used to make fuels.

Bioethanol is made by fermentation of sugars.

Bacteria are used to make cheese and yoghurt.

Micro-organisms

The idea that micro-organisms appeared spontaneously was disproved by scientists such as Spallanzani and Pasteur.

Micro-organisms are used to make food.

Micro-organisms must be handled carefully to avoid contamination and infection.

Yeast is a single-celled fungus that is used to make bread, beer and wine.

Micro-organisms are grown in fermenters to make useful products.

The fungus *Fusarium* makes mycoprotein (Quorn).

The fungus *Penicillium* makes the antibiotic penicillin.

Unit quiz

1. What kind of organism is yeast?

2. What does yeast make when it respires anaerobically?

3. Name **two** food products that are made using bacteria.

4. What is the name of the sugar in milk, which is changed to lactic acid during the production of yoghurt?

5. What is meant by the term biogenesis?

6. In which century did Spallanzani do his experiments that questioned the idea of biogenesis?

7. Explain how Pasteur's swan-necked flasks helped to disprove the theory of biogenesis.

8. What is a fermenter?

9. Why do fermenters often have a stirrer?

10. Why do fermenters producing mycoprotein not have a stirrer?

11. What **two** gases are present in biogas?

12. What is bioethanol?

13. How is agar jelly used to grow micro-organisms?

14. Explain why a metal loop is held in a Bunsen flame before being used to add bacteria to agar jelly.

15. Explain why we should not culture micro-organisms at body temperature.

Literacy activity

Theodore Schwann

Theodore Schwann lived in Germany between 1810 and 1882. He was a physiologist – a scientist who studies life processes.

At this time, scientists were in the middle of a fierce debate about the theory of spontaneous generation. Although Spallanzani's experiments had showed that no micro-organisms developed in broth if this was sealed off from the air, many people said that this was because air had an 'essential quality' that was needed for the microbes to live, not because it had stopped any microbes from getting in. Schwann attempted to take Spallanzani's experiments a bit further by passing air through acid, or by heating it, and then showing that no microbes appeared in sealed flasks of sterile broth containing this air. Even this, though, did not silence the supporters of the spontaneous generation theory, who just said that the acid and heat had removed the 'essential quality' from the air that was needed for microbes to appear and to live.

Nevertheless, Schwann's experiments helped Pasteur to plan and carry out his much more conclusive experiments, which were done just a few years later. Schwann also has many other claims to fame, for example, discovering that all living things are made of cells.

QUESTIONS

1. What is a physiologist?
2. Explain why Schwann thought his experiment disproved spontaneous generation.
3. On what grounds did supporters of spontaneous generation disagree with Schwann's conclusions?
4. Suggest how Schwann's work may have inspired Pasteur in the design of his experiments using swan-necked flasks.

Exam practice

1 Yeast is used in many processes to produce food and drink products.

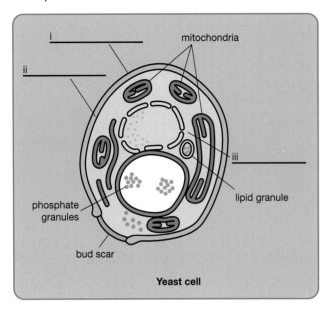

Yeast cell

a Copy the diagram and fill in the missing names for the parts of the cell. [3]

b Yeast can respire with or without oxygen. Copy and complete the following passage choosing from the words below to fill in the gaps.

sugar   heat   carbon dioxide
expands   rise   respiration

In the process of making bread, yeast is used to provide _____ _____. This is gained as a product of its _____. The yeast uses the _____ added to the dough mixture to produce energy. The resulting gas is contained within the dough and _____ when the bread is cooked. This causes the bread to _____ and gives it a fluffy texture. The yeast is killed off by the _____ in the cooking process. [6]

2 Yeast is also used to make alcoholic products such as beer and wine. Copy the following sentences, putting them into the correct order.

A Hops are then added to give the beer flavour.
B The starch in barley grains is broken down into a sugary solution by enzymes in the germinating grains, in a process called malting.
C The sugary solution is extracted and then fermented. [3]

3 Micro-organisms are used in the production of medicinal products such as penicillin. An industrial fermenter like the one shown below is used in this process.

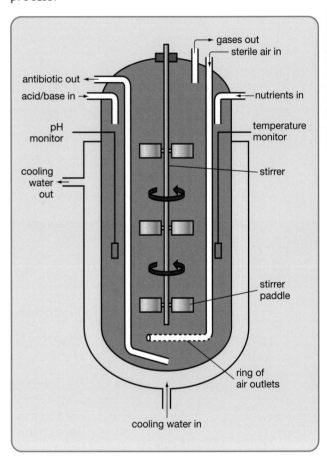

Answer the following questions.

a **i**   Why is the liquid stirred? [1]
    ii   For what purpose is air pumped in? [1]
    iii Why must the air be sterile? [1]
    iv How is the temperature controlled? [1]

b Agar is used in the culturing of bacteria in laboratories. Specific agar can be used to grow specific types of bacteria. The agar powder is mixed with water whilst being heated and then sterilised. It can then be poured into Petri dishes and left to cool and solidify. Which of the following are the main constituents of agar?

fat   protein   mineral ions   starch
carbohydrate   vitamins [3]

(Total 19 marks)

A biogas generator was set up in the laboratory to make gaseous fuel by anaerobic fermentation of organic matter.

The generator was filled with a mixture of grass cuttings, kitchen vegetable waste and water. This was then mixed into a creamy paste called slurry.

Every day the generator was checked to see if the liquid in the manometer had moved and if the gas being produced was flammable.

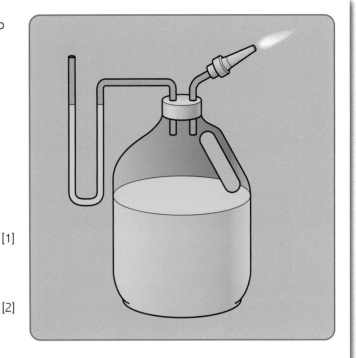

a At first the generator produced a gas that was not flammable. Suggest what this gas was. [1]

b After a few days the generator began to produce a flammable gas. Give the name **and** the chemical formula for this gas. [2]

c When the generator has stopped producing the first gas and has started producing the second, flammable gas, which type of respiration are the bacteria undergoing? [1]

d Give some advantages of biogas as a fuel source. [3]

(Total 7 marks)

The answer is half correct. The generator produces methane. The student has not given its chemical formula, CH_4.

ai) *The first gas produced from the generator was carbon dioxide.*

ii) *Methane.*

iii) *The bacteria are undergoing anaerobic respiration.*

iv) *It is a renewable resource and it is cheaper than fossil fuels or nuclear power.*

This is the correct answer, only some of the bacteria present are undergoing anaerobic respiration, those that cannot do this will die off.

These answers are correct but are not enough for the three marks. Other answers include: it is environmentally clean; its residue, called activated sludge, can be used as a fertiliser.

This is the correct answer. The generator, although not inoculated with a culture, contained bacteria that respire aerobically. The gaseous product of aerobic respiration is usually CO_2.

Overall Grade: B

How to get an A

Care should be taken when answering questions. Always refer to the number of marks available for each question. The specification says you should know about the advantages and disadvantages of given types of biogas generator. Make sure that you know about generators that could be used in the home and those that could be used to generate large amounts of methane to be used as fuel for a power station.

Chemistry 3a

DISCOVER THE PH SCALE!

The pH scale is used to measure the acidity of a solution – or the activity of its hydrogen ions. The scale was invented by the Danish chemist Soren Peder Lauritz Sorensen in the early twentieth century.

pH stands for *pondus hydrogenii*, or 'power of hydrogen'.

Most substances have a pH in the range 0 to 14, although there are exceptions. Acid mine run-off has a pH of -3.6.

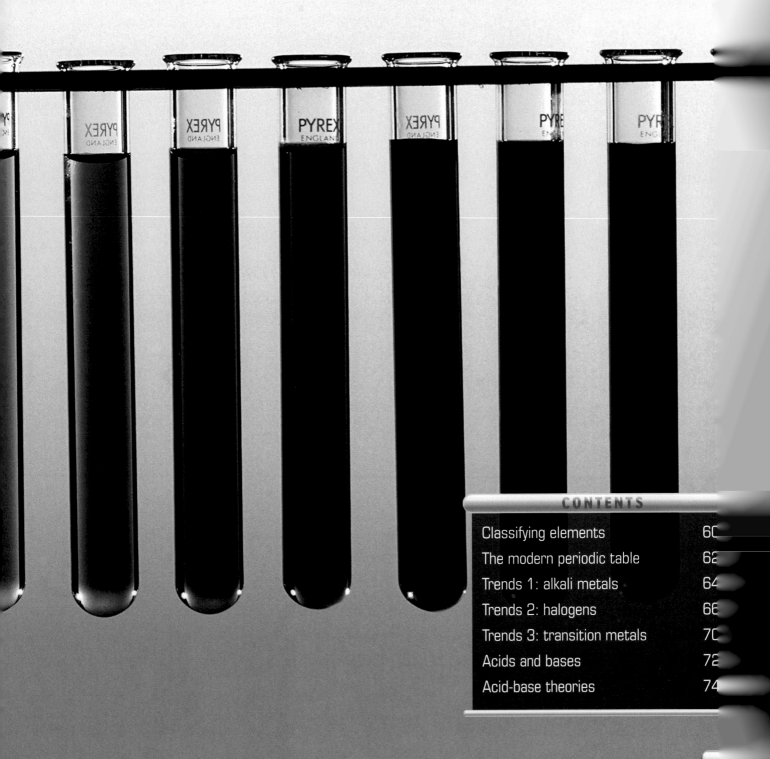

The pH value of a solution can be measured by adding pH indicator, which changes colour according to the acidity or alkalinity of the solution.

A pH meter is an electronic instrument which consists of a measuring probe connected to an electronic meter that measures and displays the pH value.

CONTENTS

Classifying elements

You will find out:
- How ideas about classifying elements have developed through history
- How the periodic table was developed
- The origins of the modern periodic table

Grouping elements

As scientists learned more about **elements** and **atoms**, they wanted to find a way to classify elements. In the 1780s, Lavoisier divided the elements he knew about into four classes. John Dalton (1766–1844) realised that **atomic mass** was an important property. In the early 1860s, John Newlands noticed that if you put the elements in order of their atomic mass, every eighth element had similar properties. He called this his 'Law of Octaves'.

FIGURE 1: John Newlands (top-left) predicted the classification of elements into eight groups in 1864, just before Lothar Meyer (top-right) and Dmitri Mendeleev (middle) independently developed a periodic table of elements in 1869–70.

Mendeleev and Meyer's race

Dmitri Mendeleev and Lothar Meyer, working independently, took these ideas further and put the elements into a table, in eight **groups** (columns). They concentrated on the chemical properties of elements for this classification, putting elements with similar properties in the same group. The result was the predecessor of the modern periodic table we use today. Mendeleev's table came out first, in 1869, and Meyer's appeared in 1870, so it is Mendeleev's name that tends to be remembered.

QUESTIONS

1. Why did Newlands name his law the 'Law of Octaves'?
2. What properties of elements did Mendeleev use to classify them?
3. What does the term 'periodic', in periodic table, mean?

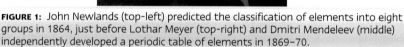
...atom ...atomic mass ...element ...group

Early periodic tables

Newlands' Octaves *(his 'periodic table' of 1864)*							
H	Li	Ga	B	C	N	O
F	Na	Mg	Al	Si	P	S
Cl	K	Ca	Cr	Ti	Mn	Fe
Co, Ni	Cu	Zn	Y	In	As	Se
Br	Rb	Sr	Ce, La	Zr	Di, Mo	Ro, Ru
Pd	Ag	Cd	U	Sn	Sb	Te
I	Cs	Ba, V	Ta	W	Nb	Au
Pt, Ir	Tl	Pb	Th	Hg	Bi	Cs

FIGURE 2: Newlands' Table of Octaves.

Newlands recognised that the elements have a repeating pattern of properties when grouped according to their atomic mass. His table of elements has eight groups and the elements at the top of the table have lower atomic masses than those lower down.

Group / Period	I	II	III	IV	V	VI	VII	VIII
1	H							
2	Li	Be	B	C	N	O	F	
3	Na	Mg	Al	Si	P	S	Cl	
4	K	Ca	*	Ti	V	Cr	Mn	Fe Co Ni
4	Cu	Zn	*	*	As	Se	Br	
5	Rb	Sr	Y	Zr	Nb	Mo	*	Ru Rh Pd
5	Ag	Cd	In	Sn	Sb	Te	I	

* Indicates a blank left by Mendeleev in his table

FIGURE 3: Mendeleev's original periodic table.

Mendeleev divided elements into eight groups (the columns) and then listed **periods** (the rows) of elements. As in Newlands' table, the elements at the top have lower atomic masses than those lower down.

The elements in columns all have similar properties. For example, group VII: fluorine, chlorine, bromine and iodine were all placed in this group by Mendeleev. These are known today as the **halogens**, and are in Group VII of the modern periodic table.

Mendeleev's problems

If you look at Mendeleev's table (figure 3), you will see that he used a double-column system. He put in elements that seemed to fit, but for which he knew something was not quite right. Most of these are the **transition elements**, which are now placed differently in the modern periodic table (see page 62).

He also realised that there were gaps – places in the table where an element should be. No known element fitted these gaps, so Mendeleev worked out that they had not yet been discovered.

The table we use today dates back to the 1940s, when Glenn Seaborg discovered plutonium in 1940 and then all the **transuranic elements**, with atomic numbers 94 to 102. He placed the actinide series below the lanthanide series as separate blocks. The importance of the table was finally recognised in 1951, when Seaborg was awarded the Nobel Prize in chemistry. Mendeleev almost got it in 1906, but missed it by one vote!

QUESTIONS

4   List **two** similarities between Newlands' Table of Octaves and Mendeleev's first periodic table.

5   List **two** differences between Newlands' Table of Octaves and Mendeleev's first periodic table.

6   List **three** key differences between Mendeleev's first table and the modern Periodic Table on page 62.

QUESTIONS

7   What **two** main problems did Mendeleev have when he was putting together the first draft of his periodic table?

8   Did he manage to solve either of these problems? If so, describe how.

The modern periodic table

You will find out:
- How elements are classified using the modern periodic table
- Why the periodic table is a useful scientific tool
- How the arrangement of elements in the periodic table relates to the electronic structure of their atoms

The most useless element…

Dubnium, **atomic number** 105, is possibly the most useless element known! Only very small amounts of it have ever been made – these are so small, they cannot actually be seen. The first samples were made through nuclear reactions involving fusion of an isotope of californium, ^{249}Cf, with one of nitrogen, ^{15}N.

$$^{15}\text{N} + {}^{249}\text{Cf} \rightarrow {}^{260}_{105}\text{Db} + 4{}^{1}\text{n}$$

… but the periodic table is useful

The periodic table is a very powerful tool for studying the elements and how they combine. Elements are grouped according to their **reactivity** and the types of reactions they undergo.

FIGURE 1: The modern periodic table.

QUESTIONS

1 Mendeleev listed elements in order of increasing atomic weight (now called relative atomic mass).

   a According to what property are the elements arranged in the modern periodic table?

   b Which particle within the atom is responsible for this property?

2 How many elements are currently included in the periodic table? Could there ever be more? Explain your answer.

…alkali earth metals …alkali metals …atomic number

Today's periodic table

Figure 1 shows the periodic table of today. It puts elements in groups according to their atomic number (the number of **protons** they have), not their atomic mass. This has only been possible since the discovery of atomic structure in the early 1900s.

Trends down the table

The groups consist of elements with the same arrangement of electrons in their outer shells. So, for example, in the **alkali metals** in group I, lithium has a single electron in its outer shell, so do sodium and potassium, and so on. As you go down the group, the number of electrons increases – the extra electrons are all in the inner shells, while the outer shell still has one single electron. As that single outer electron gets further away from the nucleus, it is held on to far less tightly, so elements further down the table are much more reactive than those at the top.

The opposite is true for the elements on the right-hand side of the table that gain electrons when they react: the bigger the atom, the further away from the nucleus the outer shell is, so the harder job it has to attract electrons to gain a full outer shell. So, for example, reactivity in group VII, the **halogens**, decreases as you go down the group.

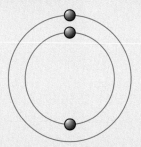

FIGURE 2: Lithium has three electrons, two in the inner shell and one in the outer shell

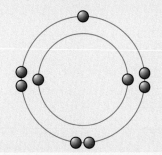

FIGURE 3: Fluorine has nine electrons, two in the inner shell and seven in the outer shell.

Trends across the table

The reactivity of metals decreases as you go from left to right in the periodic table. The group I elements, the alkali metals, are more reactive than the **alkali earth metals** in group II. These have two electrons in their outer shell and two are harder to lose than one!

As you go across the table, the elements in groups VI and VII have an almost full outer shell of electrons. When they react they are eager to gain electrons. Again, it is easier to gain one electron than two, so the halogens are more reactive than elements in group VI.

Including new and synthetic elements

Mendeleev anticipated the existence of elements that might be found after he had devised his first periodic table, but he did not predict the existence of group VIII, the **Noble gases**, or that some elements that do not exist in nature would be made by scientists.

Most of the artificial elements are by-products of radioactive decay of elements in the lanthanide and actinide groups. They are produced by bombarding other elements with alpha particles to change the number of protons in each atom.

QUESTIONS

6   There was one group of the periodic table that Mendeleev did not predict but that was discovered before he died. Research in books or on the Internet to find out which group it was, who discovered it and what it meant to Mendeleev.

7   How is it possible to produce an element artificially?

QUESTIONS

3   Which is more likely to react with chlorine; lithium or potassium? Explain your answer using diagrams showing the electronic configuration of the atoms.

4   Where are the non-metals in the periodic table? Name **five** non-metals.

5   What properties do elements in group VIII of the periodic table share? Explain your answer.

Trends 1: alkali metals

You will find out:
- About the physical and chemical properties of the alkali metals
- That reactivity of the alkali metals increases as you go down the group
- How the arrangement of electrons in alkali metals explains their properties

Odd metals

The **alkali metals** are rather odd metals. They have low melting points and low densities – the first three, lithium, sodium and potassium, actually float on water. They have little strength; sodium is like soft putty that can be cut with a knife. None of them is very shiny either.

FIGURE 1: Sodium metal is only shiny when it is freshly cut.

Trends in physical and chemical properties

The alkali metals are all the elements in group I (the first column) of the periodic table. From the top, they are: lithium, sodium, potassium, rubidium and caesium. All are reactive metals but they get more reactive as you go down the group: lithium is the least reactive, caesium is the most reactive.

Table 1 shows the melting points, boiling points and densities of all five alkali metals.

Element	Symbol	Atomic number	Melting point °C	Boiling point °C	Density g/cm^{-3}
Lithium	Li	3	181	1347	0.53
Sodium	Na	11	98	883	0.97
Potassium	K	19	64	774	0.86
Rubidium	Rb	37	39	688	1.48
Caesium	Cs	55	29	679	1.87

TABLE 1: The alkali metals.

▌▌ QUESTIONS ▐▐

1. Look at Table 1. Work out the differences in melting points between lithium and sodium, between sodium and potassium, and so on down the group. What do you notice?

2. Do the same thing for the atomic numbers. What do you notice? How does this relate to the position of the elements in the periodic table?

3. Which of the alkali metals could melt if left out in the sun on a hot day? Why?

Rubidium and caesium don't burn in water, they explode!

...alkali metals   ...alkaline   ...exothermic   ...hydroxide

Reactions of alkali metals with cold water

If you place a piece of lithium, sodium or potassium on the surface of cold water in a wide beaker it will float. Sodium and potassium are likely to move around and fizz. Potassium may burn with a blue flame. The flame is burning hydrogen; it is a purple colour because it has some potassium ions in it.

Rubidium and caesium don't burn in water, they explode!

All of these reactions are **exothermic** but, as you will notice, the reaction is more intense and violent as you go down the group in the periodic table.

All alkali metals react with water to produce **hydroxides**. These dissolve in the water to give strongly **alkaline** solutions (pH 14). An example of the equation for one of these reactions is:

$$2Li_{(s)} + 2H_2O_{(l)} \rightarrow 2LiOH_{(aq)} + H_{2(g)}$$
lithium   water   lithium hydroxide   hydrogen gas

Reactions with non-metal ions

Alkali metals react with non-metals to form **ionic compounds** in which the metal ion carries a charge of +1. These ionic compounds are colourless or white.

Alkali metals burn in oxygen or air with coloured flames, but they react to form white **oxides**. For example:

$$4Li_{(s)} + O_{2(g)} \rightarrow 2Li_2O_{(s)}$$
lithium   oxygen   lithium oxide

These oxides react with water to form strongly alkaline metal hydroxide solutions (pH 14).

Alkali metals also burn in chlorine to form colourless ionic compounds such as lithium chloride (Li^+Cl^-). These chlorides are soluble in water and give neutral solutions (pH 7). For example:

$$2Li_{(s)} + Cl_{2(g)} \rightarrow 2LiCl_{(s)}$$
lithium   chlorine   lithium chloride

FIGURE 2: Lithium-ion rechargeable batteries took a long time to develop due to the instability of lithium metal.

QUESTIONS

4 Why are alkali metals stored under oil?

5 Write a balanced equation for the reaction between sodium and water.

6 What type of ions do the alkali metals form?

7 What happens when sodium burns in chlorine? What is formed and what is the reaction?

Explaining the trends using atomic theory

Each of the alkali metals has an outer shell containing just one single electron. This electron transfers very easily to another atom, which is why the group is very reactive. The arrangement of electrons in the different alkali metals also explains why reactivity increases down the group.

From lithium down to caesium, the atom of each element has an extra full electron shell. Each still has a single electron in its outer shell but, as the atoms get larger, this outer electron gets further away from the pull of the positive charge of the nucleus. The extra layers of negatively charged electrons decrease the pull of the nucleus still further. So the larger the atom, the more loosely held the outer electron, making it even easier for it to be transferred to another atom to form an ionic compound.

QUESTIONS

8 Use simple electron diagrams of lithium, sodium and rubidium to show why the reactivity of the alkali metals increases as you go down group I of the periodic table.

9 Explain what happens to the outer electron of a sodium atom when it reacts with water to form sodium hydroxide. Include a balanced equation and electron diagrams in your answer.

...ionic compound ...oxide

Trends 2: halogens

You will find out:
- About the physical and chemical properties of the halogens
- That reactivity of the halogens increases as you go down the group
- How the arrangement of electrons in the halogens explains their properties

Halogens – friend and foe?

The **halogen** gases, fluorine and bromine, are very poisonous and dangerous. Chlorine gas was used as a chemical weapon in World War I. But, further down the group, the liquid iodine has been used as an antiseptic.

FIGURE 1: In World War I, chlorine gas was used as a chemical weapon, with dreadful effects.

Physical properties of the halogens

All the halogens are coloured and the colour gets darker as you go down the group. Fluorine is a pale yellow gas, chlorine gas is yellow/green; bromine is a dark red liquid with a brown vapour and iodine is a black solid with an intense purple vapour.

All of the halogens exist as an element as molecules made up of pairs of atoms. The bonding that holds the atoms together is **covalent** and this is broken when halogens react.

FIGURE 2: Three of the halogens; chlorine, bromine and iodine.

Trends in melting and boiling points

The halogens are in group VII of the periodic table. Table 1 shows their melting and boiling points, which both increase as you go down the group.

Halogen	Symbol	Atomic number	Melting point °C	Boiling point °C
Fluorine	F	9	−219	−188
Chlorine	Cl	17	−101	−34
Bromine	Br	35	−7	59
Iodine	I	53	114	184

TABLE 1: The melting points and boiling points of the halogens.

▪ QUESTIONS ▪

1 How does the appearance of the halogens change as you go down the group?
2 Which halogens are gases, which are liquids and which are solids at room temperature (21 °C)?

...*covalent*   ...*displace*   ...*halide ion*

Trends in chemical properties

All the halogens are reactive non-metals, but they get less reactive as you go down the group: fluorine is the most reactive, iodine is the least reactive. Note that this is the opposite of the alkali metals' trend!

The halogens all need one electron to fill their outer shell of electrons: they gain this electron when they react. All the halogens show very similar chemical properties.

Halogens react with metals to form **ionic salts** in which the **halide ion** has a charge of −1. An example of the reaction equation is:

$$Mg_{(s)} + Cl_{2(g)} \rightarrow MgCl_{2(s)}$$
magnesium   chlorine   magnesium chloride

Halogens also form compounds with other non-metals. The bonding between these molecules is covalent, not ionic. An example is the reaction of chlorine with hydrogen to form hydrogen chloride (hydrochloric acid when dissolved in water).

$$H_{2(g)} + Cl_{2(g)} \rightarrow 2HCl_{(g)} \qquad HCl + H_2O \rightarrow H^+_{(aq)} + Cl^-_{(aq)}$$

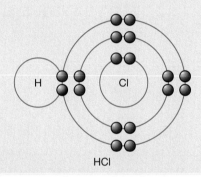

HCl

FIGURE 3: Hydrogen and chlorine share an electron so that they can both have a full outer shell.

Displacement activity

The reactivity order of the halogens can be demonstrated by seeing which ones **displace** which others from a salt in aqueous solution. If you add chlorine water to an aqueous solution of potassium bromide, chlorine displaces bromine to form potassium chloride and bromine:

$$Cl_{2(aq)} + 2KBr_{(aq)} \rightarrow 2KCl_{(aq)} + Br_{2(aq)}$$

Chlorine also displaces iodine from potassium iodide. Bromine displaces iodine from potassium iodide and iodine does not react. Fluorine displaces all other halogens.

Electron shells: size matters

Astatine is the radioactive halogen below iodine in the periodic table. It does not occur naturally, but we can predict its properties.

A halogen molecule consists of two atoms held together by a covalent bond. This becomes easier to break as you go down the group as the outer electrons are further away from the nucleus and are held less tightly. But the increase in distance from the nucleus and the shielding by many more layers of negative charge also means that the larger individual atoms do not gain electrons as easily as the smaller atoms. Overall, the reaction requires more energy, so astatine, at the bottom of the group, will be the least reactive halogen.

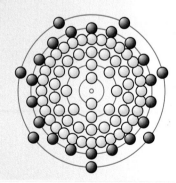

FIGURE 4: The electron shells of astatine (atomic number 85).

QUESTIONS

3   How do the halogens differ from alkali metals in the pattern of their reactivity?

4   How could you show that fluorine is more reactive than bromine?

5   Write balanced equations for the reactions between chlorine and **two** of the alkali metals.

QUESTIONS

6   Why does iodine not react as well with an alkaline metal as chlorine? Include balanced equations and electron diagrams in your answer.

Manaccanite

SELF-CHECK ACTIVITY

The year is 1791 and the place Manaccan, a small village in the far South West of Cornwall. The local vicar, the Reverend William Gregor is pursuing his hobby of studying rocks and minerals. He has already collected many local samples and catalogued them, but he now comes across a material he hasn't seen before.

"Charlotte, Charlotte," he calls out as he emerges from his workshop. His wife rushes out of the drawing room with a concerned expression on her face.
"What is it?"
"Look, look at this!" He shows her the reddish brown substance.
"Where did it come from? What is it?" she asks.
"You remember the black sand I found down in the valley?" he hurriedly explains, "You know, that turned out to be magnetic? Well, I reduced it to a calx and this is it. I do believe it is a new material!"

Gregor called the new material manaccanite, after the place where he found it. Although he didn't succeed in purifying it, his findings were published that year, but aroused little interest.

Today manaccanite is a material with a range of uses, but one of the most important ones is for building aircraft and spacecraft. In both cases strength and low weight are important and it has advantages over both steel and aluminium. It now has a different name. Here are some clues:
- It is a metal.
- Compared with Group 1 metals it is:
    stronger and harder
    denser
    reaches its melting point at a higher temperature.
- Its ions can have different charges.
- It forms coloured compounds.
It was independently discovered a few years later by another scientist who gave it its modern name. In this activity you will need to do a bit of detective work to try and find out which element it is.

CHALLENGE

Which part of the Periodic Table contains metals?

Manaccanite has a high melting point, way beyond 1200 °C. Which part of the Periodic Table contains metals with this order of melting point?

STEP 3

It has electrons in four shells. In the fourth shell it has two electrons, and the third shell is incomplete. Which part of the Periodic Table can you now narrow it down to?

STEP 4

You will now need to consider the properties of the material. It has a similar tensile strength to steel, but is 40% lighter. It is heavier than aluminium but significantly stronger. Its combination of high strength and low weight means that it is widely used in aircraft construction – around 77 tonnes are used to build an Airbus A380 'double-decker' airliner. Can you work out which element it is?

Maximise your grade

These sentences show what you need to include in your work to achieve each grade. Use them to improve your work and be more successful.

Grade	Answer includes...
F	Locate examples of metals in the periodic table.
	Locate the section of the periodic table which is exclusively metals.
	Locate information about the melting points of metals.
	Find out which section of the periodic table has metals with very high melting points.
C	Explain what is meant by electron shell structure.
	Find the section of the periodic table which has elements with shell structures that correspond to the one in the text.
A	Use the other information and conduct research to identify the correct element.
	Identify the correct element and explain your reasoning with clarity.

STEP 5

Finally, a couple of other clues to help.
- Its current name is based on the name of a group of people in Greek mythology.
- Its oxide is used to make white paint.

Trends 3: transition metals

You will find out:
- The physical and chemical properties of the transition metals
- That their reactivity increases down the group
- How the arrangement of electrons in the transition metals explains their properties

Gleaming chromium

Chromium is one of the shiniest metals. It has been used here to construct an enormous sculpture that stands in Chicago, USA. It does not tarnish like iron and is a striking modern landmark. We also use chromium in our homes to plate taps and fittings, giving our bathrooms and showers some of the same gleam.

FIGURE 1: Transition metals – strong and structural. The jelly bean sculpture in Chicago, USA, is made of chromium and this bridge in England is made from iron.

Metals as you expect them

The alkali metals are atypical, but the **transition metals**, between groups II and III of the periodic table, are much more as you would expect. They are strong, hard, shiny and are all solid at room temperature. The transition metals have properties similar to one another and to other metals, but their properties do not fit in with those of any other family of the periodic table. Most transition metals are good conductors of heat and electricity. Transition metals are generally less reactive than the metals in groups I and II of the periodic table, but there are exceptions.

EXAM HINTS AND TIPS

Remember: the exception to the metal rule is mercury: it has a melting point of −38.8 °C and is a liquid at room temperature

QUESTIONS

1 What are the physical properties of metals, as illustrated by the transition metals?
2 Name as many transition metals as you can.
3 List **three** things you have used today that are made from transition metals.

...electron arrangement   ...shell

But they still have some surprises (H)

As with other periods of the periodic table, looking at how electrons are arranged in the atoms of the transition elements helps to explain how they react with other elements. In the elements you have looked at so far, the outer **shell** of electrons is full if it has eight electrons. Transition elements have high atomic numbers. They have a lot of electrons and they are able to put more than eight in the shell that is one in from the outer shell.

The atoms of transition metals can have up to 18 or 32 electrons in their second-to-outermost shell. For example, iron (Fe) has 26 electrons arranged 2-8-14-2. Cobalt (Co) has 27 electrons arranged 2-8-15-2. The outer shell in both elements is full with two electrons – the extra electron in the cobalt atom is placed in the second shell in. This continues across the period until the inner shell is full with 18 electrons. This occurs in zinc, which has 30 electrons arranged 2-8-18-2.

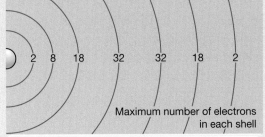

Maximum number of electrons in each shell

FIGURE 2: No shell can have more than 32 electrons – usually 18 or 32 is the maximum number.

Most elements use electrons from their outer shell to bond with other elements. Transition metals can have a full outer shell of two electrons but have an incompletely filled second-to-outermost shell. During reactions transition metals can accept and donate electrons from this inner shell.

Comparing the transition metals with the alkali metals

Transition metals have much higher boiling points and melting points than the metals in group I of the periodic table.

The melting points and boiling points of transition metals are much higher than those of the metals in group I (see page 64 for a comparison). Transition metals generally have many more electron shells than the alkali metals, so their atoms are bigger and they lose or gain electrons much less readily. This makes them much less reactive than the alkali metals.

	Titanium (Ti)	Chromium (Cr)	Manganese (Mn)	Iron (Fe)	Copper (Cu)	Zinc (Zn)
Melting point °C	1668	1857	1246	1538	1083	420
Boiling point °C	3287	2672	1962	2861	2567	907
Density g cm^{-3}	4.54	7.19	7.33	7.87	8.92	7.13

TABLE 1: Physical properties of some of the transition metals.

QUESTIONS

4 What is the electron arrangement in atoms of **a** copper, **b** zinc and **c** iron?

5 Are transition metals good conductors of heat and electricity? Explain your answer.

6 Name **three** transition metals not included in Table 1.

7 Choose **three** transition metals and list **two** uses for each.

Colourful compounds

The transition metals react with other elements to produce a huge range of compounds, many of which are brilliantly coloured. The colours arise because these compounds absorb light energy. The light energy that is absorbed promotes an unpaired electron in the second-to-outermost electron shell of the metal ion. It moves to the outer shell. The colour of the compound depends on the wavelength of light energy that is absorbed.

FIGURE 3: Copper sulfate is deep blue.

QUESTIONS

8 Research the industrial uses of **three** compounds made from transition metals.

Acids and bases

You will find out:
- The definitions of an acid and a base
- Some common reactions of acids and bases
- Which acids and bases are strong and which are weak

Natural acids

Acids and **bases** occur in nature. Ants squirt out a mixture of formic acid and other chemicals to ward off predators. The digestive system of most animals involves an acid stage – humans' stomachs produce hydrochloric acid to lower the pH to between 1 and 2.

FIGURE 1: Ants have an acid chemical weapon – that's why an ant bite hurts!

What are acids and bases?

For a substance to act as an acid or a base, water must normally be present. Acids produce **hydrogen ions** in **aqueous** solution. Remember that the hydrogen ion is a proton. In water, the hydrogen ion, the proton is **hydrated** and is shown in chemical equations as $H^+_{(aq)}$.

An acid is defined as a **proton donor**.

A base is defined as a **proton acceptor**.

Substances can be strong acids or weak acids or strong bases or weak bases. Examples of each are shown in Table 1.

Strong acid	Weak acid	Strong base	Weak base
Hydrochloric acid	Ethanoic acid	Sodium hydroxide	Sodium hydrogen carbonate
Nitric acid	Citric acid	Potassium hydroxide	Ammonia
Sulfuric acid	Carbonic acid		

TABLE 1: Examples of strong and weak acids and bases.

QUESTIONS

1 Think of some substances that you encounter every day that are either an acid or a base.

2 Write the definition of an acid and a base.

3 Name a strong and a weak base, then a strong and a weak acid.

...acid   ...alkali   ...aqueous   ...base   ...dissociation   ...hydrated   ...hydrogen ion

Why strong and weak?

The strength of acids and bases is explained by the extent to which the acid molecules split up (**ionise**) into ions in water. The ionisation of acids and bases in water is shown as equilibrium reactions.

Strong acids and bases are almost completely ionised in water, so the equilibrium lies far to the right.

Here are the **dissociation** reactions of a strong acid, nitric acid, and a strong base, sodium hydroxide.

$$HNO_{3(aq)} \rightarrow H^+_{(aq)} + NO_3^-_{(aq)}$$
$$NaOH_{(aq)} \rightarrow Na^+_{(aq)} + OH^-_{(aq)}$$

Weak acids are only partially ionised in water so form fewer ions in solution.

It is important not to confuse the words *strong* and *weak* with the terms *concentrated* and *dilute*. Concentration indicates how much of the original acid is dissolved in the solution. You can have a concentrated solution of a weak acid, or a dilute solution of a strong acid.

Acid reactions

Reactions with metals

Hydrochloric acid reacts with the metal calcium to form calcium chloride solution and hydrogen gas.

$$Ca_{(s)} + 2HCl_{(aq)} \rightarrow CaCl_{2(aq)} + H_{2(g)}$$

Sulfuric acid gives calcium sulfate solution and hydrogen gas.

$$Ca_{(s)} + H_2SO_{4(aq)} \rightarrow CaSO_{4(aq)} + H_{2(g)}$$

Reactions with bases

The reaction between an acid and a base is called a **neutralisation** reaction. Acids are neutralised by reaction with metals, oxides, hydroxides or carbonates to form salts and other products.

Metal oxides can react with acids to form salts. These metal oxides are known as basic oxides. The reaction produces a salt and water. For example:

$$CuO_{(s)} + H_2SO_{4(aq)} \rightarrow CuSO_{4(aq)} + H_2O_{(l)}$$

An **alkali** is a base that is soluble in water. In aqueous solutions they produce **hydroxide ions**, $OH^-_{(aq)}$. Alkalis, like all bases, react with an acid to give a salt and water. For example:

$$2NaOH_{(aq)} + H_2SO_{4(aq)} \rightarrow Na_2SO_{4(aq)} + 2H_2O_{(l)}$$

QUESTIONS

4 Write a balanced equation for the reaction between copper oxide (CuO) and hydrochloric acid.

5 What is a strong acid and what is a concentrated acid? When are they the same and when are they not?

6 What is an alkali and how does it react with an acid?

Neutralisation and pH

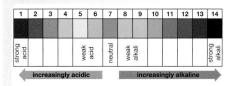

FIGURE 2: Acids and alkalis are measured on a pH scale.

If you add acid to an alkali (an aqueous solution of a base), the pH starts at 13 and falls gradually at first. As the neutralisation point is almost reached at pH 7, the change becomes more dramatic. This is the point where **titration** shows that neutralisation has occurred. With excess acid, the pH falls further and then levels out to about pH 1.

If you add alkali to an acid, the pH starts at about 1 and rises a little at first. Near the neutralisation point at pH 7, the change becomes more dramatic, and with excess alkali the pH continues to rise and then levels out to about 13.

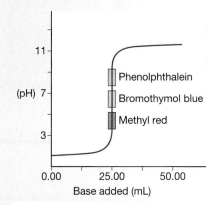

FIGURE 3: Plotting change in pH when an acid is neutralised by a base.

QUESTIONS

7 Find out the formulae of citric acid and carbonic acid and write balanced equations for their ionisation.

8 Describe a titration experiment you have done, or seen demonstrated.

...hydroxide ion   ...neutralisation   ...proton acceptor   ...proton donor   ...titration

Acid–base theories

You will find out:
- About Arrhenius, Lowry, Brønsted and Lewis and their contributions to acid-base theory
- Why some ideas are accepted more readily than others

Explaining acids and bases

Today we learn about acids and bases at school, but before the 1880s, nobody understood why **acids** and **bases** behaved the way they do.

In 1883, a young Swedish researcher, Svante Arrhenius said in his PhD thesis that ionic compounds **dissociate** and become free ions in solution. He said that acids produce **hydrogen ions** and bases produce **hydroxide ions**. This was revolutionary – earlier in the 1800s, Michael Faraday had thought about ions, but thought they were only produced when an electric current was passed through a solution.

Arrhenius' new idea didn't go down well – he almost lost his chance of a scientific career.

FIGURE 1: Svante Arrhenius (1859–1927).

Acceptance came later (H)

Arrhenius' work was not accepted immediately but, like all great scientists, he did not even think of giving up. He sent his thesis to other notable chemists in other countries – and some were impressed. The great chemist Wilhelm Ostwald recognised the brilliance of the theory and offered Arrhenius a post to work with him in Germany. Arrhenius developed his theories further and they were accepted in the early 1900s. In 1903, he was awarded the Nobel Prize.

Limitations of Arrhenius' theory (H)

Arrhenius' explanation of acids and bases only applied to **aqueous systems**. It does not explain why some compounds containing hydrogen, such as HCl, dissolve in water to give acidic solutions and why others, such as CH_4 (methane), do not. Also, the theory can only classify substances as bases if they contain the hydroxide ion (OH^-), and cannot explain why some compounds that do not contain OH^-, such as Na_2CO_3, act like bases.

■ QUESTIONS ■

1 What was Arrhenius' theory about acids and bases?
2 How long did it take for Arrhenius' theory to be accepted? Does this surprise you?

...acid   ...aqueous system   ...base   ...dissociate

Brønsted and Lowry   (H)

Some of the problems of Arrhenius' theory were overcome by a development of the acid-base theory in 1923, when the Danish chemist Johannes Brønsted and the English scientist Thomas Lowry published different papers with much the same theory.

FIGURE 2: Johannes Brønsted (1879–1947).

They proposed that an acid could be defined as 'a substance that can donate a proton (H^+)'.

They defined a base as 'a substance that can accept a proton (H^+)'.

These new definitions include acids and bases that are ions or neutral molecules. It also explains the role of water in acid-base reactions: H_2O accepts H^+ ions from acids to form H_3O^+ ions. Brønsted and Lowry's theory also applies to solutions with solvents other than water and to reactions that occur in the gas or solid phases.

This model of acids and bases does not mean the earlier model was wrong – it extends it and allows more compounds to be defined as acids. It also enables us to describe the strength of an acid or a base. The strength of an acid or a base depends on how well the compound dissociates in water: strong acids and bases dissociate almost completely.

Example of a strong acid

Hydrochloric acid is an example of a strong acid. It ionises almost completely when it dissolves in water. So it is a very good proton donor.

$$HCl_{(aq)} + H_2O_{(l)} \rightleftharpoons H_3O^+_{(aq)} + Cl^-_{(aq)}$$

0.004% at equilibrium   99.996% at equilibrium

Example of a weak acid

Ethanoic acid is an example of a weak acid. It ionises only slightly when it dissolves in water and so is a poor proton donor.

This is an equilibrium reaction. The majority of the solution is unionised ethanoic molecules:

$$HC_2H_3O_{2(aq)} + H_2O_{(l)} \rightleftharpoons H_3O^+_{(aq)} + C_2H_3O_2^-{}_{(aq)}$$

98.7% at equilibrium   1.33% at equilibrium

FIGURE 3: Strong and concentrated acids fume and are dangerous to handle

Lewis acids   (H)

Another scientist who made an important contribution to our knowledge of the chemistry of acids and bases was the American chemist Gilbert Lewis (1875–1946).

A **Lewis acid** is defined to be any molecule that accepts a single pair of electrons. A **Lewis base** is any molecule that donates a single pair of electrons. Thus, H^+ is a Lewis acid, since it can accept a pair of electrons, while OH^- and NH_3 are Lewis bases, both of which donate a pair of electrons.

$$H^+ + :\ddot{O}: H^- \rightarrow H_2O$$

Today, we usually say electrons rather than a pair of electrons, as sometimes it is just one!

FIGURE 4: Gilbert Lewis at work.

====== QUESTIONS ======

3   What theory did Brønsted and Lowry propose about acids and bases?
4   How was this theory different to that of Arrhenius?
5   Look at figure 1 of Arrhenius at work. Give **three** differences you would see between this and a scientist at work today.

====== QUESTIONS ======

6   Summarise Lewis' definition of an acid and a base.

Unit summary

Concept map

The way elements are classified developed over time. John Newlands, Lothar Meyer and Dmitri Mendeleev all contributed important ideas.

Mendeleev was the first to put the elements into a periodic table. This was the basis of the modern periodic table we use today.

Trends in chemical properties are seen down the groups and across the periods of the table.

The periodic table

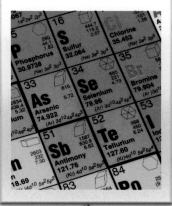

Group I is the alkali metals; typical metals with high boiling and melting points. Reactivity increases down the group. Group VII are the halogens – coloured gases, liquids and solids. Reactivity decreases down the group.

More typical metals are the transition elements found between Groups II and III. These are hard and shiny and are good conductors.

The theories to explain acids and bases developed as a result of the work of Svante Arrhenius, Johannes Brønsted, Thomas Lowry and Gilbert Lewis.

Acids and bases

Acids are defined as chemicals that produce hydrogen ions, donate protons or donate free electrons. They react with bases and are neutralised.

There are strong acids, strong bases, weak acids and weak bases. Strong acids and bases ionise almost completely in water. Weak acids and bases ionise less well.

The strength of an acid and its concentration are different. The concentration of an acid describes the amount of acid used to make up the solution. It is possible to have a dilute solution of a strong acid and a concentrated solution of a weak acid. The same applies for bases.

Unit quiz

1 What tool is used to classify all the elements we have today?

2 Why is this tool useful for studying how elements react?

3 What are the vertical and horizontal rows of this tool called?

4 Who was involved in developing this tool?

5 Name **three** alkali metals.

6 Name **three** halogens.

7 Name **six** transition metals.

8 What is special about the electron shells in the transition metals?

9 What is the definition of an acid?

10 What is the definition of a base?

11 Who put forward theories about acid and bases?

12 What is **a)** a strong and **b)** a weak acid?

13 What is **a)** a concentrated and **b)** a dilute base?

14 What is a neutralisation reaction?

Literacy activity

New periodic table invented

A new periodic table has been developed. It shows how chemical elements are distributed in nature, sorting them by electrical charge rather than atomic number.

Bruce Railsback of the University of Georgia in Athens, USA redesigned the periodic table after becoming tired with pointing at the original version in class.

The Earth's minerals consist mostly of electrically charged elements, or ions. These behave differently from the original periodic table's neutral atoms. Railsback grouped ions with similar charge according to where they are found. Some elements appear several times with different charges. Sulfur appears four times: S, S^{2+}, S^{4+} and even S^{6+}.

Geologists know that a mineral's properties – such as its melting point, or how easily it dissolves in water – depend on the size, charge and structure of its ions. Ions can be grouped into families with similar chemical behaviour, which are therefore found in similar natural environments.

The five families in Railsback's table represent minerals in soil, those in the Earth's crust and mantle, those dissolved in water, those in the atmosphere and those forming the basic nutrients of life.

QUESTIONS

1 How does the traditional periodic table sort elements and what criteria does the new one use?

2 Why do you think different scientists want to have different versions of the periodic table?

3 Apart from the criteria used for sorting, list **two** other differences between Railsback's table and the accepted one.

Exam practice

1 Copy the table below and put a tick if the property is true for that group of metals. The first one has been done for you.

	Transition metals	Group 1 metals
Good catalyst	✔	
Low melting point		
High reactivity		
Form coloured solids		
Low density		
Strong		
Ions may have different charges		

[6]

2 For this question choose an answer from the simple periodic table below.

Group 1	Group 2	Transition metals	Group 3	Group 4	Group 5	Group 6	Group 7	Group 0

a These elements have molecules made of two atoms and have coloured vapours.

b This group's atoms have a charge of 1+ and their reactivity increases as you go down the group.

c These elements are all metals and their ions may have different charges.

d This group forms ions with a charge of 1- and forms molecular compounds with non-metals.

e They are called the halogens.

f They have three electrons in their highest occupied energy level (outer shell). [6]

3 A piece of lithium is placed in water containing universal indicator.

a Give three observations that would be made. [3]

b Write a word equation for this reaction. [2]

c If a piece of potassium were placed on water, how would the observations be different? Explain this in terms of electrons. [3]

4 The graph shows the results obtained from a titration. Some 1.0 mol/dm^3 hydrochloric acid has been added to 20 cm^3 of a household cleaner. Use the graph to help answer these questions.

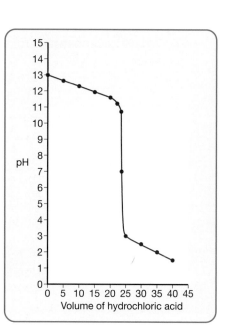

a What was the pH of the cleaner? [1]

b What volume of acid just neutralised the cleaner? [1]

c Name a suitable indicator for this titration. [1]

d Is the household cleaner more or less concentrated than the hydrochloric acid? Explain your reasoning. [2]

5 The graph shows the solubility of substance Z.

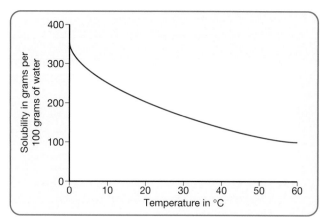

a Is Z a solid or a gas? Explain your reasoning. [2]

b How many grams of Z will dissolve in 100 g of water at 10 °C? [1]

c What extra mass of Z would dissolve in 100 g of water if it was cooled from 60 °C to 20 °C? [2]

(Total 30 marks)

A sample of water is being tested in the laboratory. 20 cm³ of the sample and 20 cm³ of distilled water are each shaken with 1 cm³ of soap solution in a boiling tube. The results are shown in the table.

	Water sample	Distilled water
Height of lather/mm	3	28
Appearance	cloudy	clear

a **i**   Is the sample hard or soft water? [1]
   ii Why does the sample appear cloudy after it has been shaken with soap solution? [1]
   iii What ions dissolved in the water sample could cause this to happen? [2]

b **i**   Describe in detail **two** ways of removing the hardness from a sample of water. [4]
   ii Give **one** advantage of hard water. [1]
   iii Give **two** disadvantages of hard water. [2]

c This diagram shows a simplified flow diagram of the treatment water receives before reaching your home.
   i   What is the purpose of filtration? [1]
   ii What is the purpose of chlorination? [1]
   iii What will remain in the water even after this treatment? [1]

(Total 14 marks)

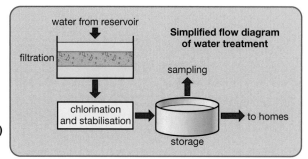

Simplified flow diagram of water treatment

water from reservoir

filtration

sampling

chlorination and stabilisation

storage

to homes

---

a *i*   *The sample is hard because it has gone cloudy and has not given a good lather.*
   ii *The sample has made scum. This forms when soap reacts with ions in the water.*
   iii *This might be from Ca²⁺ ions or Mg²⁺ ions which have got into the water through contact with rocks such as chalk and limestone.*

The student must have read the mark scheme! Good answers giving more than was needed for the marks.

Another good answer but the student missed the fact that **two** methods were needed in part i. A second way is to use an ion-exchange column. This contains H⁺ and Na⁺ ions which exchange places with the Ca²⁺ ions or Mg²⁺ ions as they pass through the column.

b *i*   *Hardness can be removed by treating the water with sodium carbonate (soda crystals). These react with the Ca²⁺ ions or Mg²⁺ ions causing them to precipitate out as calcium and magnesium carbonate.*
   ii *An advantage is that Ca²⁺ ions are good for your health. They are needed for strong bones and teeth and a healthy heart.*
   iii *Two disadvantages are that it needs much more soap to get a good lather, and that water heated in washing machines, kettles and boilers produces scale which may lead to them not working properly.*

Another thorough answer.

c *i*   *Filtration removes solid particles.*
   ii *Chlorination kills micro-organisms.*
   iii *Dissolved substances will still be present. Mostly this is good, giving the water a nice taste, but it might mean the water is hard or contains harmful nitrates.*

Overall Grade: A

How to get an A
Despite the fact that the student has missed out 2 marks on one part, this is still a first-rate answer and still gets an A. The student has learnt the work in detail and there are no gaps in his/her knowledge. Your notes and revision books are always useful but you must also look back at the Specification to see exactly what it is you must learn. Practise all the questions you can find and you will be able to write clear, full answers like this.

Chemistry 3b

DISCOVER WATER!

A water molecule contains one oxygen atom and two hydrogen atoms. The atoms are held together by strong covalent bonds. Without water there is no life. We are mostly water and all the chemical reactions in our cells need water. Many substances dissolve in water and most of the chemical reactions that support our lives take place there.

The purest water is water produced by distillation.

Water has very high surface tension, giving it the ability to form into almost spherical, clearly defined droplets.

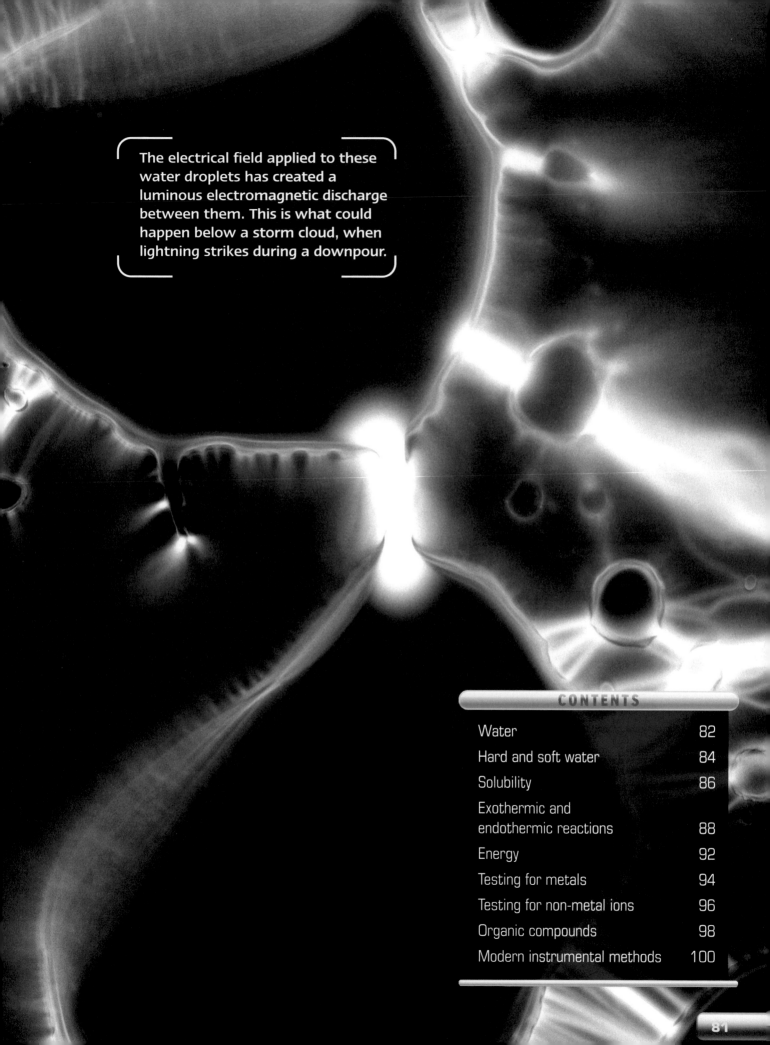

The electrical field applied to these water droplets has created a luminous electromagnetic discharge between them. This is what could happen below a storm cloud, when lightning strikes during a downpour.

CONTENTS

Water

You will find out:
- How water sources are chosen
- About the water cycle
- How water can be purified
- How distillation works

Snowflakes

Snowflakes are single crystals of ice. They form in clouds when water vapour condenses directly into ice. No two snowflakes are exactly the same.

FIGURE 1: Every snowflake is unique.

The blue planet

Viewed from space, the Earth appears to be a blue planet that is covered in water. Most of the world's water is found in oceans. Unfortunately the levels of dissolved salts are so high that drinking seawater would make you very ill. Other water is locked up in glaciers and icecaps. Only a very small amount of the water can actually be used. This water is continually being circulated in the **water cycle**. This process is driven by energy from the Sun.

Water is essential for life. People must drink water that is quite pure. If too many salts or too many **micro-organisms** are present in the water, it can cause diarrhoea, vomiting and even death. Special steps are taken to turn raw water into safe, drinking water.

Water can also be purified by **distillation**.

FIGURE 2: Most of the Earth's surface is covered by water.

How do we choose our water sources?

Water companies only choose suitable sources to supply our water. These sources should be away from any potential pollution problems. Rivers, ground water (water from underground supplies) and reservoirs can all be suitable.

FIGURE 3: A reservoir. What must water sources like this one be away from?

QUESTIONS

1 Why is Earth sometimes referred to as the 'blue planet'?
2 Where is most water on Earth found?
3 Why should people not drink seawater?

...disinfect   ...distillation   ...fluoridation

The water cycle

We have a very limited supply of water that is recycled again and again. In fact, the water that we are drinking today is the same water that was present thousands of years ago. The water cycle is driven by energy from solar radiation.

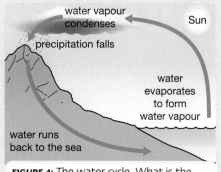

FIGURE 4: The water cycle. What is the energy source for this cycle?

As the Sun warms the water in the sea, some of this water evaporates to form water vapour. The water vapour condenses to form clouds. Eventually the air cannot hold any more water and it falls back to the ground as precipitation. Most of the water falls back into the seas, while some falls on to the land before running back to the sea, and the whole process starts again.

How is raw water changed into drinking water?

Water must be **purified** before it is safe to drink. First, any large pieces of debris such as sticks or leaves are removed. Then the water is filtered to remove any suspended particles such as small pieces of clay. The water is passed through filter beds consisting of layers of sand and activated charcoal. The charcoal helps to improve the taste of the water and also to remove unpleasant odours. Finally, the water is **disinfected**. Raw water may contain micro-organisms such as viruses, bacteria, protozoa and cryptosporidia. These tiny organisms can multiply very quickly and can cause illness or even death if consumed in large quantities. Chlorine is a very strong oxidising agent that is added to water to reduce the numbers of micro-organisms to acceptable levels.

How does distillation work?

Some countries have very limited supplies of fresh water but very plentiful supplies of fuel. In these countries water is purified by distillation. Seawater is heated to give the water molecules more kinetic energy so they move more quickly. Eventually some of the water molecules gain so much energy that they are able to escape from the liquid to form water vapour. Cold water flowing through the condenser cools the

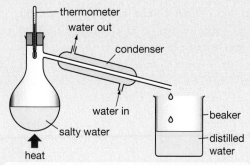

FIGURE 5: Have you set up distillation apparatus like this?

water vapour. It condenses to form liquid water again. Very pure water collects in the beaker. We call it distilled water. Distillation of seawater on a large scale is only practical where fuel is available very cheaply.

EXAM HINTS AND TIPS

You must be able to explain how raw water is changed into drinking water.

Should we allow the fluoridation of drinking water?

In some areas fluoride is added to drinking water – this is called **fluoridation**. It is added to improve dental health by decreasing the incidence of tooth decay. However, too much fluoride can also cause problems. It can cause tooth enamel to become mottled and stained. In addition, some civil liberties groups are concerned that where water is fluoridated people have no choice and are forced to consume the fluoride whether they agree with it or not. Scientists believe that the benefits of adding fluoride to the water supply outweigh the potential risks, but clearly an informed debate is needed.

FIGURE 6: Do you think fluoride should be added to drinking water?

QUESTIONS

4 How could global warming affect the speed at which water evaporates from the sea?

5 Draw a flow diagram to show the steps involved in turning raw water into drinking water.

6 What does a condenser do?

QUESTIONS

7 Do you think that fluoride should be added to drinking water? Explain your answer.

Hard and soft water

You will find out:
- How hard water is formed
- About the advantages and disadvantages of hard water
- About the different types of hard water

Beer

Beer is a popular alcoholic drink. It is made by a fermentation reaction. The main ingredients are barley, water and yeast. Flavourings such as hops, which have a bitter taste, are often added. Different types of water are used to make different types of beer. Hard water is used to produce dark beers such as Guinness, while soft water is used to make lighter beers such as pale lager.

FIGURE 1: Different types of water are used to make different types of beer.

How is hard water formed?

Have you noticed that distilled water can taste slightly different from tap water? Distilled water can be described as **soft water** because it does not contain **dissolved** calcium or magnesium salts.

Some tap water can be described as hard. **Hard water** has relatively large amounts of calcium salts and smaller amounts of magnesium salts dissolved in it.

Water is a good **solvent**. As rain falls from clouds, some carbon dioxide can dissolve in the rainwater to form carbonic acid. As the carbonic acid moves through rocks and soils that contain calcium and magnesium minerals it dissolves these minerals and the water becomes hard.

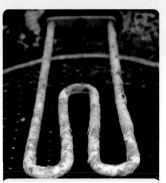

FIGURE 2: Hard water can lead to limescale.

Hard water has disadvantages and advantages. The problems associated with hard water include the deposits of **limescale** that hard water can leave on appliances such as kettles, irons, washing machines and central heating systems. As the limescale builds up, the appliance becomes more inefficient and will eventually need to be replaced. In addition, it is difficult to get hard water to form lather with soap.

Benefits of hard water include a link between hard water and a reduced risk of heart disease. It also helps to produce stronger teeth and bones. Many people also think that hard water tastes nicer.

Hard water can be softened by removing calcium ions and magnesium ions. This can be done by adding **washing soda** (sodium carbonate) or by passing the water through an **ion-exchange column**.

FIGURE 3: Hard water helps reduce the risk of heart disease.

QUESTIONS

1 Which minerals cause water to be hard?
2 Describe **one** disadvantage of hard water.
3 What are the advantages of hard water?
4 How can hard water be softened?

...dissolve   ...hard water   ...ion-exchange column

Is my tap water hard or soft?

The simplest way to check whether your tap water is hard or soft is to test how quickly the water reacts with soap to form lather. If the water forms a good lather with a small amount of soap it contains few calcium ions or magnesium ions and is soft.

If the water does not form lather readily, it is hard. The calcium ions and magnesium ions react with the stearate ions in soap to form calcium stearate or scum.

calcium sulfate + sodium stearate → calcium stearate + sodium sulfate
(soap)   (scum)

Scum forms an unpleasant layer around the sink. Only when enough soap has been added to remove all the dissolved calcium and magnesium ions does lather form.

Why is sodium carbonate added to many washing powders?

Many washing powders contain sodium carbonate or washing soda. This reacts with the calcium ions and magnesium ions in hard water and allows the detergent to work better. This equation shows how sodium carbonate can remove calcium ions from hard water:

sodium carbonate + calcium sulfate → sodium sulfate + calcium carbonate
$$Na_2CO_{3(aq)} + CaSO_{4(aq)} \rightarrow Na_2SO_{4(aq)} + CaCO_{3(s)}$$

Washing-up liquids contain soapless detergents. These are useful because they do not form a scum with the calcium ions and magnesium ions in hard water.

Why does your water softener need to be recharged?

Water softeners remove calcium ions and magnesium ions from hard water to give soft water. An ion-exchange column is one way they do this. The column consists of resin beads coated in sodium ions. When hard water passes through the column, the calcium ions and magnesium ions exchange places with the sodium ions. The water flowing out from the column is soft because it now contains low levels of calcium ions and magnesium ions, although it does contain quite high levels of sodium ions. However, once the calcium ions or magnesium ions have replaced all the sodium ions in the column, the ion-exchange stops working and the column needs to be 'recharged'. This is done by flushing the column through with salty water.

Some ion-exchange columns use hydrogen ions instead of sodium ions.

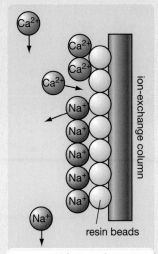

FIGURE 4: What are ion-exchange columns used for?

Different types of hard water

There are two types of hard water.

Permanently hard water is caused by dissolved calcium and magnesium sulfates and chlorides. These compounds become more soluble as the temperature of the water increases, so permanent hardness is not removed by boiling.

Temporary hard water is caused by dissolved calcium or magnesium hydrogencarbonates.

■ Carbonic acid is formed when water reacts with carbon dioxide.

water + carbon → carbonic
dioxide   acid
$$H_2O_{(l)} + CO_{2(g)} \rightarrow H_2CO_{3(aq)}$$

■ Limestone contains calcium carbonate.

■ Carbonic acid reacts with calcium carbonate to form calcium hydrogen-carbonate which is soluble in water.

carbonic + calcium → calcium
acid   carbonate   hydrogen-
**   carbonate**
$$H_2CO_{3(aq)} + CaCO_{3(s)} \rightarrow Ca(HCO_3)_{2(aq)}$$

The compounds dissolved in temporarily hard water become less soluble as the temperature of the water increases, so if the water is boiled they precipitate out of solution leaving the water softer.

▐▐▐▐▐ QUESTIONS ▐▐▐▐▐

5   How does sodium carbonate reduce the hardness of water?

6   Why is it difficult to form lather with hard water?

7   Why should formula milk for young babies not be made up with water from an ion-exchange column?

▐▐▐▐▐ QUESTIONS ▐▐▐▐▐

8   Why does temporarily hard water cause more problems than permanently hard water?

...limescale   ...soft water   ...solvent   ...washing soda

Solubility

Champagne

Champagne is traditionally drunk to mark special occasions. It is named after a region in France where the fizzy wine is produced. The bubbles in champagne are formed from the gas carbon dioxide which has been dissolved in the wine.

FIGURE 1: What puts the fizz in champagne?

Water as a solvent

Solvents are liquids that **dissolve solutes** to form **solutions**. Water is very good at dissolving ionic substances such as salts, but not good at dissolving covalently bonded substances such as fats or oils.

Solubility is a measure of the maximum amount of a solute which will dissolve in a given amount of solvent (usually 100 g) at a particular temperature.

Different substances have different solubilities. Solubility changes with temperature. The graph in figure 2 shows how the solubilities of copper sulfate and potassium nitrate change as the temperature increases. Notice that copper sulfate becomes slightly more soluble as the temperature increases, while there is a very big increase in the solubility of potassium nitrate with increasing temperature. Most solids become more soluble as the temperature increases. However, gases – for example, oxygen – become less soluble with increasing temperature.

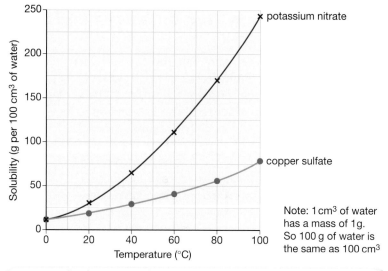

Note: 1 cm^3 of water has a mass of 1 g. So 100 g of water is the same as 100 cm^3

FIGURE 2: What happens to the solubility of copper sulfate and potassium nitrate when the temperature increases?

QUESTIONS

1 What do we call a mixture of a solvent and a solute?
2 Would you expect the salt potassium chloride to dissolve well in water?
3 Why do we often measure how much solute will dissolve in 100 g of water?
4 How much copper sulfate dissolves in 100 g of water at 60 °C?

...crystallisation   ...dissolve   ...saturated solution   ...solubility

Why is water a good solvent?

The chemical formula of water is H_2O. This tells us that every water molecule consists of two hydrogen atoms and one oxygen atom. The oxygen end of the molecule has a slightly negative charge, while the hydrogen end of the molecule has a slightly positive charge.

Ionic substances, such as sodium chloride, consist of positive and negative ions held together in a giant lattice. If solid sodium chloride is placed in water, sodium ions and chloride ions on the surface of the solid are surrounded by water molecules and are carried into solution. More ions in the solid are 'exposed' and are carried off in the same way. The process continues until all the solid has dissolved.

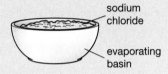

(slightly negative charge)

δ−

(slightly positive charge)

FIGURE 3: Each water molecule has a slightly positive end and a slightly negative end. It is described as polar.

Why do crystals form?

If you take a beaker of water and keep adding sodium chloride salt to the water until no more will dissolve, you will end up with a **saturated solution**. If you leave this beaker on a warm windowsill, some of the water will evaporate. The metal sodium ions have a positive charge while the non-metal chloride ions have a negative charge. Because these ions have opposite charges, the ions attract each other and they join to from crystals. This process is called **crystallisation**.

sodium chloride

evaporating basin

FIGURE 4: If some of the solvent evaporates, crystals will develop by crystallisation.

Why does temperature affect gas solubility?

As the temperature of water increases, the amount of gas which will dissolve in it decreases. Why is this?

As the temperature increases, the gas molecules gain kinetic energy. This means that more gas particles have enough energy to escape from the liquid and this reduces the concentration of dissolved gases. Fizzy drinks such as lemonade are fizzy because they contain bubbles of carbon dioxide gas. More carbon dioxide dissolves in the liquid at low temperatures. This explains why cold lemonade is bubbly, while warm lemonade which will contain less carbon dioxide tastes 'flat'.

FIGURE 5: If you want your lemonade to be bubbly, why should you be sure to chill it?

Why can power plants kill trout?

The temperature of the water in rivers is very important to aquatic life. If the water is cold, lots of oxygen can dissolve in the water and aquatic life such as fish can respire well. Power plants often use water as a coolant. The heated water this produces is then released into streams.

FIGURE 6: Trout are particularly sensitive to oxygen levels; water temperatures of around 20 °C can suffocate these fish.

Why does pressure affect gas solubility?

As the pressure of the gas increases, the amount of gas that will dissolve also increases. Gas molecules dissolve in water when they collide with the surface of the water. As the pressure increases, gas molecules collide with the surface of the water more often and so more gas particles dissolve.

QUESTIONS

5 How do you make a saturated solution?

6 Why is a water molecule described as a polar molecule?

7 Why should you put a bottle of lemonade in the fridge for a while before you open it?

8 Why does a bottle of cola go flat if the lid is left off?

QUESTIONS

9 How could the release of heated water into a river affect the amount of oxygen dissolved in the river water?

10 How could this affect aquatic life such as trout?

...solute ...solution ...solvent

Exothermic and endothermic reactions

You will find out:
- About exothermic and endothermic reactions in terms of bond breaking and bond formation
- What the activation energy of a reaction is
- How catalysts increase the rate of a reaction

The Thermit reaction

In the Thermit reaction, powdered aluminium is mixed with powdered iron(III) oxide. The mixed powders are then heated to start the reaction.

Once the reaction gets under way it gives out so much heat energy that the products of the reaction – iron and aluminium oxide – are liquid or molten. The reaction is used to produce molten iron that is then used to weld together broken railway tracks.

FIGURE 1: The Thermit reaction releases a lot of energy.

Why do some reactions release energy and others take in energy?

Have you ever noticed that when you touch the side of a beaker that contains an acid reacting with an alkali it feels warm, yet if you put sherbet on your tongue it feels cold? Some **reactions** give out **energy** while other reactions take in energy. This energy is normally in the form of heat.

During chemical reactions, existing chemical **bonds** are broken and new ones are formed. Energy is needed to break bonds and energy is released when new bonds are formed. In **exothermic** reactions, more energy is released when new bonds form to make the products of the reaction than was taken in to break the bonds in the reacting substances.

We can use an **energy profile diagram** to show the change in energy as a reaction happens. Figure 2 shows that, overall, energy is released by exothermic reactions.

In **endothermic** reactions, more energy is taken in to break existing bonds in the reactants than is released when new bonds form to make the products of the reaction. The energy profile diagram in figure 3 shows that, overall, energy is taken in by an endothermic reaction.

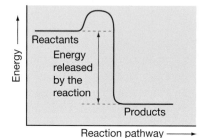

FIGURE 2: Exothermic reactions release energy.

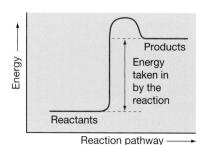

FIGURE 3: Endothermic reactions take in energy.

QUESTIONS

1 What happens during an exothermic reaction?
2 What happens during an endothermic reaction?
3 Is the Thermit reaction an exothermic reaction or an endothermic reaction?

...*activation energy*   ...*bond*   ...*bond energy*   ...*catalyst*   ...*endothermic*

Is burning methane exothermic or endothermic? (H)

A chemical bond has a **bond energy**. This is the average amount of energy required to break one mole of that type of bond.

Table 1 shows the values of some bond energies. We can see that to break one mole of C–H bonds 413 kJ of energy must be supplied. When one mole of C–H bonds is formed 413 kJ of energy will be released.

We can use the values in table 1 to calculate the energy change when one mole of methane is burnt.

- When it burns, methane reacts with oxygen to form carbon dioxide and water vapour:

Bond	Bond energy $(kJmol^{-1})$
C–H	413
O=O	496
O–H	463
C=O	743

TABLE 1: : Some bond energies.

methane + oxygen → carbon dioxide + water vapour

$$CH_4 + 2O_2 \rightarrow CO_2 + 2H_2O$$

- *Step 1:* calculate the amount of energy required to break the existing bonds in the reactants:

  4 moles of C–H bonds = 4 x 413 kJ = 1652 kJ
  2 moles of O=O bonds = 2 x 496 kJ = 992 kJ

  The total amount of energy required to break the bonds in the reactants = 1652 kJ + 992 kJ = 2644 kJ

- *Step 2:* calculate the amount of energy released when the new bonds are formed in the products:

  4 moles of O–H bonds = 4 x 463 kJ = 1852 kJ
  2 moles of C=O bonds = 2 x 743 kJ = 1486 kJ

  The total amount of energy released when the bonds in the products are formed = 1852 kJ + 1486 kJ = 3338 kJ

Overall, in this reaction, more energy is released when new bonds are formed than is taken in to break the existing bonds. So the burning of methane is exothermic. In fact, the burning of fuels is always exothermic, but different fuels release different amounts of energy.

Getting a reaction started

The minimum amount of energy required to start a reaction is called the **activation energy**. The energy profile diagram in figure 4 shows the activation energy of the reaction, that is, the energy required to break the bonds in the reactant particles and start the reaction. The bigger the activation energy, the more energy must be supplied for the reaction to start.

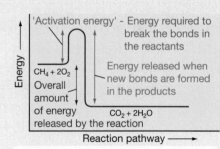

FIGURE 4: How can you tell that this is an exothermic reaction?

How do catalysts speed up the rate of reaction?

Catalysts are substances that increase the rate of a chemical reaction but are not themselves used up in the reaction. Catalysts increase the rate of a reaction by offering an alternative reaction pathway that has a lower activation energy.

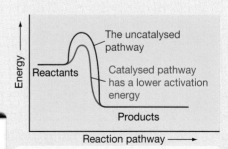

FIGURE 5: How does a catalyst speed up the rate of chemical reaction?

QUESTIONS

4 Calculate the amount of energy released when one mole of water (H_2O) is formed.

5 Calculate the amount of energy required to break the bonds in one mole of methane (CH_4).

6 What is the activation energy of a reaction?

7 How do catalysts increase the rate of a chemical reaction?

…energy   …energy profile diagram   …exothermic   …reaction

Bio Willie

SELF-CHECK ACTIVITY

Willie Nelson is a name well known for many years, especially in the USA, for Country and Western music. Having performed to countless fans in venues large and small, and sold millions of records, tapes and CDs, many thought that Willie would gradually wind down and enjoy life. In fact his name is once again being promoted, but this time for something completely different – biodiesel.

Ordinary diesel fuel is derived from crude oil and although it is widely used the world over, it has a number of disadvantages, such as supply and pollution. One of the alternatives is biodiesel, and Willie Nelson has put his name to it. Willie found out about biodiesel in Hawaii. He ended up buying a new Mercedes Benz and putting vegetable oil in the tank: "The tailpipe smells like French Fries!" he said.

Biodiesel is derived from crops and is usually blended with conventional diesel. The most common mix is B20, which is 20% biodiesel and 80% ordinary diesel. It is possible to use pure biodiesel but this starts to get slushy at around 0 °C.

Biodiesel cuts emissions of smog-forming pollutants and global warming gases. However, it increases the amount of nitrogen oxide released, and huge areas of land would have to be turned over to crops for biodiesel to impact on our consumption of crude oil.

Nevertheless, Bio Willie is selling well and truckers have been some of the most enthusiastic purchasers. One of the big attractions for Willie and many other Americans is that biodiesel reduces America's need to buy crude oil from abroad. It may also give a helping hand to farmers as they grow the sunflowers, peanuts or soybeans (some of the crops from which biodiesel can be made).

CHALLENGE

STEP 1

Why is supply a problem in the long-term for conventional diesel? Why is there concern about pollution from it?

Which gas is produced when any hydrocarbon burns in air? Why is this a problem? How does using biodiesel help in terms of pollutants?

In what way would the growing use of biodiesel be good for America's farmers? What might happen if there was a total switch to biodiesel?

If biodiesel is so good, why not use it in a pure form instead of mixing it with conventional diesel?

Evaluate the use of biodiesel in terms of environmental impact.

Maximise your grade

These sentences show what you need to include in your work to achieve each grade. Use them to improve your work and be more successful.

Grade	Answer includes...
F	Know that biodiesel is a fuel.
	Explain that biodiesel can be used as an alternative to conventional diesel.
	State what gas is produced when hydrocarbons burn in air.
	Explain an advantage of biodiesel compared with conventional diesel.
C	Explain several advantages of biodiesel compared with conventional diesel.
	Compare the advantages of conventional diesel and biodiesel.
A	Evaluate the environmental impact of biodiesel.
	Comprehensively evaluate the environmental impact of biodiesel.

Energy

You will find out:
- How food provides us with energy
- How to measure the amount of energy released during a reaction

Hidden sugar

Scientists have found that lots of people in Britain are consuming too much sugar in their diets. This sugar is not only bad for people's teeth but consuming too many calories can also contribute towards long-term health problems. However, cutting down on the amount of sugar that you are eating is not always easy. Many foods contain 'hidden sugar', for example a can of fizzy drink contains around seven teaspoons of sugar. You would be a bit surprised if you saw someone add seven teaspoons of sugar to a cup of coffee but we give fizzy drinks to young children.

FIGURE 1: Do you know how much hidden sugar there is in a fizzy drink?

The right amount of energy

Have you noticed that many food labels contain nutritional information such as the amount of salt in the food? These labels often show how much energy there is in the food. Food is a type of fuel. Although we normally measure **energy** in joules, for historic reasons we often measure the amount of energy in foods in **calories**. One calorie is equal to 4.2 joules. This information is useful because it helps us to get the right amount of energy from the food we eat. If we did not get enough energy from our food we would feel tired and could become ill or even die. If we get too much energy from our food we could become very fat or **obese**. People who are obese are more likely to develop serious health problems including heart disease and diabetes. Generally, foods rich in fats, oils and carbohydrates contain large amounts of energy. Carbohydrates consist of carbon, hydrogen and oxygen atoms. Sugars, such as glucose are simple carbohydrates while starches are much larger and more complex carbohydrate molecules. During respiration, glucose reacts with oxygen to produce carbon dioxide and water vapour and to release energy. During this reaction, existing bonds are broken and new bonds are formed. Overall, energy is released so this is an exothermic reaction.

glucose + oxygen → carbon dioxide + water + energy

Our bodies use this energy to:
- keep our hearts beating
- maintain our body temperature
- move and work.

FIGURE 2: Foods that contain lots of fats, oils and carbohydrates tend to contain lots of energy.

QUESTIONS

1 How many joules are equal to one calorie?
2 What happens if you don't get enough energy from the food you eat?
3 What happens if you get too much energy from the food you eat?
4 Which diseases are linked with being very overweight?

...calories ...calorimetry ...energy

How does calorimetry work?

Calorimetry uses changes in the **temperature** of water to measure the energy released by fuels or foods.

We can use calorimetry to compare the energy contents of different foods. In figure 3, the food is burnt and the energy that is released is used to heat water. The greater the increase in the temperature of the water, the higher the energy content of the food.

Using calorimetry

Calorimetry can also be used when a solid reacts with a solution or when two solutions react together. The reaction is carried out in an **insulated** beaker. The insulation is important because it reduces the amount of heat energy entering or leaving from the surroundings.

We can use our results to work out the energy change for the reaction using this equation.

energy change = mass x specific heat capacity x change in temperature

Figure 4 shows how calorimetry can be used to work out the energy change for the reaction between copper sulfate solution and zinc powder. We will assume that 1 cm³ of copper sulfate solution has a mass of 1 g.

The **specific heat capacity** of a substance is the amount of energy which is required to raise the temperature of 1 g of the substance by 1 °C. We will use a value for the specific heat capacity of copper sulfate solution of 4.2 J g^{-1} °C^{-1}.

So the energy change for this reaction is:

= 50 g x 4.2 J g^{-1} °C^{-1} x 35 °C

= 7350 J

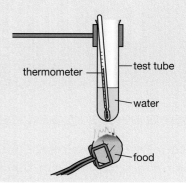

FIGURE 3: A simple way to compare the amount of energy in different foods.

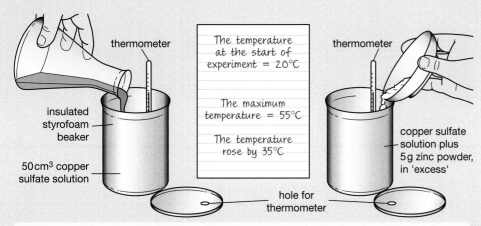

> The temperature at the start of experiment = 20°C
>
> The maximum temperature = 55°C
>
> The temperature rose by 35°C

FIGURE 4: Using a simple calorimeter to measure the energy released in a reaction.

Healthy eating

Recent healthy eating campaigns have encouraged the government to introduce new legislation to improve the quality of food sold in school canteens. Sugary junk foods such as chocolate and sweets will no longer be available.

In addition, meals will need to contain less salt, sugar and saturated fat and more fresh fruit and vegetables. Some schools are worried that these ingredients might be more expensive.

FIGURE 5: Should junk foods be banned?

QUESTIONS

5 What does calorimetry measure?

6 What type of reaction gives out energy overall?

7 What type of reaction takes in energy overall?

QUESTIONS

8 Is it right to ban the sale of chocolate in schools when it is available in government canteens?

...insulated   ...obese   ...specific heat capacity   ...temperature

Testing for metals

You will find out:
- How to use traditional methods to identify metal ions in compounds
- How to carry out a flame test
- Why precipitates form

Coloured candle flames

A recent novelty is a range of candles which have beautiful coloured flames. These candles contain small amounts of metal salts. When the candles are lit, the salts burn with coloured flames.

Flame tests

Scientists often need to identify the **metal ions** in compounds. For example, a scientist might want to analyse a water sample to see if it is polluted.

Think of the different coloured lights you see when fireworks explode. When the metal salts in fireworks are heated they release different coloured lights.

FIGURE 1: How do these candles burn with coloured flames?

- Lithium salts produce **scarlet**-red flames.
- Sodium salts produce yellow-orange flames.
- Potassium salts produce **lilac** flames.
- Calcium salts produce brick-red flames.
- Barium salts produce apple-green flames.

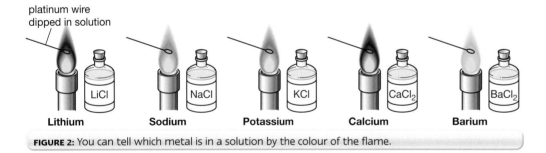

platinum wire dipped in solution

| LiCl | NaCl | KCl | CaCl$_2$ | BaCl$_2$ |

Lithium **Sodium** **Potassium** **Calcium** **Barium**

FIGURE 2: You can tell which metal is in a solution by the colour of the flame.

Using sodium hydroxide solution to identify metals

Some metal ions can be identified by observing their reaction with sodium hydroxide solution:

- solutions of copper(II) ions give pale blue **precipitates**
- solutions of iron(II) ions give grey-green precipitates
- solutions of iron(III) ions give red-brown precipitates
- solutions of magnesium ions and aluminium ions both give white precipitates.

If we get a white precipitate with sodium hydroxide solution, how can we tell if the solution contains aluminium ions or magnesium ions? If more sodium hydroxide solution is added to a magnesium precipitate it does not change. However, if more sodium hydroxide solution is added to an aluminium precipitate, the white precipitate will dissolve to form a colourless solution.

QUESTIONS

1 How do fireworks give out light of different colours?
2 What is the colour of the light given out when potassium salts are heated?
3 An unknown metal salt produces a green flame when heated. Which metal is in the unknown salt?
4 If you add sodium hydroxide solution to a solution containing iron(II) ions what would you see?

EXAM HINTS AND TIPS

Make sure you can recall the flame test and sodium hydroxide precipitate colours mentioned in this section.

Conducting a flame test

Flame tests are a powerful way of identifying the metal ions present in a compound. They are particularly useful for identifying group 1 and group 2 metal ions in compounds.

First the sample is placed on a watchglass. A very clean platinum wire is dipped into concentrated hydrochloric acid (to clean it further) and then into the sample. The wire is then put into a hot, blue Bunsen burner flame.

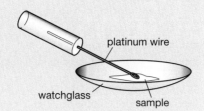

platinum wire

watchglass

sample

FIGURE 3: What is used to clean the platinum wire before a flame test?

Identifying copper carbonate and zinc carbonate

The compounds copper carbonate and zinc carbonate display distinctive colour changes when they are heated:

copper carbonate → copper oxide + carbon dioxide
$$CuCO_3 \rightarrow CuO + CO_2$$

Copper carbonate is a green powder; copper oxide is a black powder.

zinc carbonate → zinc oxide + carbon dioxide
$$ZnCO_3 \rightarrow ZnO + CO_2$$

Zinc carbonate is a white powder; zinc oxide is yellow when it is hot, but as it cools it changes colour and turns white. Unfortunately this technique can only be used to identify these two compounds.

A closer look at precipitates

A precipitate is formed when two solutions react together to form an insoluble solid. In the sodium hydroxide test for copper ions, copper(II) ions react with hydroxide ions to produce copper(II) hydroxide. Copper(II) hydroxide does not dissolve – it is a precipitate.

$$Cu^{2+}_{(aq)} + 2OH^-_{(aq)} \rightarrow Cu(OH)_{2(s)}$$

Iron(II) ions react with hydroxide ions to produce iron(II) hydroxide. Iron(II) hydroxide does not dissolve – it is a precipitate.

$$Fe^{2+}_{(aq)} + 2OH^-_{(aq)} \rightarrow Fe(OH)_{2(s)}$$

Iron(III) ions react with hydroxide ions to produce iron(III) hydroxide. Iron(III) hydroxide does not dissolve – it is a precipitate.

$$Fe^{3+}_{(aq)} + 3OH^-_{(aq)} \rightarrow Fe(OH)_{3(s)}$$

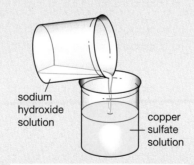

sodium hydroxide solution

copper sulfate solution

FIGURE 4: Precipitates are insoluble.

Potassium salts don't always burn with a lilac flame

When a metal ion is heated in a Bunsen flame it uses the heat energy to promote an electron from its usual energy level to an excited energy level. When the electron falls back down, light is given out. The colour of the light given out can be used to identify the metal ion in the compound.

When flame tests are carried out on samples of potassium salts, the results can sometimes be surprising. Occasionally potassium salts appear to give a yellow-orange flame, rather than the expected lilac colour. This is because potassium salts are often contaminated with small amounts of sodium. The colour from the sodium is so intense that even a little sodium contamination can have a big impact on the colour observed.

FIGURE 5: 'Lo-salt' contains potassium chloride and sodium chloride.

QUESTIONS

5   Why must the wire used in a flame test be very clean?

6   How could you tell that a sample of metal carbonate is zinc carbonate?

7   How is a precipitate formed?

QUESTIONS

8   Why might a sample of Lo-salt appear to burn with an orange flame rather than a lilac flame?

Testing for non-metal ions

You will find out:
- How to use traditional methods to identify non-metal ions in compounds

Barium meals

Doctors use X-rays to see what is happening inside a patient's body. X-rays of the stomach are not very clear, so patients who might be suffering from stomach problems like ulcers or tumours may be given a 'barium meal'. X-rays cannot pass through barium, so the doctor gets a clearer picture of what is happening inside the patient. Soluble barium compounds are very poisonous. Yet a barium meal which contains the compound barium sulfate is completely safe. Barium sulfate is **insoluble**, so it passes through the body without being absorbed.

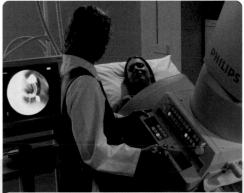

FIGURE 1: Why are some X-ray patients given a barium meal?

Identifying non-metal ions

Scientists often need to identify the **non-metal ions** in compounds. For example, a scientist might want to identify a particular mineral or rock.

Testing for sulfate ions

We can find out whether a sample contains sulfate ions by dissolving it in water and adding dilute hydrochloric acid followed by a few drops of dilute barium chloride solution.

If the sample contains sulfate ions, a white **precipitate** of barium sulfate is formed.

Testing for halide ions

The elements of group 7 of the Periodic Table are known as the **halogens**. They react with many metals to form ionic salts called **halides**, e.g. chlorides, bromides and iodides.

Solutions of metal halides in water contain metal ions and halide ions. We can find out whether a sample contains any of these halide ions by dissolving the sample in water and adding dilute nitric acid followed by a few drops of dilute silver nitrate solution.

If a precipitate forms, the colour can be used to identify the halide ion present:

- chloride ions form a white precipitate
- bromide ions form a cream precipitate
- iodide ions form a yellow precipitate.

Testing for nitrate ions

We can find out whether a sample contains **nitrate** ions by adding dilute sodium hydroxide solution to the sample, followed by a little aluminium powder and finally heating the mixture.

If the sample contains nitrate ions, **ammonia gas** will be produced. This gas turns damp red **litmus paper** blue.

Testing for ammonium ions

We can find out whether a sample contains **ammonium ions** by adding sodium hydroxide solution to the sample. Ammonium ions react with hydroxide ions to form ammonia gas. Ammonia turns damp red litmus paper blue.

Testing for carbonate ions

We can find out whether a sample contains carbonate ions by adding dilute acid. If carbonate ions are present they react with the acid to form the gas carbon dioxide which turns limewater cloudy.

:: QUESTIONS ::

1. How would you test for the presence of sulfate ions in a sample?
2. A sample of an acidified metal halide reacts with silver nitrate solution to produce a cream precipitate. Which halide ion is present in the sample?
3. How can ammonia gas be identified?

...ammonia gas   ...ammonium ions   ...halide   ...halogen   ...insoluble

What's going on in the tests?

Testing for sulfate ions

We have seen how barium chloride solution can be used to test for the presence of sulfate ions. This equation summarises the reaction:

$$Ba^{2+}_{(aq)} + SO_4^{2-}_{(aq)} \rightarrow BaSO_{4(s)}$$

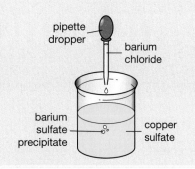

FIGURE 2: The sulfate ions in the copper sulfate solution react with the barium ions in barium chloride to form a white precipitate of barium sulfate.

Testing for halide ions

When silver nitrate solution is added to a solution of halide ions, a silver halide precipitate is formed. These equations sum up the reactions between silver nitrate solution and the different halide ions:

$$Ag^+_{(aq)} + Cl^-_{(aq)} \rightarrow AgCl_{(s)}$$
$$Ag^+_{(aq)} + Br^-_{(aq)} \rightarrow AgBr_{(s)}$$
$$Ag^+_{(aq)} + I^-_{(aq)} \rightarrow AgI_{(s)}$$

Testing for nitrate ions

When sodium hydroxide solution is added to a sample of nitrate ions and aluminium powder and the mixture is heated, ammonia gas is produced.

This reduction reaction can be summarised by this equation:

$$NO_3^-_{(aq)} \xrightarrow[\text{NaOH solution}]{\text{Al}} NH_{3(g)}$$

Testing for ammonium ions

When sodium hydroxide solution is added to ammonium compounds, ammonia gas is produced. This equation summarises the reaction:

$$NH_4^+_{(aq)} + OH^-_{(aq)} \rightarrow NH_{3(g)} + H_2O_{(l)}$$

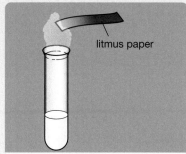

FIGURE 3: Ammonia gas turns damp red litmus paper blue.

EXAM HINTS AND TIPS

Make sure you can recall the tests mentioned in this spread.

Scientists often need to identify the non-metal ions in compounds

Identifying silver halides

When a solution containing halide ions is acidified and then reacted with silver nitrate solution, the colour of the silver halide precipitate formed can be used to identify which halide ion is present.

This sounds simple, but in practice it is quite difficult because it can be very hard to tell whether a precipitate is white, cream, or yellow. Scientists often use ammonia solutions to be sure they have identified a halide correctly.

- White silver chloride precipitate dissolves readily in dilute ammonia solution.

- Cream silver bromide solution does not dissolve in dilute ammonia solution, but does dissolve in concentrated ammonia solution.

- Yellow silver iodide precipitate is insoluble in both dilute and concentrated ammonia solutions.

QUESTIONS

4 Give the symbol equation for the reaction between copper sulfate, $CuSO_4$ and barium chloride, $BaCl_2$.

5 Give the symbol equation for the reaction between silver nitrate, $AgNO_3$ and sodium chloride, NaCl.

6 Give the symbol equation for the reaction between ammonium ions and hydroxide ions.

QUESTIONS

7 Draw a flow diagram to explain how you would tell samples of sodium chloride and sodium bromide apart.

Organic compounds

You will find out:
● What the empirical formula of an organic compound is
● How the empirical formula can be found by experiment

Carbon

Organic compounds all contain the element carbon. There are millions of different organic compounds. From the food that we eat to the clothes that we wear, organic compounds are an essential part of our lives.

FIGURE 1: Organic compounds are very important to us.

Propane

Camping stoves often run on propane. When propane is heated in a good supply of oxygen, it reacts to form carbon dioxide and water vapour.

propane + oxygen → carbon dioxide + water
$$C_3H_{8(g)} + 5O_{2(g)} \rightarrow 3CO_{2(g)} + 4H_2O_{(g)}$$

Alkanes and alkenes

Ethane (C_2H_6) and ethene (C_2H_4) are both **hydrocarbons**.

FIGURE 2: Why does propane make a good fuel?

Ethane is a **saturated** hydrocarbon (it contains only a single C–C bond) and belongs to the **alkane** family. Ethene is an **unsaturated** hydrocarbon (it contains a C=C double bond) and belongs to the **alkene** family.

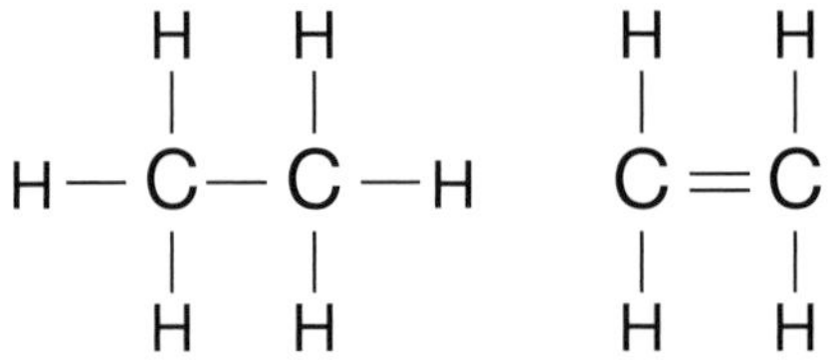

FIGURE 3: What differences can you see between the bonds in ethane and ethene?

We can differentiate between members of these two families of organic compounds by adding **bromine water** to the samples. Alkanes show no reaction with bromine water, while alkenes quickly changes the bromine water from orange-brown to colourless.

QUESTIONS

1 Name the element found in all organic compounds.
2 What happens when organic compounds are heated?
3 Name the products of the reaction between propane and oxygen.
4 Name a saturated hydrocarbon.

...alkane   ...alkene   ...bromine water   ...empirical formula   ...hydrocarbon

Empirical formulae

The **empirical formula** of a compound is the ratio of the elements in the compound in their simplest form.

For example, ethene has the molecular formula C_2H_4. The ratio of the elements in each molecule of ethene, in its simplest form, is one carbon atom to two hydrogen atoms. So the empirical formula of ethene is CH_2.

A closer look at fuels

Fuels are burnt to release energy. Examples of fuels include petrol and ethanol. These are both organic compounds.

Ideally a fuel should release lots of energy when it is burnt, be very abundant and non-polluting.

- Petrol is obtained from crude oil. Burning petrol releases lots of energy but our resources of crude oil are limited. Additionally the combustion of petrol produces carbon dioxide which contributes to the greenhouse effect.

- Ethanol is made by the fermentation of vegetable matter. However enormous amounts of land would be required to grow enough vegetable matter to meet the world's demand for fuel. This land could not then be used for homes or to grow food.

FIGURE 4: Is this corn better used as food or for making ethanol?

Organic compounds all contain the element carbon

Finding the empirical formula of a compound (H)

We can calculate the empirical formula of a compound by burning a sample of the compound completely and then analysing the products of the reaction.

Suppose 2.2 g of an unknown hydrocarbon compound is burnt completely in oxygen to form 6.6 g of carbon dioxide and 3.6 g of water vapour.

If we divide the mass of the compounds produced by the **relative formula mass** of these compounds, we can calculate the numbers of moles of carbon dioxide and water vapour that are produced.

- Carbon dioxide has a relative formula mass of 44.

$$12 + (16 + 2) = 44$$

Water has a relative formula mass of 18.

$$(1 \times 2) + 16 = 18$$

Carbon dioxide: $6.6 \div 44 = 0.15$ moles
Water: $3.6 \div 18 = 0.2$ moles

- As each water molecule contains two hydrogen atoms, we should multiply our value for water by 2 to find the number of moles of hydrogen (0.4 moles).

- So the ratio of carbon to hydrogen atoms in the products is 0.15:0.40, or in the simplest form of the ratio 3:8.

- Therefore the empirical formula of the unknown hydrocarbon compound is C_3H_8.

QUESTIONS

5 Give the empirical formula of ethene.

6 What is the empirical formula of butene, C_4H_8?

QUESTIONS

7 What is the empirical formula of a compound?

8 3.6 g of an unknown hydrocarbon is burnt completely in oxygen to form 9.9 g of carbon dioxide and 8.1g of water vapour. What is the empirical formula of the unknown hydrocarbon?

Modern instrumental methods

You will find out:

- How modern instrumental methods have enabled scientists to identify elements and compounds

Helium

Helium is the second most abundant element in the Universe, but it was first identified not on Earth but in the Sun. In fact the element's name comes from the Greek word for the Sun, helios. The element was identified by scientists developing **spectroscopy**.

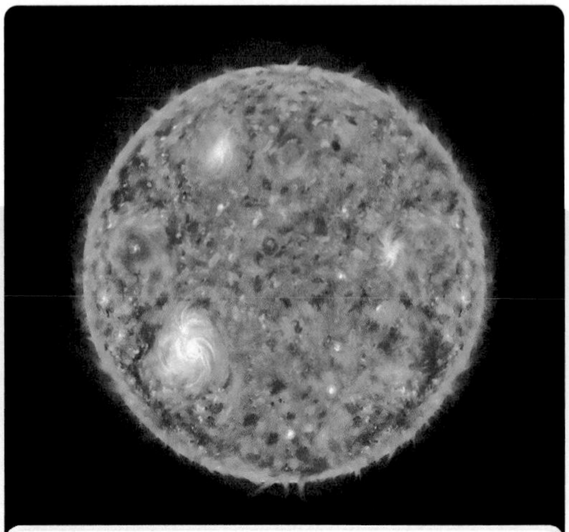

FIGURE 1: The element helium was first identified in the Sun.

Why are modern analytical methods better? (H)

Traditional laboratory methods of **analysis** can be slow and require a large **sample** of the material to be available. They are also very labour intensive. The development of a range of instrumental methods that are faster, more **accurate**, more **sensitive** and require smaller amounts of sample has revolutionised our ability to **identify** chemicals.

Some techniques are used to identify elements, for example, atomic absorption spectroscopy.

Other techniques are used to identify compounds, for example, infrared and ultraviolet spectroscopy, gas/liquid chromatography (glc) and high pressure liquid chromatography (hplc).

Some methods, such as mass spectroscopy, can be used to identify either elements or compounds.

In addition, modern instrumental techniques do not just identify the elements or compounds present, they can also help you determine how much of each is present in a sample.

The choice of method depends on the speed and sensitivity required. Usually the most cost-effective method is used.

QUESTIONS

1. What are the advantages of using modern instrumental methods over traditional methods of analysis?
2. What is atomic absorption spectroscopy used for?
3. What is ultraviolet spectroscopy used for?
4. What factors should be considered when choosing a method of analysis?

...*accurate* ...*analysis* ...*identify* ...*sample*

How have improvements in electronics and (H) computing helped scientists?

Modern instruments are often connected to computers. These computers process enormous amounts of information very quickly.

Atomic absorption spectroscopy

Atomic absorption spectroscopy is a powerful technique for identifying the presence of specific elements in a sample. Visible light has a range of wavelengths, from the violet end to the red end of the visible **spectrum**. If light is shone through a sample, some wavelengths of light are absorbed by atoms. This leaves dark bands in the spectrum where light has been absorbed. For example, if red light is absorbed there will be a dark band in the red region of the spectrum.

Different elements absorb radiation of different wavelengths and so produce different spectra. The amount of radiation absorbed can be used to work out the amount of that element present in the sample.

Atomic absorption spectroscopy in the steel industry

Steel is a mixture of iron and other elements. The properties of steel can be changed by controlling the amounts of the other elements, such as chromium and nickel added to the iron. This makes it possible to produce steel with exactly the right properties for a particular application.

Steel furnaces use a mixture of molten iron straight from the blast furnace and scrap iron. The furnace controllers analyse this mixture to see how much chromium and nickel is there already. They can then calculate how much should be added to produce steel. Traditional techniques of analysing steel would take days. Today's modern instrumental methods can give the answers in less than an hour.

Infrared spectroscopy

Infrared spectroscopy is usually used to identify organic molecules. Different bonds absorb radiation of slightly different wavelengths. By seeing which wavelengths have been absorbed, the bonds present in the molecule can be identified.

Ultraviolet spectroscopy

Ultraviolet spectroscopy is used to measure the concentration of nitrate ions in water. Ultraviolet light with a range of wavelengths is passed through the sample and some of the radiation is absorbed. A compound is identified by comparing the ultraviolet spectrum for the sample with the spectra produced by known samples.

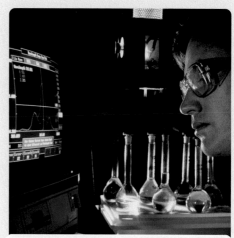

FIGURE 2: Typical sensitivity of atomic absorption spectroscopy might be as low as one part of metal (lead, for example) in a million million parts, so pollution of water by heavy metals can be detected.

EXAM HINTS AND TIPS

You should be able to explain how atomic absorption spectroscopy is used in the steel industry.

Forensic science

Forensic scientists help law enforcement agencies such as the police by providing technical information to help solve crimes. The development of modern instrumental methods has been extremely important in this area. For example, mass spectroscopy can be used to analyse hair and fingernail samples to check whether someone has been using illegal drugs.

Modern instrumental methods are also widely used to monitor levels of pollution.

QUESTIONS

5 Why are computers linked to machines such as mass spectrometers?

6 How does atomic absorption spectroscopy work?

7 Why is it an advantage to use atomic absorption spectroscopy rather than traditional methods of analysis in the steel industry?

QUESTIONS

8 Today's modern instrumental methods are faster, more accurate, more sensitive and require smaller amounts of sample. How can these methods help to reduce crime levels?

Unit summary

Concept map

Water is a good solvent for ionic substances.

Water

As the temperature increases, solids tend to become more soluble in water, while gases tend to become less soluble.

Hard water contains calcium or magnesium ions.

As the pressure increases, gases become more soluble in water.

The food that we eat provides us with energy.

Energy

Overall, exothermic reactions release energy, while endothermic reactions take in energy.

The energy in food is measured in calories. 1 calorie is equal to 4.2 J.

We can measure the energy in food using a technique called calorimetry.

We can identify non-metal ions including sulfates, halides, nitrates and ammonium ions using traditional methods.

Identifying chemicals

Modern instrumental methods of analysis are faster, more accurate, more sensitive and require smaller amounts of sample.

We can use flame tests to identify the metal ions in compounds.

Unit quiz

1   Which chemical is added to raw water to kill micro-organisms?

    fluoride   chlorine
    magnesium   calcium

2   Which gas makes the bubbles in fizzy drinks?

    carbon monoxide   nitrogen
    carbon dioxide   oxygen

3   Which of these ions would make water hard?

    calcium   sodium   hydrogen   iron

4   What is the name of the compound found in washing soda?

    sodium hydrogen carbonate
    sodium hydroxide
    sodium carbonate
    carbon dioxide

5   What is the name given to the minimum amount of energy which is required to start a chemical reaction?

    lift off activation energy   exothermic
    energy   explosive energy

6   The energy in foods is measured in calories. How many joules are equal to one calorie?

    1.0   10.0   4.2   2.4

7   Which technique is used to measure the heat flow that occurs when a reaction takes place?

    titration   displacement
    distillation   calorimetry

8   A flame test is carried out on a sample of a sodium salt. What colour would you expect to see?

    lilac   apple-green
    yellow-orange   scarlet-red

9   What colour precipitate forms when sodium hydroxide solution is added to a solution that contains copper(II) ions?

    white   grey   blue   brown

10 Which of these techniques can be used to identify the elements in a sample?

    ultraviolet spectroscopy
    infrared spectroscopy
    atomic absorption spectroscopy

Literacy activity

Body Mass Index

If you consume more energy than your body requires, your body stores this extra energy as fat. If you are very overweight or obese you are more likely to develop serious long-term health problems.

The Body Mass Index, BMI, is a useful way of calculating whether adults are the right weight. Body Mass Index is calculated using the equation:

$$\text{BMI} = \text{weight in kg} / (\text{height in m})^2$$

If your BMI is under 18.5, you are underweight.

If your BMI is between 18.5 and 24.9, you are a normal weight.

If your BMI is between 25.0 and 29.9, you are overweight.

If your BMI is over 30.0, you are obese.

This table shows some information about four adults.

Name	Weight (kg)	Height (m)	BMI
Abi	66.0	1.68	
Ed	80.0	1.82	
Alex	92.0	1.80	
Sam	95.0	1.72	

QUESTIONS   1   Copy and complete the table by calculating the BMI of each person. Give your answer to 3 significant figures.

                 2   Use the information in the table to classify each person as underweight, normal weight, overweight or obese.

1 This is a simple energy level diagram.

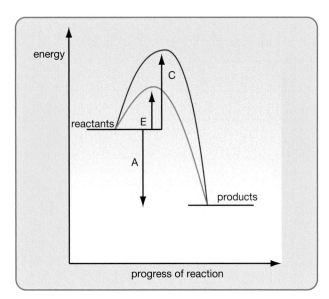

a Which arrow shows the activation energy without a catalyst? [1]

b Which arrow shows the activation energy with a catalyst? [1]

c Which arrows show the energy taken in as bonds are broken? [1]

d Which arrow shows the overall energy change for the reaction? [1]

e Is the reaction exothermic or endothermic? [1]

2 Copy out the boxes below and match the flame colour to the ion by joining the boxes with a line.

Sodium	lilac
Potassium	green
Calcium	yellow
Barium	brick-red

[4]

3 a How should you test for an ammonium salt? Give details of the test and state the result expected. [3]

b How would you test for a nitrate? Give details of the test and state the result expected. [3]

4 A series of test tube reactions were carried out on a sample. The results are shown below. Read these, then answer the questions.

Test	Result
1. Dilute hydrochloric acid was added.	No gas was formed.
2. Barium chloride solution was then added to the tube from test 1.	A white precipitate formed.
3. A few drops of sodium hydroxide was added to a fresh sample.	A white precipitate formed.
4. Sodium hydroxide was added to the results from test 3 until no further change occurred.	The white precipitate remains.

a What ion can be ruled out after test 1? [1]

b What ion does test 2 confirm the presence of? [1]

c Which three ions could be present based on test 3? [2]

d Which positive ion can be ruled out after test 4? [1]

e What further test would be needed to be certain about the metal ion? [1]

5 A student is given an organic compound and asked to analyse it in the laboratory. He does the only test he knows and finds that the sample decolourises bromine water.

a What does this tell the student? [1]

b i The student says that to find out more he would use an instrumental method such as mass spectroscopy. Give the names of two other instrumental techniques that could be used. [2]

ii Give two advantages of such instrumental methods. [2]

(Total 26 marks)

When ethanol (alcohol) burns in the air, energy is given out. The overall energy change can be calculated by using bond energy data. The equation can be shown as:

$$H - \underset{\underset{H}{|}}{\overset{\overset{H}{|}}{C}} - \underset{\underset{H}{|}}{\overset{\overset{H}{|}}{C}} - O - H \ + \ 3O = O \ \longrightarrow \ 2O = C = O \ + \ 3H - O - H$$

a i Use the bond energy data here to complete
the table below. This has been started for you.   [7]

Bond	C–H	C–O	O–H	C–C	O=O	C=O	H–O
Bond energy kJ/mol	412	358	463	348	496	743	463

ii Calculate the overall energy
change for this reaction.   [1]

iii Is the reaction endothermic
or exothermic?   [1]

b A student wants to compare energy
obtained when a crisp and bread are
burned. He burned each substance
and used the energy to heat 100 g of
water. The results are in the
table.

i Complete the table.   [4]

ii Which food provides
the most energy?
Explain your answer.   [2]

iii What is the problem with eating energy-rich foods like crisps?   [1]

Bonds broken			Bonds made		
Type	Number	Energy kJ/mol	Type	Number	Energy kJ/mol
C–H	5	5 x 412= 2060	C=O	4	4 x 743 = 2972
	Total			Total	

	Mass burnt /g	Temperature of water before heating / °C	Temperature of water after heating / °C	Temperature rise / °C	Temp. rise per gram burnt °C/g
Crisp	1.2	20	56		
Bread	2.2	21	44		

(Total 16 marks)

---

a i

Bonds broken			Bonds made		
Type	Number	Energy kJ/mol	Type	Number	Energy kJ/mol
C–H	5	5 x 412= 2060	C=O	4	4 x 743 = 2972
C–C	1	348	O–H	6	6 X 463 = 2778
C–O	1	358			
O–H	1	463			
O=O	3	3 X 496 = 1488			
	Total	4717		Total	5750

ii The overall change is 10 467 kJ/mol.

iii The reaction is exothermic.

a ii The overall change is the **difference** between the energy taken in to break bonds and the energy given out when bonds are formed. This is 5750 – 4717 = 1033 kJ/mol.

b i

	Mass burnt /g	Temperature of water before heating / °C	Temperature of water after heating / °C	Temperature rise / °C	Temp. rise per gram burnt °C/g
Crisp	1.2	20	56	36	30
Bread	2.2	21	44	23	10.5

ii The crisps have the most energy. They produce the
highest temperature rise per gram of food burnt.

iii Energy-rich foods like crisps are bad for you.

biii Yes ... but how? Eating foods which provide
more energy than you need can lead to obesity.

bii This is the correct answer.

aii This is the correct answer.

Overall Grade: B

How to get an A

Quite good answers but there were some easy marks the student failed to gain. When calculating overall energy changes you have to find the difference between the energy needed to break all bonds in the reactants and the energy given out when all the bonds form in the products.

DISCOVER SPIRAL GALAXIES!

Many objects move with circular motion, from huge galaxies containing thousands of millions of stars down to bacteria swimming. In all these, there is always some force that stops the object just moving off in a straight line. We are able to observe the way both galaxies and bacteria move by using the way light is refracted through lenses.

Out in space, well away from stars and galaxies, it is totally black. It is totally silent too, even close to the stars. The sound of all those nuclear explosions is unable to travel across the vacuum between stars.

Our galaxy, the Milky Way, is a spiral galaxy. Our Sun is about a third of the way out along one of the arms, orbiting around the centre of the galaxy. Our Earth is in orbit around the Sun, travelling at nearly 30 000 km/s.

Most galaxies contain thousands of millions of stars. Can you imagine the total amount of light given out by thousands of millions of stars like our Sun?

CONTENTS

Just a moment

You will find out:

- That the moment is the turning effect of a force
- What is meant by 'centre of mass'
- How to locate the centre of mass of symmetrical objects

Lifting bridges

The lifting bridge shown in the photograph is quite common across some canals. It is strong enough to drive a herd of cows over, and weighs several tonnes. Yet one person can lift it to allow a narrow boat to pass underneath. How can one person move it? **Moments** give us the answer.

FIGURE 1: How can one person lift this bridge?

What are moments?

Sometimes we use **forces** to make things turn, such as when we push on a door to open it, or use a spanner to undo a nut. The **turning effect** that the force has is called its moment.

- Imagine you are pushing open a heavy door. Pushing gently won't open the door, but pushing harder will. The moment is bigger if the force used is bigger.

- Imagine you are trying to undo a really tight nut. A longer spanner works much better than a shorter one. The moment is bigger if the distance between the force and the pivot (or **axis of rotation**) is bigger.

We can calculate the size of any moment using this equation:

moment = force x perpendicular distance from the line of action of the force to the axis of rotation
(newton metre, Nm)   (Newton, N)   (metre, m)

FIGURE 2: How can the moment be increased in each of these situations?

Balanced or unbalanced?   (H)

If the turning effect of the forces trying to turn an object clockwise is exactly the same size as the turning effect of the forces trying to turn the object anticlockwise, then the object won't turn at all. We can say that an object does not turn if:

total clockwise moment = total anticlockwise moment

Example: Find the size of the force needed to stop the ruler shown on the right from rotating.

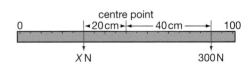

clockwise moment =
300 × 40 = 12 000 Ncm

For the ruler to balance,
anticlockwise moment =
12 000 Ncm = X × 20

X = 12 000 ÷ 20 = 600 N

(NB: It is alright to use cm instead of m for the distances, so long as you use cm for all the distances.)

░░ QUESTIONS ░░

1 What is the turning effect of a force called?
2 What **two** things make the turning effect of a force bigger?
3 Give **one** example of your own of somewhere we might use the turning effect of a force.
4 Suggest how a heavy person and a light person could sit at different ends of a see-saw so the see-saw did not turn.

...anticlockwise moment ...axis of rotation ...centre of mass

Centre of mass

If we imagine all the mass of an object concentrated at a point, that point is called its **centre of mass**. It may help to imagine the object collapsing down to a point. For example:

- a sphere would collapse down to the centre of the sphere, so the centre of mass is at the centre of the sphere
- a ruler would collapse down to a point halfway along the ruler, so the centre of mass is halfway along the ruler
- a cone would collapse to a point near the wide end, so the centre of mass is nearer the wide end than the point.

For any symmetrical object, the centre of mass is always on the axis of symmetry. If there is more than one axis or plane of symmetry, the centre of mass will be where they cross.

Making things balance

You cannot balance a ruler suspended by a string like the one above – it turns. The weight of the ruler is like a force acting downwards from the centre of mass of the ruler. The moment of the weight makes the ruler turn clockwise. We can balance the ruler by putting another weight on it that has an anticlockwise moment.

Example: The ruler shown below has a weight of 1 N. Find out what size force you would have to put at the 0 cm mark of this ruler to make it balance.

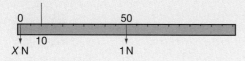

For the ruler to balance:

clockwise moment = anticlockwise moment

$1 \times 40 = X \times 10$

$X = 40 \div 10 = 4\,\text{N}$

Watch Out When an object doesn't turn, the total clockwise moment is exactly the same size as the total anticlockwise moment.

QUESTIONS

5 Describe in your own words what the centre of mass is.

6 Where would the centre of mass of a cylinder be?

7 A ruler has a mass of 50 g. Imagine it is suspended from the 40 cm mark. Where could you put a 20 g mass to make the ruler balance?

REMEMBER

The centre of mass is the point where we can imagine all the mass is concentrated.

What happens next?

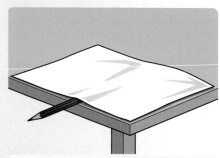

FIGURE 3: What happens when the exposed part of the pencil is hit firmly?

Imagine a pencil and paper were set up on a table as shown in figure 3. Discuss what would happen if the part of the pencil overlapping the edge of the table was hit firmly. When you have decided what you think will happen, your teacher may demonstrate the experiment to you, or may allow you to try it. Can you explain what you observe?

QUESTIONS

8 A metre rule is suspended from a string at the 30 cm mark. It balances horizontally with a 150 g mass at the 0 cm mark and a 50 g mass at the 100 cm mark. What mass would you have to replace the 150 g mass with to make the rule balance horizontally if it were suspended from the 60 cm mark?

Moments and stability

You will find out:
- What factors affect the stability of an object
- How to find the centre of mass of a thin sheet of material
- How to describe that the position of the centre of mass affects stability

You can't do that!

Have you ever tried standing with your back to a wall, your heels touching the wall, then tried to pick something up from the floor just in front of your feet? Or can you stand upright beside a wall, arms by your sides, both feet together, and the side of one foot touching the wall? Try. Can you explain what happens?

What is stability? (H)

Stability tells us how likely an object is to topple over. **Stable** objects are those that do not topple over easily. The more **unstable** an object is, the more easily it topples. How stable an object is depends on its shape and where its **centre of mass** is.

- In figure 2, the vase on the left is much less likely to topple than the vase on the right. An object is more stable if its base is wider.
- In figure 3, the vase on the left is less likely to topple. An object is more stable if its centre of mass is lower.

Equilibrium

When an object is not toppling over, scientists say it is in **equilibrium**. All three Bunsen burners in figure 4 are in equilibrium, but they are not all equally stable.

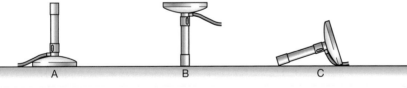

FIGURE 4: Are all these Bunsen burners in equilibrium?

- Bunsen A is in **stable equilibrium**. If you tip it slightly, it will return to the position it is in now.
- Bunsen B is in **unstable equilibrium**. If you tip it slightly, it will topple over.
- Bunsen C is in **neutral equilibrium**. If you roll it slightly, it will stay in the new position.

FIGURE 1: Why can't you do this?

FIGURE 2: Which vase is more stable?

FIGURE 3: Which vase is more stable?

WOW FACTOR!

Lifeboats are 'self-righting'. Sealed-in buoyancy makes the centre of mass so low that they are only stable the right way up.

■ QUESTIONS ■

1. Describe in your own words what is meant by an 'unstable object'.
2. State the **two** factors that affect the stability of an object.
3. What is the difference between stable equilibrium and unstable equilibrium?
4. Suggest **two** changes you could make to a lorry to make it more stable.

...centre of mass ...equilibrium ...gravity ...neutral equilibrium ...resultant moment ...stability

Finding the centre of mass

You know that a ruler will only balance horizontally if you suspend it from its centre point. If you suspend it from any other point, it will tip up until its centre point (its centre of mass) is below the point you suspend it from. When suspended, any object that is free to move will turn until its centre of mass is below the point of suspension. We can use this to find the position of the centre of mass of any thin sheet, or 'lamina'.

- Make a hole at the edge of the sheet. Suspend the sheet from this hole.
- Use a plumb line to show a vertical line running down from the point of suspension.
- Use three crosses to mark, then draw, this line.
- Repeat for two other points of suspension.
- The centre of mass is where the three lines cross.

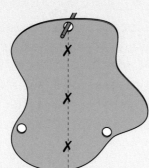

FIGURE 5: Why is it better to use three holes than two?

Explaining stability (H)

For any object, we can always imagine **gravity** as a force pulling downwards on its centre of mass.

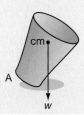 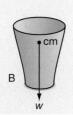 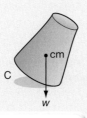

FIGURE 6: Which of these vases will topple?

Figure 6 shows three weighted vases.

- Vase A: the weight acting downwards from the centre of mass causes a **resultant moment** about the edge of the base of the vase, which makes the vase topple.
- Vase B: the weight acts down through the base and the vase does not topple.
- Vase C: The weight acts down through the base, causing a resultant moment about the edge of the base, which tips the vase upright again.

| | QUESTIONS | |

5   Use moments to explain why putting a weight in the bottom of a vase makes the vase more stable.

6   Use moments to explain why it is harder to balance a long pencil upright than it is a short pencil.

EXAM HINTS AND TIPS

Remember that an object will topple if its weight acts downwards outside its base.

Ferry disasters

FIGURE 7: Can you use moments to explain why this happened?

In March 1987 the car ferry *Herald of Free Enterprise* capsized as she left the Belgium port of Zeebrugge. 193 people died. An official report said the bow doors of the ferry had been left open. Water came in and sloshed about on the car deck as the ferry attempted to turn, making her extremely unstable. The report said that even a few centimetres of water on the car deck would have been enough to capsize the ferry. In 1994 a similar accident, caused by the bow doors leaking, caused the German-built ferry *Estonia* to sink with the loss of 852 lives.

| QUESTIONS |

7   Use moments and centre of mass to explain how water on the car decks made the *Herald of Free Enterprise* and the *Estonia* so unstable.

...stable   ...stable equilibrium   ...unstable   ...unstable equilibrium

Circular motion

You will find out:

- How force and acceleration act on an object moving in a circle
- How centripetal force is needed to keep an object moving in a circle
- How to identify what provides the centripetal force

Hammer throwing

Hammer throwing is a popular sport in Scottish Highland Games. An athlete whirls the heavy 'hammer' round and round, then releases it. The winner is the athlete whose hammer goes the furthest, in the right direction. Imagine what hammer throwing feels like. What forces act on the hammer? And on the athlete? What is the connection between whirling the hammer and the distance it travels?

FIGURE 1: What forces are in action here?

Circular motion and force

When there is no **resultant force** on an object, the object will remain stationary or will continue to move at a constant speed in a straight line. A resultant force acting on the object always makes it change speed or direction or shape.

When an object moves at a constant speed in a circle, its direction is changing all the time. This tells us that there must be a force acting on the object all the time. Without this force, the object would fly off in a straight line, like the hammer does when the hammer thrower lets go of it. For an object moving with **circular motion**, the force always acts towards the centre of the circle. This force is called the **centripetal force**.

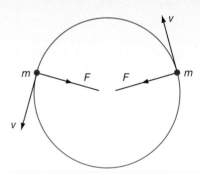

FIGURE 2: Centripetal force always acts towards the centre of the circle.

Circular motion and acceleration

Whenever there is a resultant force acting on an object, the object **accelerates** in the direction of the force. When an object accelerates, its **velocity** changes. The velocity of an object tells us about its speed and its direction. Velocity can be changing even if the speed stays the same. This is what happens for an object moving in a circle. The centripetal force towards the centre of the circle causes an acceleration, called the **centripetal acceleration**, towards the centre of the circle. The speed of the object does not change, but its direction (and its velocity) changes all the time.

FIGURE 3: Which way are the force and the acceleration acting here?

▌▌ QUESTIONS ▌▌

1. Describe in your own words how you know there is a resultant force on an object moving in a circle.
2. Which of these are always changing for an object moving in a circle? Speed, velocity, direction.
3. Explain how an object moving in a circle can be accelerating, even when its speed is constant.

...*accelerate*   ...*centripetal acceleration*   ...*centripetal force*   ...*circular motion*

How big is the centripetal force?

Imagine you are using a force to make an object move in a circle. Perhaps you are learning to throw the hammer. What will affect the size of the centripetal force you need to use?

It's hard to whirl the hammer round, but a child could whirl round a tennis ball on a string.

- As the mass of the object increases, the centripetal force you need increases.

As you whirl the object faster and faster, it gets harder and harder to stop it flying off.

- Therefore, as the speed of the object increases, the centripetal force you need increases.

Imagine a dog runs round and round you at top speed on a very short lead, then on a very long lead. When he's on a short lead he goes round you lots and lots of times in a minute. His direction is changing very quickly and you have to use a big force to stop him getting away. When he's on a long lead, it's much easier to hang on to him.

- As the radius of the circle decreases, the centripetal force you need increases.

FIGURE 4: What things increase the centripetal force needed to stop the dog getting away?

What provides the centripetal force?

Sometimes **tension** in a string provides the centripetal force for objects moving in a circle. But sometimes we can't see what is providing the centripetal force.

For vehicles driving around bends, the **friction** between the tyres and the road provides the centripetal force that stops the vehicle skidding off in a straight line. On race tracks the bends are banked – the road tilted up slightly – so that a component of the weight of the vehicle acts down the slope and adds to the force due to friction, helping to keep the fast-moving cars on the road.

> ### EXAM HINTS AND TIPS
>
> Remember: An object in circular motion always has a centripetal acceleration – towards the centre – because its direction is always changing.

> ### EXAM HINTS AND TIPS
>
> Remember: An object moving with circular motion will fly off in a straight line if the centripetal force stops acting.

QUESTIONS

4 State **two** things that would make the centripetal force needed smaller.
5 Explain why fast cars cannot go round as sharp bends as slow cars.
6 Discuss what provides the centripetal force for clothes in a spin dryer.

Centripetal force always acts towards the centre of the circle

Centrifuges

Centrifuges are useful in many areas of science for separating liquids that are mixtures of components with different masses. As the centrifuge tube is spun, the heavier particles move to the bottom of the centrifuge tube.

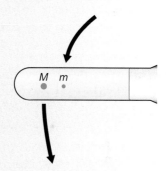

FIGURE 5: Why do these particles move apart as the centrifuge is spun?

Circular motion explains why this happens. As the tube is spun faster, the centripetal force increases. Suppose at a given speed the centripetal force is just strong enough to keep a particle of mass m in circular motion. It won't be strong enough to keep a particle of larger mass M in circular motion, so the particles of larger mass tend to fly away from the circle, ending up in the bottom of the tube.

QUESTIONS

7 A child in a car holds a helium balloon on a string. Discuss which way the helium balloon moves as the car turns a corner, and why.

Gravity and orbits

You will find out:

- That gravitational forces keep planets and moons in orbit
- The factors that affect the size of the gravitational force between two masses

Saturn's moons

Each spacecraft that flies close to Saturn discovers more moons. In 2005 scientists reported that Saturn had 47 confirmed moons. Why does Saturn have so many moons when the Earth has only one? And why do planets have moons at all? Why don't the moons just orbit the Sun, like the planets do? We can use **gravity** to answer these and other questions.

The solar system (H)

The solar system consists of planets, asteroids and comets orbiting around the Sun. Can you name all nine planets in order, starting with Mercury nearest the Sun? You may also know that the orbits of the planets are slightly squashed circles called **ellipses**. Gravity is the force that keeps the planets in their **orbits**.

We can think of the planets as moving in circles around the Sun, with gravity providing the **centripetal force** needed to keep them in **circular motion**. Without the force due to gravity, they would just fly off into deep space, moving in straight lines. Moons orbit planets because the **gravitational force** between the moon and the planet is bigger than the gravitational force between the moon and the Sun. The moon just cannot get away from the planet.

FIGURE 1: Why do some planets have lots of moons?

FIGURE 2: Use these initial letters to name the planets in order, starting from the Sun: M, V, E, M, J, S, U, N.

Watch Out Until recently, Pluto would also have been listed as a planet, but it has now been officially downgraded to a 'dwarf planet' or pluton.

More about gravity

Gravity is a force that acts between all objects with **mass**. It is a two-way force, pulling the objects together. When gravity on Earth makes an apple fall downwards, the gravitational force is actually pulling on the Earth as well as on the apple, to move them closer together. We only see the apple move because the light apple moves much more easily than the much more massive Earth! Anyway, as we are standing on the Earth, we wouldn't see it move. Also, apples falling the other side of Earth would be pulling it the other way.

'Hold tight, we're going up!'

⏹ QUESTIONS ⏹

1. What provides the centripetal force for planets orbiting the Sun?
2. What would happen to the planets if the gravitational force stopped acting?
3. Describe in your own words why moons orbit planets instead of orbiting the Sun.
4. What do we mean when we say that gravity is a 'two-way force'?

---

centripetal acceleration ...centripetal force ...circular motion ...ellipse ...free fall

How big is the gravitational force?

The size of the gravitational force between two objects depends on the mass of the objects and on the distance between them.

- The gravitational force increases when the mass of one or both of the objects increase.

This is why the **weight** (the gravitational force between an object and Earth) is bigger for a 1 kg mass than it is for a 1 g mass. It is also why objects weigh less on the Moon than they do on Earth – the mass of the Moon is less than the mass of the Earth.

- The gravitational force decreases as the distance between the objects increases.

This explains why the Earth orbits around the Sun, but does not orbit around all the other stars in the Universe. All the stars except the Sun are so far away that the gravitational force between them and the Earth is too small to have a noticeable effect.

FIGURE 3: Has this astronaut really escaped from gravity?

Free fall

The astronaut in figure 3 is in **free fall**. Sometimes people call this 'zero gravity' or 'weightlessness'. This is very misleading because it makes it sound as though gravity is not acting on the astronaut – and it is. You would have to be more than a thousand times as far away as Pluto to escape the Sun's gravity. The astronaut and his spacecraft have exactly the same **centripetal acceleration** towards the Earth, so the astronaut does not feel any pull towards his spacecraft and is able to float around inside it. You can experience the same effect on the vertical-drop rides at some theme parks.

Tides

Tides are caused by the gravitational attraction between the Earth and the Moon. The gravitational force decreases with increasing distance, so the water nearest the Moon is pulled more strongly towards the Moon than the mass of the Earth itself, causing high tide on the side of Earth nearest the Moon.

The Moon and the Earth are also revolving around a common centre of mass, causing the oceans to be 'flung outwards', just as passengers are 'flung outwards' as a car goes round a bend. This causes the high tide on the opposite side of the Earth.

The gravitational force from the Sun has much less effect, but can make tides higher or lower, depending on the relative positions of the Sun and the Moon.

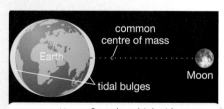

FIGURE 4: How often does high tide occur in any particular place?

QUESTIONS

5 Describe **two** ways in which the gravitational force between two objects could be decreased.

6 Explain why our Moon orbits the Earth, not the Sun.

7 Discuss whether or not an astronaut in free fall will change speed.

QUESTIONS

8 Use the Internet to find out more about the tides. Explain what you find out to a partner.

Satellites

You will find out:

- About types and uses of artificial satellites
- How to describe the different types of satellite orbit
- How to use centripetal force and speed to explain satellite orbits

Artificial satellites

The first artificial **satellite** was launched by the Russians in 1957. Now there are thousands of satellites orbiting Earth, as well as thousands of pieces of broken satellites and other 'space junk'. A NASA scientific observatory satellite, launched in 1991, weighed over 17 tonnes, but most modern satellites only weigh a few tens of kilograms because lighter satellites are cheaper to build and to launch into space.

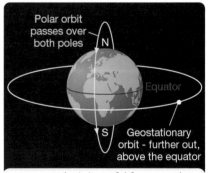

FIGURE 1: Do you know what 'satellite TV' is?

What is a satellite?

A **satellite** is any object in space that **orbits** around a larger body. So the Moon is Earth's **natural satellite**. Often when we talk about satellites we mean **artificial satellites** – the devices scientists have launched into orbit around Earth. These have many different uses. For example:

- communications satellites, used for sending telephone and television signals around the world
- Global Positioning System (GPS) satellites, used for navigation
- monitoring satellites used for weather forecasting, tracking animal migration, and monitoring factors affecting the environment, such as deforestation
- scientific research satellites, used for studying Earth, the solar system and beyond
- military satellites, sometimes called 'spy satellites'.

All these satellites have two things in common: they all contain solar panels, or some other energy source, to make the instruments on board work, and they all have a means of sending electrical signals back to Earth.

Different orbits

There are two types of satellite orbit. A satellite in **geostationary orbit** stays above the same point on the Earth's surface all the time, usually a point near the equator. Communications satellites are in geostationary orbit, so the television company always knows where to send the television signals to. Monitoring satellites usually orbit much closer to the Earth's surface, orbiting in circles passing over the North and South Poles. This way they can monitor all of the Earth's surface every few hours. This type of orbit is called a **polar orbit**.

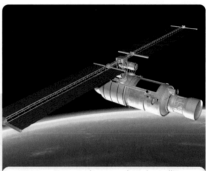

FIGURE 2: Why is it useful for a weather satellite to be in a polar orbit?

```
QUESTIONS
```

1 Describe in your own words what an 'artificial satellite' is.
2 Name **four** different types of satellite.
3 State **two** things that satellites have in common.
4 Describe the difference between 'geostationary orbit' and 'polar orbit'.

EXAM HINTS AND TIPS

Remember: 'Geo' means 'earth' and 'stationary' means 'still'. So a satellite in geostationary orbit seems to stay still above the Earth's surface.

...artificial satellite ...centripetal force   ...geostationary orbit   ...gravitational force

Understanding orbits

To understand how satellites stay in orbit, we have to think about the **centripetal force** needed to keep the satellite moving in a circle, and the **speed** the satellite is travelling at.

Imagine a satellite is orbiting at a particular height above the Earth. If it goes too fast, the centripetal force will not be large enough to stop the satellite flying off in a straight line, and disappearing into space. If it goes too slowly it will not have enough kinetic energy to prevent the centripetal force pulling it back down to the Earth's surface.

The centripetal force on a satellite is provided by the **gravitational force**. This decreases as the satellite gets further from Earth, so the satellite has to go slower to stop it flying off into space.

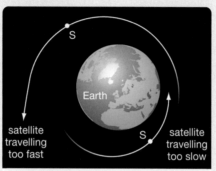

FIGURE 3: A satellite must not travel too fast or too slowly.

Geostationary orbit

Geostationary satellites orbit the Earth at a height of almost 36 000 km, completing one orbit every 24 hours, so they always stay above the same point on the Earth's surface. Follow this thought experiment to find out why they have to be at exactly the right height.

FIGURE 4: A satellite in geostationary orbit.

- The satellite is in geostationary orbit, travelling at speed v. The centripetal force is exactly the right size to keep it in orbit.

- Imagine the satellite moves a bit further away. The centripetal force will decrease.

- The satellite will have to slow down to prevent it flying off into space.

- If the satellite slows down, it will not be able to complete a whole orbit in 24 hours. It will no longer be in geostationary orbit.

WOW FACTOR!

A satellite in geostationary orbit travels at just over 11 000 km/h. Satellites in polar orbit go much faster!

Measuring the Earth's gravity

The gravitational force due to the Earth is not the same everywhere on the Earth's surface. Features such as ocean ridges and mountain ranges make it stronger in some places than in others. Scientists are using a pair of satellites to map the variations. The satellites orbit Earth 220 km apart. Their distance apart, accurate to a few thousandths of a millimetre, and their exact speed are measured using GPS and a beam of microwaves bounced between the two satellites. As the gravitational force on each satellite varies, the satellites move closer together or further apart. Scientists hope the information from these two satellites will help them predict the pattern of ocean currents, helping them to understand how these affect climate.

QUESTIONS

5 What provides the centripetal force for a satellite orbiting Earth?

6 Why does a satellite fall back to Earth if it travels too slowly?

7 Discuss what would happen to a satellite in geostationary orbit if it moved closer to Earth. Think about these things in order: centripetal force, speed, time taken to complete one orbit.

QUESTIONS

8 Discuss the advantages and disadvantages of making the pair of satellites orbit the Earth further apart or closer together.

Telstar

SELF-CHECK ACTIVITY

CONTEXT

In 1962, television was about to enter a whole new world – that of moving pictures and sound being sent from one continent to another. Telstar was the satellite built to do this job. It was spherical and about one metre in diameter. It had a mass of 77 kg and was powered by solar cells.

It was launched in April 1962 and placed above the Earth so that it orbited once every 2 hours 37 minutes. Its function was to enable pictures and sound to be sent from the USA to France and Britain. It didn't transmit directly to people's homes, but to the TV company to allow them to receive, edit and re-transmit to viewers.

As it was in a low orbit it could only connect the USA with Britain and France for about 20 minutes, and then vanished for well over 2 hours. This was a problem for two reasons. Firstly it meant that there were long periods when nothing could be transmitted, and secondly it meant that the aerial had to track the satellite as it travelled across the sky.

The place in Britain where the signal was received was at Goonhilly in Cornwall. The huge aerial with its parabolic reflector had to pan across the sky and then move back, ready for the next pass.

In fact, Telstar did not last long. The transistors in the circuits were damaged by radiation released by weapons tests and although engineers managed to get it working again, it wasn't to be for long. Within less than a year of launching, it was out of use, but it had shown the way for global links.

Goonhilly is still relaying TV signals from across the Atlantic (and elsewhere) but the satellites used these days are all geostationary ones. They are much further out than Telstar and orbit the Earth at the same rate that the Earth rotates; they are, therefore, always in the same place relative to a point on the surface of the Earth.

CHALLENGE

STEP 1

Telstar was in a much lower orbit than modern geostationary satellites. Compare its speed to that of those later satellites.

STEP 2

Low orbiting satellites are less effective at providing a TV link between continents. Why do you think Telstar had to be placed in a low orbit?

STEP 3

Some modern weather image satellites are put in a low orbit. Why might it be an advantage for that kind of satellite?

STEP 4

Why did the aerial used at Goonhilly have to have such a large reflector?

STEP 5

Why would satellites like Telstar not be suitable for providing satellite TV directly to people's homes? You should be able to think of several reasons.

Maximise your grade

These sentences show what you need to include in your work to achieve each grade. Use them to improve your work and be more successful.

Grade	Answer includes...
	Describe how the speed has to be different for a satellite in a lower orbit.
F	Suggest why Telstar was placed in a lower orbit.
	Research and record the speed of Telstar compared to that of a satellite in geostationary orbit.
	Suggest why a low orbit might be appropriate for a weather satellite.
C	Suggest why a large reflector had to be used to detect the signal.
	Explain in detail why a large reflector had to be used to detect the signal.
A	Suggest why a satellite like Telstar could not be used to broadcast directly to people's homes.
	Identify and explain several reasons why a satellite like Telstar could not be used to broadcast directly to people's homes.

Light and mirrors

You will find out:
- How to construct ray diagrams for the images formed by mirrors
- How to describe the images formed by plane and curved mirrors
- About uses of concave and convex mirrors

Hall of Mirrors

Have you ever been in a Hall of Mirrors? The mirrors can make you look much fatter or thinner than you really are, or much taller or shorter. They can even change just part of your reflection so you look as though you have very long legs, or a very long neck. How magical they are!

FIGURE 1: Why do the mirrors in a Hall of Mirrors give such strange reflections?

Drawing ray diagrams

Figure 2 is a ray diagram showing a ray of light hitting a plane mirror, (a mirror that is flat). The ray diagram has these important features.

- The normal is a line drawn perpendicular (at right angles) to the reflecting surface at the point of incidence (where the incident ray hits the mirror). The normal helps you to draw and measure angles accurately.
- The incident ray is the ray of light going towards the mirror. The angle between this ray and the normal is called the angle of incidence.
- The reflected ray is the ray of light going away from the mirror. The angle between this ray and the normal is called the angle of reflection.
- Whenever light reflects from a mirror, the angle of incidence is equal to the angle of reflection.

Describing images

Think about how you could describe your image (your reflection) formed by a plane mirror.

- The image is the same way up as the object (you). We say it is upright, not **inverted** (upside down).
- The image is the same size as the object. We say it is not magnified, or that the magnification is 1.
- The image is the same distance from the mirror as the object.
- The image is not really there. If you were to put a screen behind the mirror you would not see an image of you on the screen. We say it is **virtual**, not **real**.

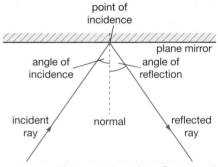

FIGURE 2: Which way does the reflected ray move if the angle of incidence increases?

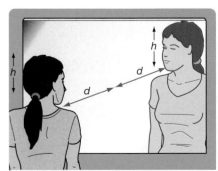

FIGURE 3: Can you use the correct scientific language to describe this reflection?

⊪ QUESTIONS ⊪

1   Name **six** things that should be included in a ray diagram. Give a description or definition for each one to a partner.

2   Write down all **four** characteristics that describe the image formed by a plane mirror. Use the correct scientific language.

...concave   ...convex   ...focal length   ...focus

What happens if the mirror is curved?

Figure 4 shows how parallel rays of light change direction when they hit a curved mirror.

- A **concave** (or converging) mirror has a reflecting surface that curves inwards, like a cave or the bowl of a spoon. Parallel rays hitting it come together, or converge.

- A **convex** (or diverging) mirror has a reflecting surface that curves outwards, like the back of a spoon. Parallel rays hitting it spread out, or diverge.

- When parallel incident rays are reflected from a curved mirror, the **focus** is the point that all the reflected rays pass through, or that all the reflected rays seem to have come from.

- The distance between the focus and the mirror is called the **focal length** (*f* in figure 4) of the mirror. The focal length is half the radius of curvature of the mirror.

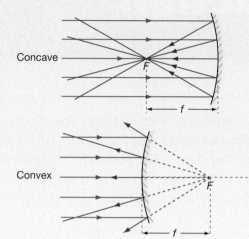

Concave

Convex

FIGURE 4: Reflection in curved mirrors.

Using curved mirrors (H)

The image in a convex mirror is always upright, and smaller than the object. This makes convex mirrors very useful for driving mirrors, or as shop security mirrors, as they have a very wide field of view – you can see a much larger area in them than you would in a plane mirror.

FIGURE 5: Can you identify the plane, convex and concave mirrors in these photographs?

The magnification of a mirror is found using the formula:

$$\text{magnification} = \frac{\text{height of image}}{\text{height of object}}$$

If the object is a long way away from a concave mirror, the image is inverted and smaller than the object. This is useful for collecting and focusing a signal, for instance in a satellite dish or telescope. If the object is closer to a concave mirror than its focus, the image is upright and larger than the object. Make-up mirrors are concave.

▌▌▌▌ QUESTIONS ▌▌▌▌

3   Describe what is meant by the 'focus' of a curved mirror.

4   Jan's eye is 3 cm wide, but in her make-up mirror it looks 3.6 cm wide. What is the magnification of her mirror?

5   Discuss with a partner how the images in a Hall of Mirrors are formed.

The angle of incidence is equal to the angle of reflection

Atomic hammers

Space telescopes use curved mirrors to collect light and form images. The mirrors have to be ultra-smooth to produce images without any distortions. Polishing the mirror sometimes rubs away too much of the surface. American scientists have found they can 'hammer' the surface smooth, without damaging any coating on the mirror, using a beam of atoms of an inert (unreactive) gas, such as argon, fired at the mirror in a vacuum. The strength of the 'hammer' can be changed by changing the energy of the beam of gas atoms.

▌▌▌▌ QUESTIONS ▌▌▌▌

6   A torch has a bright light bulb placed at the focus of a concave mirror. Discuss what the torch beam will be like.

Refraction

You will find out:

- What refraction is and why it happens
- What happens to light passing through convex and concave lenses
- How to draw ray diagrams for lenses

Bull's eye!

Have you ever seen windows like this, where the image you see through them is distorted? This happens because the glass has different thicknesses in different places, so rays of light passing through the window are bent. Even plain windows in very old houses often give distorted images because it used to be much harder to make large, flat panes of glass.

FIGURE 1: Why is this image distorted?

What is refraction?

Have you seen how a stick in water looks bent, or a coin in the bottom of a mug can be made to 'disappear'? These effects happen because light changes direction as it passes from water to air.

Figure 2 shows how a ray of light changes direction as it passes through a glass block or through a **prism**. This is called **refraction**.

- Refraction happens at every boundary between two different materials. It does not happen inside the glass block itself.
- The light ray bends towards the **normal** as it goes from air into glass. It bends away from the normal as it goes from glass to air.

Why does refraction happen?

You have probably heard that light always travels at the same speed – at the **speed of light**! This is not quite true. It is harder for light to travel through glass than through air. So light actually slows down a tiny bit as it goes through glass.

Look at figure 3. Imagine you are driving the car along the light beam. When one side of the car hits the glass block, that side of the car will slow down, while the other side of the car keeps going just as fast as before. The car will turn towards the glass block, towards the normal, just as a ray of light does.

The **refractive index** of the glass tells us how much the light changes direction as it enters or leaves the glass. The bigger the refractive index, the more the light changes direction.

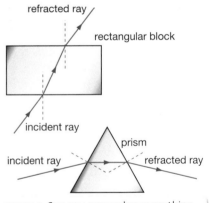

FIGURE 2: Can you remember something else that happens to light passing through a prism?

FIGURE 3: What will happen when the car hits the block?

⏸ QUESTIONS ⏸

1. Which way is light refracted as it passes from glass to air?
2. What happens to the speed of light as it goes from air to glass?
3. Water refracts light in exactly the same way as glass does. What does this tell you about the speed of light in water?

...concave   ...converging   ...convex   ...diverging   ...focal length   ...magnification   ...normal

How do lenses work?

Lenses are like a collection of prisms. The light changes direction at both boundaries of the lens. Look at figure 4. You can see that a **convex** lens is a **converging** lens; it makes the rays of light come together. A **concave** lens is a **diverging** lens; it makes the rays of light spread out.

Figure 5 shows the standard way of drawing rays passing through a lens, imagining the ray of light changing direction only once in the centre of the lens. You can find the **focal length** of a lens by shining parallel rays of light through it and finding where the refracted rays cross over, or where they seem to come from.

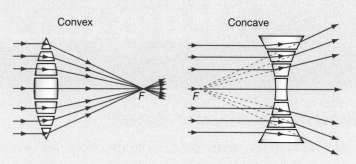

FIGURE 4: Lenses are like a lot of prisms joined together.

Drawing ray diagrams

We can use **ray diagrams** like the ones in figure 6 to find the type of image formed by a lens. If we draw the ray diagram to scale, we can find the position and size of the image too.

- Draw the **principal axis**. Draw the centre line of the lens at right angles to the principal axis. Mark C, the centre of the lens, and F, the focus. Draw the lens.
- Draw the object at the correct distance from the lens. Measure the distance from the centre line of the lens, not the edge.
- Draw a ray from the top of the object straight through point C on the lens.
- Draw a ray from the top of the object to the lens, parallel to the principal axis, then through the focus.
- The top of the image is where these two rays cross.
- Repeat the process drawing two rays from the bottom of the object (and other points if you need to). Draw the image.

You can calculate the **magnification** of a lens using the formula:

$$\text{magnification} = \frac{\text{height of image}}{\text{height of object}}$$

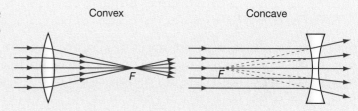

FIGURE 5: Why are the rays to the focus of the concave lens drawn as dotted lines?

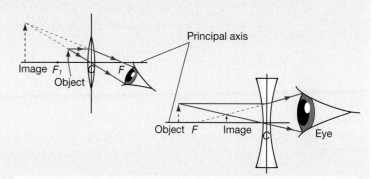

FIGURE 6: Formation of images by convex and concave lenses.

▦ QUESTIONS ▦

4 What is the other name for a convex lens?

5 Describe how to find the focal length of a concave lens.

6 Draw a ray diagram for an object 2 cm tall, placed 3 cm from a convex lens with focal length 2 cm. Find the size and position of the image, and the magnification of the lens.

Using lenses

You will find out:
- About some uses of convex and concave lenses
- How to describe the images formed by convex and concave lenses for objects at different distances from the lens

What can you see?

Over half the people in the UK wear spectacles or contact lenses, and many more need to. If you are one of them, or you know someone who does, you will know how inconvenient it is when glasses get lost or broken. Whether you wear glasses or not, you have almost certainly used something that includes lenses, such as binoculars, a telescope, a microscope or a camera.

Correcting vision

People who are **short-sighted** cannot see distant objects clearly. Their eyeball is too long and the image forms in front of their retina. A **concave lens** makes rays of light from a distant object diverge, so that the image forms further back, on the retina.

People who are **long-sighted** cannot see near objects clearly. Their eyeball is too short and the image would form behind their retina. A **convex lens** makes rays of light from a near object converge, so that the image forms further forward, on the retina.

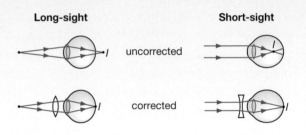

FIGURE 1: What type of lens is being used to correct each type of problem?

A magnifying glass

You can see from the diagrams in figure 2 that how much a **magnifying glass** magnifies an object depends on the **focal length** of its lens, that is, on how curved the lens is. The more curved the lens, the shorter its focal length, and the more the magnifying glass magnifies whatever you are looking at. For any lens, we can calculate the **magnification** using the usual formula:

$$\text{magnification} = \frac{\text{height of image}}{\text{height of object}}$$

Figure 3 shows water acting like a lens. The bowl of water is acting like a very curved magnifying glass, with a short focal length and a high magnification. Before microscopes were invented, scientists discovered that they could use tiny drops of water on glass slides as very powerful magnifying glasses. Try it, if you have the chance.

FIGURE 2: Which lens would make the best magnifying glass?

FIGURE 3: Water can magnify too!

⚏ QUESTIONS ⚏

1. Describe what we mean when we say someone is 'long-sighted'.
2. What type of lens corrects short-sightedness, and how does it work?
3. How does the focal length of a magnifying glass affect its magnification?
4. What is the magnification of a lens that makes a bug that is 4 mm wide look 6 mm wide?

...concave lens ...convex lens ...focal length ...inverted ...long-sighted

Changing the image (H)

You can see from figure 4 that a concave lens always forms the same type of image, wherever the object is placed. The image is always **virtual**, **upright** and smaller than the object (magnification is always less than 1).

This is not true for a convex lens. Hold a magnifying glass at arm's length and look through it. What type of image do you see? The type of image formed in a convex lens depends on the distance between the object and the lens.

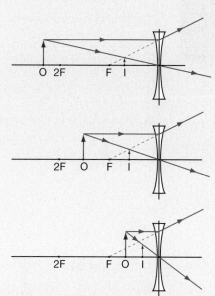

FIGURE 4: Can you describe the image formed by a concave lens?

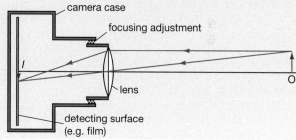

FIGURE 5: When will the image be the same size as the object?

Using convex lenses

The image formed by a camera is **real** and **inverted**. In figure 5 you can see that the distance between the image and the lens increases as the object gets closer to the lens. To focus the camera on closer objects, you move the lens outwards, so that the distance between the lens and the detecting surface increases. Most modern cameras do this automatically for you, but you can often see the lens moving.

In your eye, you cannot change the distance between the lens and the retina. Your eye forms clear images of objects at different distances by using muscles around the edge of the lens to change the focal length of the lens. As you get older the lens does not change shape as easily, which is why most people become long-sighted as they age.

FIGURE 6: How could you form clear images for objects at different distances from the camera?

▌▐▌ QUESTIONS ▌▐▌

5 What is meant by a 'virtual' image?

6 Where must you place the object so that a convex lens gives an image with a magnification of more than 1?

7 Explain in your own words what is meant by 'focusing' a camera.

...magnification ...magnifying glass ...real ...short-sighted ...upright ...virtual

Listen! Look!

You will find out:
- How sounds are caused, and how they travel
- How to describe sounds
- How to compare sounds using oscilloscope traces

Sound or noise?

We usually call sounds that we don't like 'noise', but people disagree about what sounds are 'noise'. For example, would you call church bells on Sunday morning noise or a pleasant sound? Noise pollution is generally defined as sounds that are loud enough or go on long enough to cause damage to hearing. Can you think of some situations where it is important to be able to measure sound?

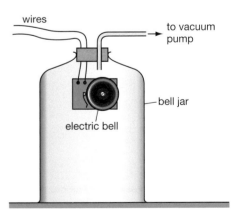

FIGURE 1: Why does this noise monitor need to wear ear defenders?

Looking and listening

Sounds are caused by things **vibrating**. Put your fingers on your throat as you speak, look at a tuning fork as it is 'singing', or touch the front of a loudspeaker when loud music is playing. The vibrations make the air particles vibrate – sound is transmitted as a wave of vibrating air particles.

A sound wave has places where the air particles are squashed together (**compression**) and places where they are spread out (**rarefaction**). Sound travels as a **longitudinal wave**; the air particles vibrate backwards and forwards in the same direction as the sound energy travels.

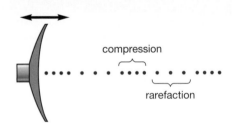

FIGURE 2: Can you describe the difference between a longitudinal wave and a transverse wave?

Have you seen the experiment shown in figure 3? As the air is pumped out of the bell jar, the sound from the ringing bell gets quieter and quieter until you can no longer hear it. Sound cannot travel through a **vacuum** – there are no vibrating particles to transmit the sound energy.

Describing sounds

To describe a sound we need to know three things.

- The **amplitude**, or volume, – how loud or quiet the sound is. Amplitude is measured in **decibels (dB)**. A whisper is about 10 dB, a pneumatic drill about 3 m away is about 100 dB. Listening to sounds above about 85 dB for more than 8 hours a day can permanently damage your hearing.
- The **frequency**, or **pitch** – how high or low the sound is. Frequency is measured in cycles per second (**Hertz, Hz**). Humans can hear frequencies in the range 20–20 000 Hz.
- The **quality** of the sound – whether or not the sound is pleasant to listen to.

FIGURE 3: How can you tell the bell still produces sound when the air is pumped out?

(labels on figure 3: wires; to vacuum pump; bell jar; electric bell)

⁞⁞ QUESTIONS ⁞⁞

1. What causes sound?
2. What is a longitudinal wave?
3. Explain in your own words why sound cannot travel through a vacuum.
4. Give an example of a high amplitude, low frequency sound.

... amplitude ...compression ...decibels (dB) ...frequency ...Hertz (Hz) ...longitudinal wave

Using an oscilloscope to compare sounds

We can use the trace on an **oscilloscope** to 'see' a sound wave. It does not actually show us the sound wave itself (because the oscilloscope trace is a transverse wave and the sound wave is longitudinal), but it does allow us to see how the amplitude and frequency of a sound wave changes.

- The vertical height of the trace shows amplitude.
- The horizontal width of the trace shows frequency, or pitch.

Look at figure 4. Trace A has a higher amplitude than trace B; it is the trace of a louder sound. The horizontal axis of each trace represents time. You can see that trace C completes two cycles in the same time as trace D completes one cycle. Trace C will complete twice as many cycles in one second as trace D. So trace C is for a sound with twice the frequency of the sound making trace D.

The **time base** of an oscilloscope tells us how long the horizontal axis of the oscilloscope represents. We can use this to calculate the exact frequency of a sound. If the whole trace shown for trace C represents 0.01 second, we can see that each complete cycle of sound C takes 0.005 second. So sound C in 1 second would complete 200 cycles, and has a frequency of 200 Hz.

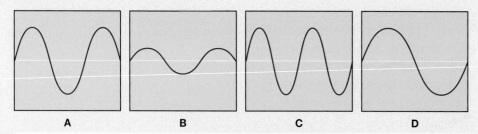

A   **B**   **C**   **D**

FIGURE 4: What would the trace look like for a sound that was getting louder?

Musical instruments

Different musical instruments sound different even when they play the same note. That is because each instrument produces the main note and also lots of other notes (called harmonics), with whole-number multiples of the frequency of the main note. All these notes add together to give the unique quality of sound of each instrument.

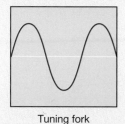

Tuning fork

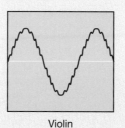

Piano

Violin

FIGURE 5: How can you tell these instruments are all playing the same note?

QUESTIONS

5. Describe the oscilloscope trace for a sound that gets quieter, then louder.
6. Copy trace D in figure 4, and draw another trace over it for a sound with half the amplitude and half the frequency.
7. An oscilloscope trace shows five complete cycles in 0.1 second. What is the frequency of the sound wave?

What are decibels?

Decibels measure the energy transmitted by a sound. The way human hearing works means that decibels are worked out on an unusual scale. Whispering is about 10 dB and a pneumatic drill 3m away is about 100 dB, but that does not mean that the sound from a pneumatic drill has only ten times the energy of a whisper. Decibels are worked out using a logarithmic scale, which means that when the number of decibels goes up by 10, the sound is ten times louder. So a conversation at about 50 dB is not five times louder than a whisper. The number of decibels has increased by 40, so the conversation is $10 \times 10 \times 10 \times 10$ (10^4), that is 10000, times louder than the whisper.

QUESTIONS

8. The pain threshold is about 120 dB, and 140 dB can cause immediate deafness. How do these volumes compare with the loudness of a pneumatic drill?

Did you hear that?

You will find out:

- What ultrasound is
- About examples of reflection and refraction of sound
- Some ways in which ultrasound can be useful

Bats are amazing!

Bats are some of the UK's smallest mammals, weighing about the same as a 20 p coin. They are amazing creatures. They can find and catch flying insects in total darkness without bumping into anything, and can even tell the difference between a twig and a twig with a moth on it! How do they do it? Children sometimes claim they can hear bats squeaking, and that's an important clue.

FIGURE 1: Bats are great to watch, and they certainly never get tangled in your hair!

Sound you can't hear

Humans can hear sounds in the **frequency** range 20 Hz to 20 000 Hz, but sound is caused by things **vibrating**, and things can vibrate at any speed. Elephants and crocodiles can hear 'rumbles' that are far too low for us to hear, and dogs and many other animals can hear **ultrasound**, sounds that are too high-pitched for our ears to detect. Bats find their way around using ultrasound squeaks. As we get older, we gradually become less able to hear high sounds, which is why many children can hear bats but most adults cannot.

Reflection and refraction of sound

Both sound and ultrasound signals can be reflected. We call the **reflection** of a sound an **echo**. Echoes are easiest to hear near hard surfaces, such as buildings, tunnels or empty houses, because sound reflects best from hard surfaces.

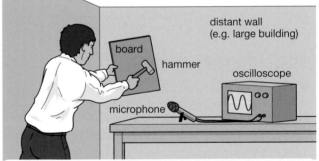

FIGURE 2: This man is measuring the speed of sound in air, by timing how long it takes for an echo to get back to him.

Remember that **refraction** is when a wave, such as light, changes speed when it goes from one material to another. Sound and ultrasound can be refracted too. They travel faster in solids than in air, because it is easier for the vibrations to pass from particle to particle within a solid. That is why you can hear railway lines humming before you can hear a train coming. Have you noticed that you can hear sounds from further away at night? That is because sound travels more slowly through colder air. At night-time the air close to Earth is colder than the air higher up, so sound is refracted down towards the Earth's surface.

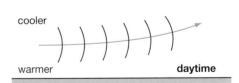

FIGURE 3: Why does the sound signal bend away from the Earth during the daytime?

⊞ QUESTIONS ⊞

1 What is ultrasound?
2 Why are children more likely to be able to hear bats than adults are?
3 In the oscilloscope trace from the experiment shown in figure 2, which will have the larger amplitude, the original sound or the echo?
4 What is refraction?

...amplitude ...echo ... frequency ...media

Ultrasound reflections (H)

Whenever an ultrasound signal reaches a boundary between two different materials (**media**), some of the signal is reflected and some is refracted and passes on through the new material, but at a different speed.

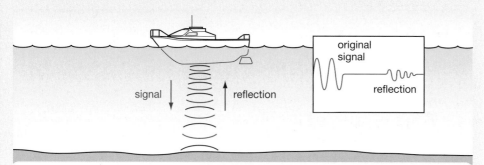

signal ↓   ↑ reflection

original signal

reflection

FIGURE 4: Which would give a louder reflected signal, a shoal of fish or the seabed?

Figure 4 shows how ships can use ultrasound to measure the depth of the water they are in.

- The reflected signal always has a smaller **amplitude** than the original signal. Only a small part of the original signal is reflected back to the boat.

- The horizontal distance between the original signal and the reflection tells the monitor how long the signal took to travel to the seabed and back again. Knowing that the speed of sound in sea water is approximately 1530 m/s, the distance to the seabed can be calculated.

Other uses of ultrasound

If there are two boundaries, on each side of a layer of rock for example, some of the ultrasound signal will be reflected from each boundary, giving two reflected signals. The time between the two reflected signals can be used to calculate the distance between the boundaries. This is useful for:

- measuring thicknesses of pipes, or layers of paint
- finding oil or gas in different rock formations

There are many medical uses of ultrasound, including scanning unborn babies (fetuses) to check they are healthy, measuring blood flow through the heart and major blood vessels, detecting kidney stones and some cancers.

Ultrasound can also be used to clean machinery that is difficult or impossible to dismantle and jewellers use ultrasound to clean jewellery. Ultrasound is used to vibrate the machinery or jewellery so that the dirt is shaken off.

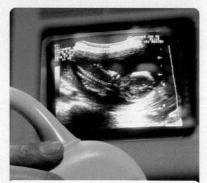

FIGURE 5: Ultrasound can be used to check the development of a fetus.

Ultrasound is sound signals too high-pitched for our ears to detect

Exploding tumours?

In 2003 a company from Northern Ireland announced that it had destroyed cancer cells in mice without drugs, surgery or radiation. They had found that applying an electric field to the cancer tumour made the cells particularly good at absorbing ultrasound signals instead of transmitting or reflecting them. They were able to use a blast of low energy ultrasound to make the tumour cells 'explode'. Much more work is needed, but the company hopes to be able to start trials in humans soon.

QUESTIONS

7 Suggest some reasons why it is a good thing to be able to use a low energy ultrasound signal.

8 How does the electric field help?

QUESTIONS

5 Suggest how bats use ultrasound to find prey and to avoid obstacles.

6 Ultrasound can be used to measure an aeroplane's height above the ground. Suggest why the depth meter from a ship could not be used as an altitude meter for an aircraft.

Unit summary

Concept map

The turning effect of a force is called its moment. It is calculated from:
moment = force × perpendicular distance from the line of action of the force to the axis of rotation.

The gravitational force between two objects increases as the mass increases and as the distance between them decreases.

Satellites can be in geostationary orbits or polar orbits.

When an object is not turning, total anticlockwise moment = total clockwise moment.

A stable object does not topple easily, has a wide base and a low centre of mass.

Moments and circular motion

The centripetal force needed to keep an object moving in a circle increases as the mass or the speed of the object increases, and as the radius of the circle decreases.

Gravity provides the centripetal force needed to keep planets and satellites in orbit.

An object in circular motion always has a centripetal force and a centripetal acceleration acting towards the centre of the circle.

A ray diagram must show the normal, and the incident, reflected or refracted rays.

Light

Convex lenses are used in magnifying glasses and cameras and for correcting long-sight. Concave lenses are used to correct short-sight.

We describe an image by saying if it is: upright or inverted, real or virtual, and how big its magnification is.

A convex lens is a converging lens. A concave lens is a diverging lens.

Concave mirrors make rays of light converge. Convex mirrors make rays diverge.

Light bends towards the normal as it enters glass, and away from the normal as it leaves.

Refraction is caused by light changing speed as it passes from one material to another.

Sound is caused by objects vibrating. It travels as a longitudinal wave. It cannot travel through a vacuum.

Sound and ultrasound

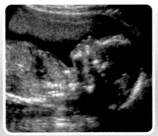

Ultrasound reflections are used to measure depth or thickness, for medical scanning and industrial cleaning.

We describe a sound by describing its amplitude, its frequency or pitch, and its quality.

Sounds can be compared using an oscilloscope trace. The vertical scale shows amplitude, the horizontal scale shows frequency.

Sound and ultrasound can be reflected and refracted.

Ultrasound is too high pitched for humans to hear. Humans hear sounds in the range 20–20 000 Hz.

Unit quiz

1 A metre rule suspended from its centre point has a 15 N force at the 60 cm mark. What force must be put at the 0 cm mark to make the ruler balance?

2 Describe the difference between stable equilibrium and unstable equilibrium.

3 Give **two** ways in which the stability of an object could be improved. Describe how they work.

4 Which of these is continually changing for an object in circular motion?

      its velocity   its speed   its direction

5 What is the acceleration for an object in circular motion called, and which way does it act?

6 Give **three** factors that affect the size of the centripetal force needed and say what effect they have.

7 What factors affect the size of the gravitational force on a satellite orbiting a planet?

8 Describe the difference between a geostationary orbit and a polar orbit.

9 List **five** words used to describe images. Say what each word means.

10 Describe how each of these mirrors affects light rays, and how the mirror can be used.

     convex mirror   **concave mirror**

11 What happens to a ray of light when it passes from glass to air?

12 Draw a ray diagram to show the image formed by a convex lens with focal length 4 cm, for an object 2 cm high placed 2 cm from the lens. Describe the image.

13 Explain why sound cannot travel through a vacuum.

14 Draw oscilloscope traces for these sounds.
   a) loud, low pitched
   b) quiet, high pitched

15 What is ultrasound? Describe **one** use of ultrasound.

Citizenship activity

Danger to marine life

Many marine mammals, such as dolphins and whales, use sound to find their way around and to communicate with each other. Some scientists believe that whales become lost and beach themselves because their hearing is damaged by ultrasound signals (used for underwater surveys) or by loud sounds from underwater explosions.

In 2004 several dead giant squid were washed ashore in the Bay of Biscay. This occurred shortly after local offshore geological surveys had been carried out using 200 dB pulses of sound waves. Forensic examinations showed that the squid all had badly damaged ears. Scientists think this caused the squid to become disorientated and rise to the surface. The squid suffocated because the shallower, warmer water could not hold as much oxygen as they needed.

The US Navy regularly carries out underwater test explosions and it has been trying to prevent these doing so much damage to fish and other marine life. It has found that surrounding an underwater explosion with a curtain of bubbles absorbs much of the energy from the explosion and limits the damage to a smaller area.

QUESTIONS

1 How do some scientists believe ultrasound or loud sounds can harm whales?

2 Discuss whether or not the dead squid were reliable evidence that sound can harm marine life.

3 The US Navy could a) carry out underwater explosions without worrying about marine life, b) continue with the explosions but try to protect the marine life, c) stop carrying out underwater explosions. Discuss which you think they should do.

4 'It is never justifiable to carry out underwater activities which kill wildlife.' What do you feel about this statement?

Exam practice

1 **a** Explain what is meant by the moment of a force. [2]

The diagram shows a 4 m long plank resting on two supports. Its weight acts at the centre, and is 200 N. The supports are each 1 m from either end.

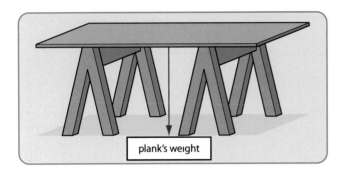

plank's weight

b A person stands on one end of the plank. To stop the plank tipping up, how close should he be to the support? The person's mass is 800 N. [4]

The person needs to stand on the end of the plank. A weight has been placed at the centre point.

c What is the smallest weight needed at the centre to allow the person to stand safely on the right-hand end of the plank? [2]

2 An astronaut is training for a space visit, and this involves experiencing different forces. To create these forces, the astronaut is placed in a pod. The pod is attached to one end of a rod, and the rod's other end is free to spin in a circle.

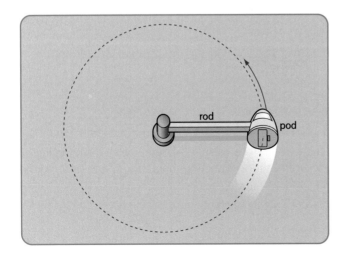

rod
pod

a Although the astronaut travels at a constant speed, he is constantly accelerating. Explain why. [2]

b Copy the diagram and draw an arrow on it to show the direction of this acceleration. [1]

c How will the size of this force change if:

   i a heavier astronaut is training in the pod
   ii the size of the arm gets longer
   iii the speed of rotation is increased? [3]

3 Communications satellites are usually put into a geostationary orbit.

a What part of the Earth does a satellite in this orbit travel over? [1]

b How long does a satellite take to complete one orbit? [1]

c What is the advantage of using an orbit like this one for communications? [2]

d Suggest, with reasons, one use for a satellite in a low polar orbit. [2]

4 The diagram shows a convex lens. An object is placed between 1 and 2 focal lengths away from the lens.

a Copy and complete the diagram to show how an image is formed. [4]

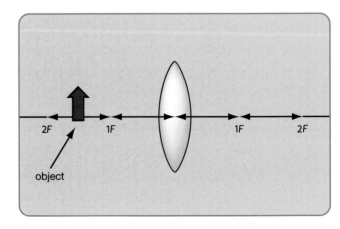

2F   1F   1F   2F

object

b Describe the image and explain why an image with these properties is formed. [3]

(Total 27 marks)

a Describe what is seen when white light is shone through a prism. [2]

b Complete the diagram to show how a prism splits white light into its separate colours. [4]

c Complete the missing words in these sentences.

The splitting of light into a spectrum is called _____.

When light changes speed as it travels from one material to a different material, it is _____. [2]

(Total 8 marks)

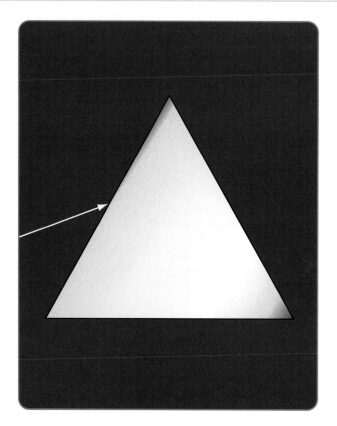

Enough for 1 mark. The student should say that a spectrum is seen.

a *The light splits into different colours.*

b

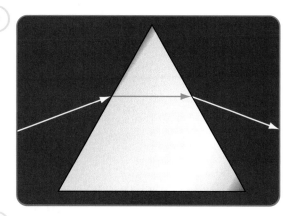

The directions of the lines are correct and many students find this tricky. For the final 2 marks, the student should show the lines getting increasingly wider as the light spreads out, finally forming a spectrum.

Neither of these is correct. The first word should be 'dispersion' and the second should be 'refraction'.

c *The splitting of light into a spectrum is called* <u>*diffraction*</u>.
When light changes speed as it travels from one material to a different material, it is <u>*reflected*</u>.

Overall Grade: C/D

How to get an A
Learn your definitions carefully. In particular, light and sound have a lot of definitions to learn so work out a way to remember these.

Physics 3b

DISCOVER THE UNIVERSE!

The artwork shows the evolution of our Universe from the Big Bang to the creation of the planets. The Universe is made up of millions of galaxies. Our Sun is just one star amongst the millions of stars in our spiral galaxy, known as the Milky Way.

A star goes through a birth, life and death cycle. The remains of dead stars become the particles from which the next generation of stars are formed.

Debris from the explosion in which a star is created can go on to form a planet millions of years later.

This is the Big Bang. Matter was created, initially as subatomic particles which then fused together to form simple atoms.

The early Universe consisted of vast clouds of hydrogen gas. Stars form when dust and gas particles are pulled together by the force of gravity.

CONTENTS

Electromagnetic force

You will find out:
- That electric currents produce magnetic fields
- That forces produced in magnetic fields can be used to make things move

The electric motor

If the electric motor had not been invented our world would be almost at a standstill. No electric trains, no lifts to take you up and down, no automatic doors. There might not even be any cars! Cars need an electric starter motor, a fuel pump, windscreen wipers, and today most cars have electric windows.

In 1819 Hans Oersted was experimenting with **electricity**. He noticed that when he passed electricity through a wire, a compass needle nearby moved towards the wire. Copper wire is not magnetic. Oersted deduced that when an electrical current flows through a wire, it creates a magnetic force field.

From this simple observation came one of the most useful devices in our world today – the electric motor.

Electromagnetic force

When a **current** flows through a **conductor** such as a copper wire, it generates a **magnetic field**. This field acts in concentric circles around the wire. If an object, like a piece of iron or another magnet comes into this field it experiences a force acting on it. This force will push or pull the object; it will be attracted or repelled. The object will move. This is called the **motor effect**.

The motor effect is used in many everyday devices and appliances. An electric motor is found in a food mixer, electric drill, hair dryer, electric fan, cranes on building sites, even in a radio-controlled super buggie. An **electric motor** is basically a copper coil inside a magnetic field. When current is passed through the coil, the two magnetic fields act on each other and the force spins the coil.

There are other devices that use this effect: the loudspeaker, the electromagnetic door lock, electromagnetic relays, electric bells and buzzers. In these devices, current flowing through a coil creates a magnetic field which acts on an iron bar or rod and forces it to move. This is called an **electromagnet**.

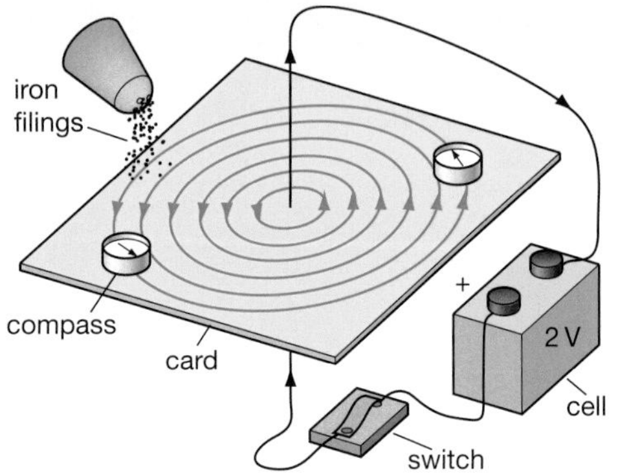

FIGURE 1: All these are powered by electric motors.

FIGURE 2: How do the iron filings and compass needles show the magnetic field around the wire?

QUESTIONS

1. What happens when a current flows through a copper wire?
2. Explain what you understand by the 'motor effect'. Why is it so important?
3. List **three** devices that use an electric motor.
4. List **three** devices that use an electromagnet.

...*conductor* ...*current* ...*electricity* ...*electric motor*

The motor effect

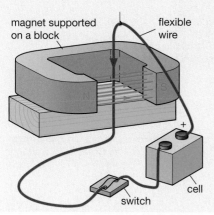

FIGURE 3: A current-carrying conductor in a magnetic field.

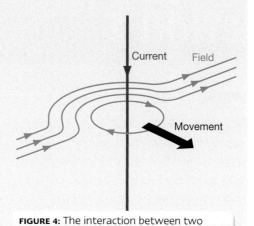

FIGURE 4: The interaction between two magnetic fields.

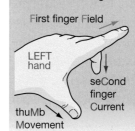
Look at the experimental set up in figure 3. A strong horseshoe magnet has been positioned with a flexible copper wire suspended through its magnetic field. The wire is connected to a battery.

- When the current is switched on, a magnetic field forms around the wire. This new magnetic field reacts with the magnetic field of the horseshoe magnet and a force pushes the wire to one side. This is the motor effect.

- If you change the direction of current by changing the battery connections, the force is still there, but acting in the opposite direction. The wire moves the other way. Figure 4 shows how the straight field lines of the magnet interact with the circular field lines around the wire.

- How can you increase this effect? Look again at figure 3. There are two key variables, the magnet and the current in the wire. The motor effect can be increased by:
  – increasing the strength of the magnetic field (by using a stronger magnet)
  – increasing the current (by adding more batteries).

As the magnet gets stronger, the magnetic field lines get closer together. Stronger current also creates a stronger magnetic field around the wire. The force acting on two sets of densely packed magnetic field lines is very strong.

Direction is everything

The relative directions of current and field lines determine the way the force will act.

- The way a magnet is positioned will alter the direction of its field lines. The direction of current can also be changed. Circular lines can run clockwise or anticlockwise.

- The direction of the force is reversed if:
  – the magnetic field is reversed
  – the direction of current is reversed.

- If the conductor (copper wire) runs parallel to the magnetic field lines, then no force will be experienced.

QUESTIONS

8   How can the direction of a magnetic field change?

9   What happens to the force on a conductor if the direction of current is reversed? Explain your answer.

10 What happens if the conductor is positioned in parallel (in line) with the magnetic field? Explain your answer.

QUESTIONS

5   Using the diagram in figure 3, explain the motor effect and how it works.

6   Why does the wire move in the opposite direction when you change the direction of the current?

7   List **two** ways of increasing the strength of the motor effect.

Electromagnetic induction 1

You will find out:
- About the generator effect
- How an a.c. generator produces electricity

The generator effect

The electric motor is a machine that keeps us moving. But it needs electricity to work, so we need an electricity generator. An electricity generator provides a source of energy that is convenient, easy to use and cheap. And it's almost as if by magic – move a wire in and out of a magnetic field and electricity flows through it!

In the previous lesson you read how Oersted discovered that electricity produced magnetism. This was important science. Everyone wanted to investigate it further. In 1831, Michael Faraday worked out that this principle also worked the other way round. He discovered how to produce electricity from magnetism.

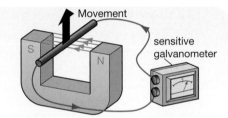

FIGURE 1: Electricity generators, large and small.

The a.c. generator   (H)

Faraday discovered that if you take a metal wire (a **conductor**) and move it so that it cuts through the field lines of a magnet, a **potential difference** is induced across the ends of the wire. This effect is called **electromagnetic induction**. It is this potential difference which acts like a battery and pushes electrons round the wire making an electric current. For current to flow, the wire must be part of a complete circuit.

FIGURE 2: What does the galvanometer show when the conductor moves through the magnetic field?

The device that generates electricity is called a **generator** (or **alternator**). It looks like an electric motor. Remember that Faraday found that the science worked both ways. Bring electricity and magnetism together and you get movement (motor effect). Bring magnetism and movement together and you get electricity. All you need to generate electricity is:

- a fixed magnet
- a coil that moves (rotates) through the magnetic field
- two slip rings and carbon brushes to carry the electricity away from the rotating coil.

Looking at figure 3, follow the rotation of one side of the coil. As the coil moves upwards it cuts through the field lines of the magnet. This creates the induced potential difference which drives electrons through the coil.

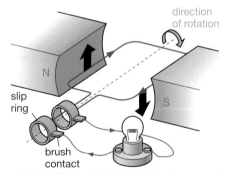

FIGURE 3: A simple a.c. generator.

The movement of electrons is an electric current. The round slip rings rotate with the coil so that the electricity can flow out of the alternator (the wire and magnet arrangement). Notice that as one side of the coil moves upwards, the other side moves downwards. This doubles the current produced.

◾◾ QUESTIONS ◾◾

1. What did Faraday discover? Why was it so important?
2. Can you explain how electricity is produced in this way?
3. What do you call the device that creates electricity?
4. Using the diagram in figure 3, describe in your own words how an generator works.

...alternator ...conductor ...electromagnetic induction

Faraday's Law

Moving a conductor through a magnetic field cuts the field lines and induces a potential difference in the conductor. This pushes electrons round the complete circuit. The principle also works the other way round: if you keep the conductor still and move the magnet, the effect is the same. The key is that the magnetic field lines are cut.

Set up the apparatus shown in figure 4. Carry out the following experiments and note down your observations.

- Move the magnet quickly into the coil. Hold the magnet still inside the coil. Pull the magnet out of the coil. How does this affect the current?
- Move the magnet slowly and then quickly. Does the current change?
- Repeat these procedures with a weaker magnet. Do you see any difference?
- Repeat again, but this time use a coil with fewer turns.
- Repeat, but use a coil with a larger diameter.

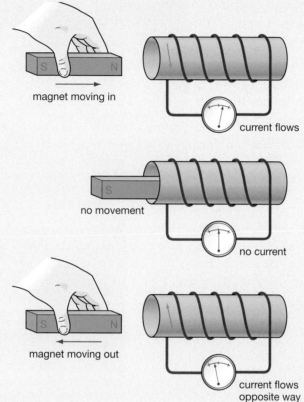

FIGURE 4: Keeping the conductor still and moving the magnet. Does this induce a potential difference in the conductor?

You will have demonstrated Faraday's Law.

The induced potential difference (hence the current) can be increased by:

- using a stronger magnet
- moving the magnet or the conductor faster
- increasing the number of turns on the coil
- increasing the diameter of the coil.

QUESTIONS

5   You can only induce current in a circuit by moving the wire through a magnetic field. True or false? Explain your answer.

6   What would be the easiest way of increasing the power produced by an a.c. generator?

7   Our UK mains electricity is 50 Hz a.c. Can you suggest which part of the generator makes it 50 Hz?

MICROPHONES

A singer's voice causes the moving coil in the microphone to vibrate, creating an induced current. This is amplified and passed through to the loudspeaker.

Lenz's Law

Lenz's Law helps us to work out which way the induced current will flow. It states that: **The direction of the induced current is such that it opposes the change producing it.**

Look again at figure 4.

- As the N pole of the magnet moves into the coil, that end of the coil must also become a N pole. Two N poles must oppose (repel) each other. Check the direction of the current – clockwise in the coil.
- As the N pole moves back out of the coil, the end of the coil becomes a S pole to oppose the direction of the magnet. A S pole will pull the N pole back towards itself. The current has changed direction – anticlockwise.

QUESTIONS

8   Explain in your own words what Lenz's Law means.

9   You generate electricity using an a.c. generator. Using figure 3, explain why it produces alternating current.

Electromagnetic induction 2

You will find out:
- The shape of alternating current
- What is meant by the term mutual induction

Tea-time surge

After a hard day's work, people relax and watch the nation's favourite soap on TV. As the programme ends, "Fancy a cuppa?" and "Maybe a bite to eat?" echo across the country. A million kettles and cookers are switched on and the demand for electricity suddenly surges. At the Dinorwig power station in North Wales the engineers are waiting for that moment. They open the sluice gates and millions of litres of water rush downhill and spin the generators. Within 12 seconds over 1500 MW of electric power is being fed into the National Grid to boil a million cups of tea.

Later that night everyone is in bed fast asleep. The demand for electricity is very low. The engineers pull some switches and the generators become electric motors which begin pumping water back uphill into the reservoir. By morning the reservoir is full and ready to deliver the **power surge** of electricity needed to cook the nation's breakfast.

FIGURE 1: The reservoir and turbines at Dinorwig pump storage power station, Wales.

Generators and motors

Generators and motors are electromagnetic machines which can work both ways. It is usual to have separate generators to produce electricity and electric motors to drive other machines. But many machines are designed to work as both. If you move a **conductor** in a **magnetic field** you generate electricity (generator). If you pass electric current through a conductor in a magnetic field, you induce movement (electric motor).

To generate electricity, it does not matter whether the **coil** moves in the magnetic field or the magnetic field moves around the coil. The key thing is that the conductor is cutting through the lines of the magnetic field.

WOW FACTOR!

Dinorwig is the fastest power station in the UK. It can turn on 2/3 capacity (1500 MW) in just 12 seconds!

QUESTIONS

1 How can the National Grid respond quickly to sudden peaks in the demand for electricity?

2 How are generators and motors 'two sides of the same electromagnetic coin'?

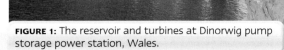

...a.c. generator   ...coil   ...conductor   ...magnetic field

Alternating current (a.c.)

You will recall that when a conductor moves through a magnetic field a potential difference is induced in the conductor. The potential difference (p.d.) exerts a force on the free electrons in the conductor and, if it is part of a complete circuit, electrons will begin to move round the circuit. An electric current is being generated.

In an **a.c. generator**, the current flows in alternate directions with each revolution of the coil. As the current alternates, so does the **voltage**.

If you connect a simple a.c. generator to an **oscilloscope**, as in figure 2, you will see a trace of the voltage being produced. For half of the coil's rotation you will see a 'plus' voltage and for the other half, a 'minus' voltage. The shape of the trace is a sine wave.

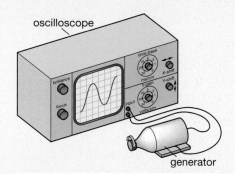

FIGURE 2: Why does a simple a.c. generator connected to an oscilloscope produce a sine wave?

Figure 3 shows an end-on view of the coils of an a.c. generator rotating inside the magnetic field, and how the position of the coil in the magnetic field relates to the voltage produced.

When the coil is vertical, for that instant, it is moving parallel to the magnetic field lines; no field lines are being cut, so there is zero voltage. When the coil is horizontal, the maximum field lines are being cut, hence maximum voltage. At the in-between positions, the voltage is increasing or decreasing, creating the trace's sine wave shape.

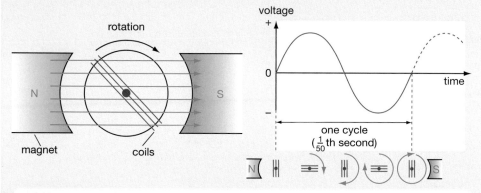

FIGURE 3: How the position of the coil in the magnetic field relates to the voltage produced.

RIGHT-HAND RULE

Fleming's right-hand rule for generators: **First finger** = direction of the magnetic field.
Second finger = current.
Thumb = direction of movement.

First finger Field
thuMb Movement
seCond finger
Current induced
RIGHT hand

Mutual induction

You will recall that pushing a bar magnet in and out of a coil produces an alternating current, and that the process also works the other way: if you run an alternating current through a coil you generate an alternating magnetic field.

If you place two coils next to each other and run an alternating current through one coil, you create an alternating magnetic field which reaches out to the second coil.

This alternating magnetic field around the second coil generates, (or induces) an alternating current in the second coil. This is called **mutual induction**.

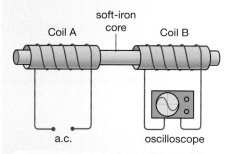

FIGURE 4: Inducing an alternating current in a second coil.

A little wonder

SELF-CHECK ACTIVITY

The year is 1821 and Michael Faraday, the famous experimenter and lecturer, is giving a lecture at the Royal Institution in London. He is explaining his latest scientific discovery to his attentive audience.

He has been working on a new idea and has constructed a piece of equipment to try it out. Faraday is fond of trying out ideas by setting up experiments and he's convinced he's on the edge of something really big.

"Look at this," he says "This is really important … but I'm not sure you're going to understand how important it is. Never mind." The children lean forward in their seats. On the bench is a piece of equipment. It has a wooden base and a metal pole going up the side, with an arm coming out at the top. At the end of the arm is a hook. On the hook hangs a long straight piece of thick bare metal wire. The bottom end of the wire dangles in a dish of mercury and in the centre of the dish is a small cylindrical piece of shiny metal. Wires connect the bottom of the pole to one end of a battery and the mercury to the other end, though a gap has been left in the wires there.

"Watch this," says Faraday and connects the wire to complete the circuit. The wire dangling in the mercury starts to move. It moves around the cylinder in the dish in a circle – and keeps on moving. It goes round and round in circles, twitching slightly but continuing in its path. "What is it?" asks one of the children, and before Faraday can answer, another asks, "What is it for?" Faraday replies, "It's an electric motor". All the children watch in amazement as the wire continues to skate in jerky circles around the bowl. "I can't start to tell you what amazing things people will do with this. Of course it needs a bit of development before it's really useful…"

CHALLENGE

STEP 1

Faraday had built a simple motor – very important for what it showed, but not a practical application. What would need to be changed to make it of practical use?

Faraday's experiment would not be allowed in a school laboratory. Why not?

Eventually the motor would stop. Why?
What transfer of energy is taking place during this experiment?
Where does the energy end up?

The cylinder of metal in the dish is a magnet; the North pole is sticking out of the dish and the South pole at the bottom. Draw the magnetic field pattern for this magnet.
The dangling wire is connected to the negative terminal of the battery via the pole and to the positive terminal via the mercury. Draw the magnetic field pattern for the wire.

Suggest **two** ways of getting the wire to travel in the opposite direction around the magnet.

Maximise your grade

These sentences show what you need to be including in your work. Use them to improve your work and to be successful.

Grade	Answer includes...
F	Explain that this motor is very weak and is unlikely to be suitable for a serious application.
	Draw the field pattern for the permanent magnet.
	Explain what energy transfer is taking place and why the motor will eventually stop.
	Draw the field pattern for the dangling wire.
C	Explain how each of these fields could be reversed.
	Explain how the fields interact to produce movement.
A	Explain with reference to the magnetic fields how the direction of rotation of the motor could be reversed.
	Draw and label a diagram of the motor with fixed wire and moveable magnet.

Faraday also built a version of the motor in which the wire was fixed and the magnet could move. Sketch and label a diagram to show how this might have been set up.

Transformers

You will find out:
- What transformers do
- How transformers work
- How the National Grid system supplies our homes with electricity

Uses of transformers

In the UK, 230 V a.c. mains electricity is used to power domestic appliances. But many appliances do not need such a high voltage to power the components inside them. A door bell, your computer or your sound system have small components that need only 12 V, or even less. **Transformers** are used to reduce ('step down') mains voltage to the required smaller voltages. Other devices may need higher voltages. A television tube requires around 30 000 V to activate its electron gun. A transformer is used to increase ('step up') mains voltage to this high level.

FIGURE 1: This is the step down transformer found in a washing machine.

What is a transformer? (H)

Transformers use the same principle of electromagnetic induction as generators. Two coils are placed close to each other, linked by a laminated soft-iron core. None of the coils actually touches. They are insulated from each other and from the iron core. The only thing that connects them is a **magnetic field**.

The coil that takes the input voltage is called the **primary coil**. The coil that gives the (higher or lower) output voltage is called the **secondary coil**. Transformers only work with a.c. voltage. The a.c. voltage in the primary coil creates an alternating magnetic field in the iron core. This alternating magnetic field affects the secondary coil, inducing an a.c. potential in it.

The input and output voltages are linked by the number of turns in the primary and secondary coils. This is given by the relationship:

$$\frac{\text{secondary voltage}}{\text{primary voltage}} = \frac{\text{number of turns in secondary coil}}{\text{number of turns in primary coil}} \text{ or } \frac{V_2}{V_1} = \frac{N_2}{N_1}$$

- If the secondary coil has more turns than the primary coil, the secondary voltage will be higher, so it is called a step-up transformer.
- If the primary coil has more turns than the secondary coil, the secondary voltage will be lower, so it is called a **step-down transformer**.

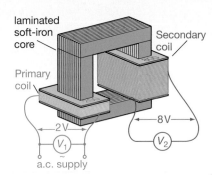

FIGURE 2: The two coils in a transformer do not touch each other. What else do you notice about them?

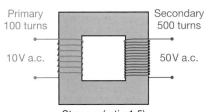

Primary 100 turns — 10V a.c. Secondary 500 turns — 50V a.c.

Step-up (ratio 1:5)

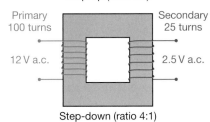

Primary 100 turns — 12 V a.c. Secondary 25 turns — 2.5 V a.c.

Step-down (ratio 4:1)

FIGURE 3: Step-up and step-down transformers.

QUESTIONS

1. Draw a diagram of a transformer. Label the soft-iron core, the primary coils and secondary coils.
2. A transformer works with any type of voltage (a.c. or d.c.). True or false? Explain your answer.
3. If the coils do not come in contact with each other, how do you get a voltage in the secondary coil?
4. How would you recognise the difference between a step-up and step-down transformer?

...magnetic field ...primary coil ...secondary coil

The National Grid system

The National Grid transports electricity from power stations to all our cities, towns and homes. You will probably have seen the tall pylons that carry the electric cables across the countryside.

To transfer electric power across such long distances engineers can use either:

- a low voltage and a high current, or
- a high voltage and a low current.

The low voltage, high current option is not helpful because the high current will heat the cables and much energy will be lost as heat. High voltage, low current is the most effective way of transporting electric power across long distances.

A power station generates electricity at 25 000 V. It needs to step-up the electricity to a much higher voltage in order to transport it efficiently. The transmission voltage in the National Grid can be as high as 400 000 V. Can you see why it is extremely dangerous to climb up an electricity pylon?

Once the electricity has reached your town you cannot use it at 400 000 V. Domestic mains electricity is 230 V. A step-down transformer is required. This time it is a two-stage process: 400 000 V is stepped down to about 11 000 V, then a second transformer reduces it further to 230 V. Most housing estates will have a local step-down transformer (sub-station) fenced off in a quiet spot. These are very dangerous places and you should never try climbing over the fence – you risk being electrocuted.

FIGURE 4: An area sub-station reduces the voltage back down to about 11 000 V.

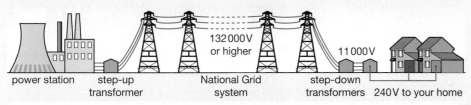

power station step-up transformer National Grid system step-down transformers 240 V to your home

132 000 V or higher   11 000 V

FIGURE 5: How many steps up and down does the electricity go through between the power station and your house?

QUESTIONS

5 How does electricity get from the power station to your home?

6 Why does the National Grid use extremely high voltages to transport electricity across the country?

7 How does 400 000 V in the Grid become 230 V mains electricity for use in your home?

8 You have kicked your football over the fence into a transformer sub-station. What should you **never** do?

What transformer (H) do you need?

The primary and secondary voltages of a transformer are related by the number of turns in the primary and secondary coils by the equation:

$$\frac{V_2}{V_1} = \frac{N_2}{N_1}$$

A step-up transformer is required to transform 25 000 V to 400 000 V. If the primary coil has 1000 turns, how many turns should the secondary coil have?

$V_1 = 25\,000$; $V_2 = 400\,000$; $N_1 = 1000$

$$N_2 = \frac{V_2 \times N_1}{V_1}$$

$$= \frac{400\,000 \times 1000}{25\,000}$$

$$= 16\,000 \text{ turns}$$

QUESTIONS

9 A transformer station has to reduce National Grid voltage to 11 000 V. If the primary coil has 36 000 turns, how many turns should the secondary coil have?

10 The local sub-station has to step down from 11 000 V to domestic mains voltage. If the transformer's secondary coil has 2000 turns, how many turns does the primary coil have?

11 A transformer has a primary coil with 50 turns and a secondary coil with 1000 turns. If you input 12 V a.c. current to the primary coil, what voltage will it step up to?

12 A television tube requires 30 000 V. A transformer with what ratio will be required if the TV works off mains voltage?

...step-down transformer ...step-up transformer

145

Eternal cycles

You will find out:
- About the life cycle of a star
- That a star can live for billions of years
- How the elements were made

Star struck

Stars are a fascinating feature of our Universe. They may seem like permanent objects in the sky, but technology has allowed us to photograph the heavens, and now we know that a star has a life cycle. A star's life is long compared to ours, but it follows a pattern similar to many of the life cycles we see here on Earth. Stars are born, they 'grow up,' exist for many years, and then they die, and there's an ongoing battle between the force of gravity and radiation pressure that makes their life cycle exciting and potentially explosive. The amazing thing is that this cycle repeats itself. The remains of the dead star become the nebula of dust and gas from which new stars are born. In our part of the Milky Way galaxy, we are in our third cycle!

FIGURE 1: When a star explodes it produces a nebula of dust and gas from which new stars will form.

Life cycle of a star

Even a star does not live forever. Eventually the **hydrogen** fuel in its core begins to run out and the nuclear energy needed to power its furnace begins to diminish. At this stage the star begins to go through a relatively fast sequence of changes. What happens next depends on the size of the star.

- A medium-sized star like our own Sun will stay a **red giant** until all its hydrogen is gone. As the hydrogen reduces, the nuclear reaction begins to slow down. Radiation pressure reduces and gravity begins to pull the red giant back into itself. It collapses into a dense and very hot **white dwarf**. Eventually it cools even further, like a dying ember, to become a **black dwarf**.

- Larger stars, five times larger than our Sun, have a more spectacular ending. As the hydrogen fuel is used up the star expands and cools to become a much larger **red supergiant**. Then it becomes unstable, collapses and explodes, releasing enormous energy in a **supernova**. The explosion blows off the outer layers of the star leaving a very dense **neutron star** or **pulsar**. If this still has enough mass, the force of its own gravity collapses it even further to become a **black hole** or **singularity**.

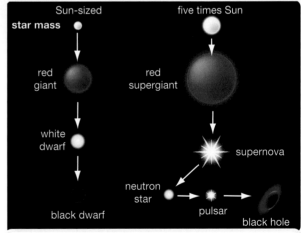

FIGURE 2: The life cycle of stars.

QUESTIONS

1 Why do stars not live forever?

2 What does the end of a star's life depend upon?

3 Describe the likely end of our own Sun. (Draw a diagram if it helps.)

4 Describe the end of a much larger star. (Draw a diagram if it helps.)

...black dwarf   ...black hole   ...gravity   ...hydrogen   ...neutron star   ...nuclear fusion   ...pulsar

Radiation pressure vs. gravity

A star is not a burning object like a fire. It's a huge, uncontrolled hydrogen bomb nuclear explosion. So why doesn't the star just explode out into space? It's our old friend **gravity** again. The nuclear explosion pushes outwards, but the force of gravity is so great that it pulls everything back in. There is a constant battle between the **radiation pressure** and gravity. As long as these two forces are in balance, the star is stable. It can remain this way for as long as 10 billion years.

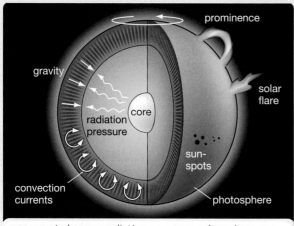

FIGURE 3: As long as radiation pressure and gravity are balanced, the star will be stable.

But how can a star burn for billions of years? Why doesn't the hydrogen just burn up in one mighty flash? The answer lies in **nuclear fusion**. When two atoms of hydrogen fuse, you get a new element, helium, the release of a huge amount of energy and two atoms of hydrogen. These two hydrogen atoms are then fed back into the nuclear fusion reaction. It's like magic: you end up with what you started with!

The word equation for this nuclear fusion is:

hydrogen $\xrightarrow{\text{nuclear fusion}}$ **helium + energy + 2 hydrogen atoms**

QUESTIONS

5   If there is a nuclear fusion reaction at the core of a star, why doesn't it explode out into space?

6   What is the interesting fact about the nuclear fusion reaction which allows stars to live for billions of years?

7   Write the word equation for the fusion of hydrogen.

Where did the elements come from? (H)

After the Big Bang there was only a large cloud of hydrogen gas. Where did all the other elements come from?

As a star goes through its life, the hydrogen in its core is used up and helium is formed. The core temperature increases and there is enough energy for the early elements – carbon, oxygen, silicon and iron – to be formed.

FIGURE 4: A supergiant's core goes supernova!

At the end of its life, the star dies in a huge explosion called a supernova. The temperature of the blast is so high that in that instant the really heavy elements, like gold, silver and lead, are formed.

All the elements are scattered into space as huge clouds of gas, dust and particles. These clouds are the seed-beds for the next generation of stars.

QUESTIONS

8   What were the first stars made of?

9   Which elements form inside a star?

10   Can you suggest why this process only goes up to iron and no further?

11   How are the other heavier elements formed?

...radiation pressure   ...red giant   ...red supergiant   ...singularity   ...supernova   ...white dwarf

How it all began

You will find out:

● About the Big Bang theory of the creation of the Universe

● How a star is born

● How a solar system forms

Heavenly bodies

In ancient times, people thought that the stars were thousands of pinpricks in the fabric of the sky and the twinkling was the light of Heaven shining through. When Galileo discovered the telescope, he realised that the stars were real heavenly bodies and that there were hundreds of thousands of them. With the early terrestrial telescopes, astronomers saw that our Sun was part of the **Milky Way galaxy** which itself was made up of millions of stars. When the Hubble Telescope came on line, it became obvious that there were millions of other galaxies, each with millions of stars, out there in the Universe.

FIGURE 1: A cluster of galaxies.

How it all began   (H)

Scientists propose that our Universe was created by the **Big Bang**. Somewhere, billions of years ago, a vast amount of energy was released in an almighty explosion. The temperature was enormous; billions of degrees. As the explosion began to cool, the energy began to change into matter. First into quarks, leptons and electrons; as the temperature cooled still further these fundamental particles came together to form subatomic particles – protons and neutrons. These finally fused together to form the first atoms of the first element – hydrogen.

■ So at the very beginning, our Universe was an expanding cloud of **hydrogen gas**.

FIGURE 2: Scientists propose that our Universe was created by an almighty explosion. What is this explosion called?

■ Then **gravity** came into play. The atoms of hydrogen gas began to gather and clump together into a ball. Slowly the ball got bigger and bigger. Gravitational forces increased with the growing size of the ball of hydrogen. The centre of the ball began to get very hot. As the ball increased in size, so did the core temperature. Finally, the temperature got so high that the hydrogen exploded like a nuclear bomb. A **star** was born.

■ If you look into the night sky with the naked eye, you will be able to see thousands of stars. With modern telescopes, astronomers are able to see further and deeper into space. There are billions of stars out there. Our Sun is part of the Milky Way galaxy, a spiral galaxy made up of a billion stars. But beyond our galaxy, there are a billion more galaxies.

FIGURE 3: Our Sun is part of the Milky Way galaxy. Can you describe the Milky Way?

▦ QUESTIONS ▦

1 How did our Universe begin? Describe the Big Bang theory.

2 What was our Universe made up of, at the very beginning? Can you explain why?

3 Describe how a star is formed.

4 'Wow, it's a big Universe!' True or false? Explain your answer.

Stars

Space isn't as empty and void as you might think. It is full of gas, mostly hydrogen, and dust and particles floating about in huge clouds called **nebulae**. Even the tiniest particle has mass, so gravity gradually begins to attract molecules of gas and dust together. With time, the cloud gradually comes together into a ball of matter.

As the size of the ball grows, the pressure inside the core increases

FIGURE 4: The Orion nebula – a huge cloud of gas, dust and particles.

and the centre becomes solid and very dense. As the particles are pulled into the mass, their potential energy is changed into kinetic energy. Molecules begin to vibrate more and the temperature in the core begins to rise. This is the beginnings of a star. It would look like a huge dull red glow hanging in space. At this stage, it is called a **protostar**.

With time, more matter is pulled in, the size increases and the core becomes hotter and hotter. At about 15 million Kelvin, hydrogen molecules spontaneously fuse and a nuclear fusion reaction ignites within the core of the protostar. It explodes brilliant white, and a star is born.

FIGURE 5: A star in the making. What is this 'red giant' stage called?

With modern telescopes such as the Hubble, astronomers have been able to confirm that our Sun is just one medium-sized star on the edge of a huge spiral galaxy of billions of stars, the Milky Way. Beyond that there are billions of other galaxies, all with their own billions of stars. And each galaxy is moving away from us at great speeds. We live in a huge and ever-expanding Universe.

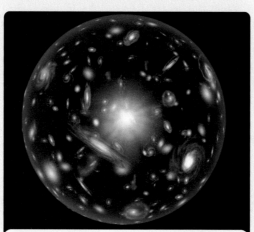

FIGURE 6: We live in a huge and ever-expanding Universe.

Planets

FIGURE 7: Slowly the gases, dust and particles begin to orbit the star, clumping together to form planets – a solar system forms.

In the explosion which creates a star, for example our Sun, there is a great deal of debris left floating about around the star. Gravity begins to kick in.

- Slowly the gases, dust and particles begin to orbit around the star. Gravity pulls them together into clumps of matter and material. In time, the clumps become huge balls of iron, nickel, silicon, carbon and oxygen, forming **planets**.

- The heavier materials like iron and nickel form the rock planets which orbit nearest the star. The lighter dust and gases orbit further out and form the giant gas planets.

- But that's not all. There is so much debris that many planets have moons orbiting round them. There are also belts of asteroids. Way out at the very edge of the **solar system** there is a final ring of gas and dust and ice. That's where comets are formed.

QUESTIONS

8 Describe the process which forms a solar system.

9 Explain why planets closer to a star are solid rock and outer planets are made of gas.

QUESTIONS

5 What part does gravity play in the formation of a star?

6 Describe the process which leads to the formation of a protostar.

7 What is the key point that triggers the birth of a star?

...nebulae ...planet ...protostar ...solar system ...star

Unit summary

Concept map

How electricity can be used to make things move

When a conductor carrying an electric current is placed in a magnetic field, it may experience a force.

The size of the force can be increased by increasing the strength of the magnetic field or increasing the size of the current.

The direction of the force can be reversed by changing the direction of current or changing the direction of the magnetic field.

How do generators work?

If an electrical conductor 'cuts' through magnetic field lines, an electrical p.d. is induced across the ends of the conductor which then drives current around the complete circuit.

The direction of the induced p.d. and current is reversed by changing the direction of motion or changing the polarity of the magnetic field.

The generator effect also occurs if the magnetic field is stationary and the coil is moved.

The size of the induced p.d. is increased by increasing the speed of movement, increasing the strength of the magnetic field, increasing the number of turns in the coil or increasing the area of the coil.

How do transformers work?

Step-up and step-down transformers are used in the National Grid.

An alternating current in the primary coil produces a changing magnetic field in the iron core and hence the secondary coil. This induces an alternating p.d. across the ends of the secondary coil.

The p.d. across the primary and secondary coils of a transformer are related by the equation $V_p/V_s = N_p/N_s$.

What is the life history of stars?

A star has a cycle of birth, life and death.

The early Universe consisted of clouds of hydrogen gas.

The force of gravity pulls the hydrogen gas into a great ball where the core begins to get very hot.

At 15 million K, hydrogen fuses in a huge nuclear explosion. A star is born.

During the stable life of a star, the force of gravity and the radiation pressure of the nuclear reaction are in balance.

A star starts with hydrogen, but during its life, all the elements are formed inside it.

A star dies when it finally explodes as a supernova. All the elements are blown into space. They form a nebula and a new cycle of star birth begins.

Our Sun is a star and part of the Milky Way spiral galaxy which has billions of stars.

The Universe consists of billions of galaxies.

Unit quiz

1 Describe the special effect when a conductor carrying electric current is placed in a magnetic field.

2 How can you increase this effect?

3 What common device was invented as a result of this discovery? Name **three** appliances which use this device.

4 What effect do you get when moving an electrical conductor through a magnetic field?

5 How can you increase this effect?

6 What do you call the device which uses this principle? Why is it such an important invention?

7 As the conductor moves through the magnetic field, when is the effect strongest and when is it weakest?

8 What do you call a device which changes low voltage to high voltage; and a device which changes high voltage to low voltage?

9 What is the equation which links primary and secondary coils with primary and secondary turns in the coil?

10 Explain why transformers are necessary when electricity is transported round the country by the National Grid.

11 What element did the early Universe consist of? Can you explain why today there are so many elements?

12 Describe the process by which a star is born.

13 What **two** forces must be in balance during the stable life of a star? Explain.

14 What happens when a star dies?

15 'Wow, it's a big Universe.' True or false? Explain.

Numeracy activity

Our solar system

Our solar system consists of the Sun plus nine planets. The planets have a flat orbit and move in an anticlockwise direction

	Mercury	Venus	Earth	Mars	Jupiter	Saturn	Uranus	Neptune
Time for 1 orbit (years)	0.2	0.6	1.0	1.8	11.7	29.1	84	165
Distance from the Sun	0.40	0.7	1.0	1.5		9.5	19	30
Mass	0.1	0.8	1.0	0.1	320	95	15	17
Average temp. (°C)	+430 to -180	+470	+15	-30	-150	-180	-210	-220

round the Sun. Astronomers long ago discovered that the planets did not wander round the Sun in a random fashion. They are all linked by incredible mathematical relationships.

Above is a table with some basic data about eight planets. Values for distance and mass are relative to Earth = 1.

In 1618 Johannes Kepler developed the laws of planetary motion by observing the orbits of planets around the Sun. He measured how long each planet took to go round the Sun and its distance from the Sun.

QUESTIONS

1 Draw a graph of the planets showing the relationship between distance and time for one orbit. Describe the shape of the graph, and the relationship between times of orbit with distance from the Sun.

2 The orbit time for Jupiter is 11.7 years. Use the graph to determine Jupiter's distance from the Sun.

3 Draw the graph of average temperature against distance from the Sun (be careful with the axis). Describe the relationship.

4 Two planets do not fit the pattern. Can you think of reasons for these two odd readings? Use the internet to help you.

5 Kepler worked out that:
(time of orbit)^2 ÷ (distance from the Sun)^3 is the same for each planet. Check this using the values given in the table.

Exam practice

1 **a** Write down the range of frequencies that can be heard by humans. [2]

b Copy and complete the table: [2]

Change to sound wave	Change to note heard
Increase in frequency	
Decrease in amplitude	

c What is the name given to sound that is too high for humans to hear? [1]

d State one medical use of this type of sound wave, and explain how the sound waves are used. [3]

2 The diagram shows equipment that can be used to show the principles of electromagnetic induction.

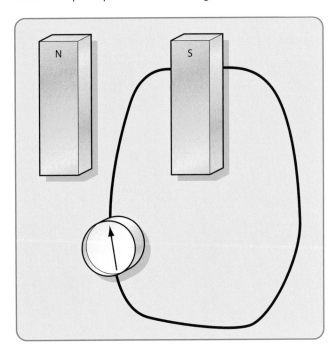

Describe how you could show:

a that a voltage is induced if the magnetic field changes near a conductor [2]

b the different factors that affect the size of the voltage [4]

c how the direction of the current can be altered. [2]

3 **a** Explain how the heavy elements found on Earth could have formed at the centre of a large star. [4]

b The diagram shows the stages in the life cycle of a star like the Sun. Copy and complete the table to write down the name of each stage. [3]

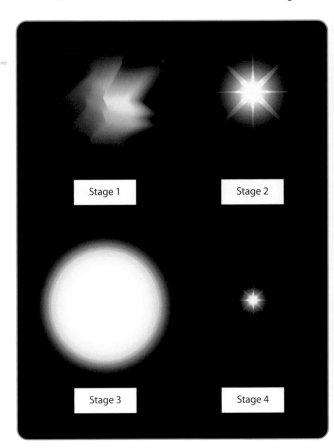

Stage in the star's life cycle	Name
Stage 1	
Stage 2 (the stage the Sun is at)	Main sequence star
Stage 3	
Stage 4	

c How does a star in stage 3 differ from a star like the Sun? [2]

(Total 25 marks)

Worked example

a Explain what is meant by a step-up transformer. [2]

b Suggest a material suitable for a transformer's core. Explain your answer. [3]

c Calculate the number of turns in the primary coil for a transformer that converts mains voltage (230 V) to 4 V. The number of turns on the secondary coil is 150. [3]

(Total 8 marks)

True for 1 mark. The second mark is for saying it increases a.c. voltages.

a *It increases voltages.*

b *Steel, because it transfers the electricity.*

c *Primary turns/secondary turns = primary voltage/secondary voltage.*
150 x 4 = 600 turns

Student gets 1 mark. The equation is correct, but did not have the values put in correctly. Primary turns = 230/4 × 150 = 8625 turns.

Steel is not suitable because it stays magnetic. Iron is used because it is a soft magnetic material and its magnetism will change with the changing magnetism created by the primary coil. The student gets no marks.

Overall Grade: D

How to get an A

Practise moving equations around. You will often need to change the subject of an equation, so use what you have been taught in maths lessons too! If you are really stuck, substitute the numbers in the equation before you change it around. You may find it easier to manipulate numbers instead.

Investigating potato chips

If a piece of raw potato is placed in pure water overnight, it gets bigger. If a piece of potato is placed in very salty water overnight, it gets smaller. Matt wanted to know how much salt he should add to the water so that the potato stays the same size.

This is what he did.

- He took six beakers and used a measuring cylinder to place 100 cm³ of distilled water into each beaker.
- He wrote 'no salt' on a label and stuck the label to the side of the first beaker.
- He then used a mass balance and carefully measured 0.20 g of salt. He added this to the second beaker and placed a label on the beaker to show the amount of salt.
- He placed 0.40 g, 0.60 g, 0.80 g and 1.00 g of salt in the remaining beakers.
- He stirred each beaker until all the salt had dissolved.
- Then he cut 18 pieces of potato. Each piece was the same size and had a mass of 1.00 g.
- He placed three pieces of potato into each beaker and then left them overnight.

- In the morning Matt removed each piece of potato.
- He carefully dried each piece and then measured its mass.

These are his results.

Mass of salt added (g)	Mass of potato at the start (g)	Mean average mass at the start (g)	Mass of potato piece at the end (g)	Mean average mass at the end (g)	Difference (g) (average mass at end – average mass at start)
0.00	1.00 1.00 1.00	1.00	1.20 1.30 1.10		
0.20	1.00 1.00 1.00	1.00	0.90 0.90 0.90		
0.40	1.00 1.00 1.00	1.00	0.90 0.80 0.70		
0.60	1.00 1.00 1.00	1.00	0.70 0.70 0.60		
0.80	1.00 1.00 1.00	1.00	0.70 0.60 0.70		
1.00	1.00 1.00 1.00	1.00	0.60 0.70 0.70		

Questions

1. Write down the range for the amount of salt used in this experiment.

2. Identify the dependent variable.

3. Is the dependent variable continuous, categoric or discrete?

4. Identify the independent variable.

5. Is the independent variable continuous, categoric or discrete?

6. Why did Matt place three pieces of potato into each of the beakers?

7. Copy and complete the table by calculating the missing values.

8. (a) What sort of graph should you use to display these results?

   (b) What should the x-axis show?

   (c) What should the y-axis show?

9. Explain how you would use your graph to work out exactly how much salt should be added to 100 cm³ of water to solve Matt's problem.

Antibiotics row

This article appeared in a newspaper.

Sick girl denied drugs by doctor

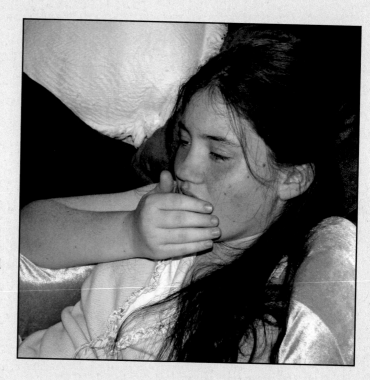

Mother of three, Shirley Taylor yesterday claimed that her oldest daughter Britney, 13, has been denied antibiotics to save the NHS money.

Mrs Taylor told our reporter how Britney, who is a patient at Tippleton Surgery, has been ill for over two weeks.

Britney has a heavy cold, sore throat and cough.

"She is really suffering. She is missing school and it's affecting her chances of passing her exams and getting a good job," claimed Mrs Taylor.

Since she became ill, Mrs Taylor has taken Britney to the Tippleton Surgery five times but each time doctors have said that her daughter did not need antibiotics.

Mrs Taylor told our reporter that the doctors were trying to save money by not giving her daughter antibiotics. "It's disgusting. I have worked all my life and now my little girl cannot get medicine when she is ill," she said.

What do you think? Have you or your family been denied antibiotics?

Text us your views.

Questions

1 Do you think this report is biased?
2 Why do you think Mrs Taylor might feel like this?
3 Why do you think the newspaper might have written an article like this?
4 If you were writing this article, what extra information would you have included?
5 Explain how articles like this can cause problems for society.

Hard and soft water

One way to find out whether a water sample is hard or soft is to test how the water reacts with soap solution. If the water forms a good lather with a small amount of soap solution, it contains few calcium or magnesium ions and is soft.

If the water does not form lather readily, it is hard.

Kevin was given five samples of tap water. Each sample was taken from a different part of the country and was labelled with a letter from A to E.

Kevin wanted to find out whether each water sample was hard or soft.

This is what he did:

- He took five identical test tubes.
- He used a measuring cylinder to place 5 cm^3 of water sample A into the first test tube and wrote an A on the side of the test tube.
- He then repeated this for the four other samples.
- Next Kevin placed one drop of soap solution into test tube A. He put a bung in the top of the test tube and shook it for one minute.
- Then he placed the test tube into a rack and looked to see whether a good lather had formed – this was a lather that covered the surface of the water sample and lasted for ten seconds.
- If no lather formed or the lather did not last for ten seconds then Kevin added another drop of soap solution and repeated the experiment until a good lather did form.
- When a good lather formed Kevin wrote down the letter of the sample and how many drops of soap solution were required for the lather to form.

Here are his results:

Sample A required one drop of soap solution to form a good lather.

Sample B required four drops of soap solution to form a good lather.

Sample C required one drop of soap solution to form a good lather.

Sample D required five drops of soap solution to form a good lather.

Sample E required one drop of soap solution to form a good lather.

Questions

1 Draw a table to show Kevin's results.
2 What is the dependent variable in this experiment?
3 What is the independent variable in this experiment?
4 Write down **one** other variable that Kevin controlled in this experiment.
5 Which of the samples were hard and which were soft? Add another column to your table to show this information.
6 Explain how Kevin could improve the reliability of the data he has collected.
7 Explain how Kevin could improve the accuracy of the way he measured the amount of soap solution added.
8 Kevin asked his teacher whether he should draw a line graph or a bar graph to display his results. If you were his teacher what would you tell him? Try to explain your answer so he can work out what to do in the future.

Paraquat poisoning

This article appeared in a newspaper.

Farmer's wife deliberately poisoned claims top scientist

In Northampton Crown Court the trial of local farmer Andy South, 68, continued yesterday. Mr South is accused of killing his terminally ill wife, Jill, 67, who died of multiple organ failure in March last year. The case has shocked residents of the village of Bilton where Mr and Mrs South had lived and worked for over forty years.

In court yesterday the expert witness, Dr. Moyra Ellis gave evidence on behalf of the prosecution. Dr. Ellis who is a leading toxicology specialist told the court how her forensic tests, using the latest instrumental methods, had revealed that high levels of the weed killer paraquat were present in tissues taken from the victim's body. Dr. Ellis explained that as well as being a very effective weed killer, Paraquat is highly toxic to people. Asked whether she

Mr South's farm at Bilton

believed that the poison had been given to Mrs South accidentally or deliberately Dr. Ellis said that she believed, due to the large amount of the poison in Mrs South's body, that it must have been given to her deliberately.

The case continues today.

Questions

1. Why would Dr. Ellis have been asked questions about her qualifications and experience in court?

2. Why would Dr. Ellis have repeated her experiments?

3. Why must a report containing all the evidence from the experiments be made available to the court?

4. Why could the defence team try to object to Dr. Ellis' statement about whether the poison had been given to Mrs South deliberately or accidentally?

Transformers

Jigna wants to investigate the prediction that the more turns of wire on the secondary coil of a transformer, the higher the output voltage.

This is what she did.

- She got two pieces of iron and two lengths of insulated wire.
- She wrapped one wire around the first piece of iron 100 times. She then connected both ends of this wire to a laboratory pack. She labelled this the primary coil.
- She then took the other piece of wire and wrapped it around the second piece of iron 10 times. She connected both ends of this piece of wire to a voltmeter. She labelled this the secondary coil.
- She placed the two coils together and set the laboratory pack to 10 V a.c.
- She turned the laboratory pack on and wrote down the number of turns on the secondary coil and the reading shown on the voltmeter.
- Next Jigna increased the number of turns on the secondary coil and repeated the experiment.
- She continued doing this until she had five sets of results.

Here are her results.

10 turns of wire gave a reading of 0.89 V.

20 turns of wire gave a reading of 1.84 V.

30 turns of wire gave a reading of 2.86 V.

40 turns of wire gave a reading of 3.80 V.

50 turns of wire gave a reading of 4.87 V.

Questions

1 What is the independent variable in this experiment?

2 Is this variable continuous, categoric or discrete?

3 What is the dependent variable in this experiment?

4 Is this variable continuous, categoric or discrete?

5 Draw a table to show Jigna's results.

6 Why should Jigna draw a line graph rather than a bar graph to display her results?

7 How could Jigna make her results more reliable?

8 Jigna noticed that the wire got very hot when she turned the laboratory pack on. Why was it important that she let the equipment cool down between each test?

9 Does the evidence support Jigna's prediction or not?

This article appeared in a newspaper.

The Street of Death

When Sam and Tricia Brown moved into their dream house on the Heron Valley estate in the village of Sixworth, they didn't give a second thought to the high voltage electricity pylon at the bottom of the garden. Today they say this pylon has ruined their lives.

The pylon, which is part of the electricity distribution system, towers above the Heron Valley estate. Mr Brown believes that the electromagnetic radiation from the power lines is the cause of his son Ricky's illness. Ricky developed leukaemia two years ago and although he is now doing better and is back at school studying for his GCSEs, he has yet to be given the all clear. However, Ricky's illness is not an isolated case. Mr Brown told our reporter how 15 people have been diagnosed with cancer in the same street over the last ten years. There are only 25 houses in the street. Even the pets are becoming ill. A dog belonging to a neighbour of Mr Brown developed a cancerous growth in its jaw and had to be put down last year.

Mrs Taylor, who began to develop headaches shortly after the family moved in to their home, said they were desperate to move but that no one wants to buy a house which has an electricity pylon at the bottom of the garden. A spokesperson for the Twelve Trees Electricity company who supply electricity to Mr Brown's home say there is no link between the electricity pylon and health problems in the area.

Questions

1 Does this article prove that Ricky Brown's illness was caused by the electricity pylon?

2 How could you prove that the incidence of cancer in this area was very high?

3 Would the existence of a higher than normal incidence of cancer cases mean that the pylon must be responsible?

4 Why might the electricity company not want there to be a link found between electricity pylons and incidences of illness?

Databank

Reactivity series of metals

Potassium — most reactive
Sodium
Calcium
Magnesium
Aluminium
Carbon
Zinc
Iron
Tin
Lead
Hydrogen
Copper
Silver
Gold
Platinum — least reactive

(elements in italics, though non-metals, have been included for comparison)

Formulae of some common ions

Positive ions

Name	Formula
Hydrogen	H^+
Sodium	Na^+
Silver	Ag^+
Potassium	K^+
Lithium	Li^+
Ammonium	NH_4^+
Barium	Ba^{2+}
Calcium	Ca^{2+}
Copper (II)	Cu^{2+}
Magnesium	Mg^{2+}
Zinc	Zn^{2+}
Lead	Pb^{2+}
Iron (II)	Fe^{2+}
Iron (III)	Fe^{3+}
Aluminium	Al^{3+}

Negative ions

Name	Formula
Chloride	Cl^-
Bromide	Br^-
Fluoride	F^-
Iodide	I^-
Hydroxide	OH^-
Nitrate	NO_3^-
Oxide	O^{2-}
Sulfide	S^{2-}
Sulfate	SO_4^{2-}
Carbonate	CO_3^{2-}

The Periodic Table

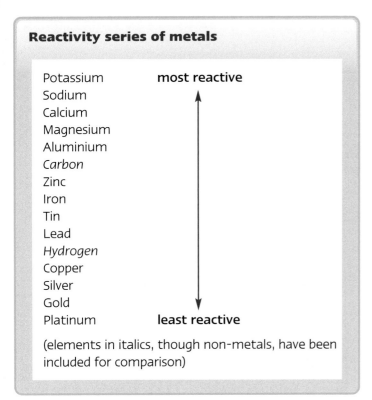

Key
relative atomic mass
atomic symbol
name
atomic (proton) number

1	2											3	4	5	6	7	0
							1 **H** hydrogen 1										4 **He** helium 2
7 **Li** lithium 3	9 **Be** beryllium 4											11 **B** boron 5	12 **C** carbon 6	14 **N** nitrogen 7	16 **O** oxygen 8	19 **F** fluorine 9	20 **Ne** neon 10
23 **Na** sodium 11	24 **Mg** magnesium 12											27 **Al** aluminium 13	28 **Si** silicon 14	31 **P** phosphorus 15	32 **S** sulfur 16	35.5 **Cl** chlorine 17	40 **Ar** argon 18
39 **K** potassium 19	40 **Ca** calcium 20	45 **Sc** scandium 21	48 **Ti** titanium 22	51 **V** vanadium 23	52 **Cr** chromium 24	55 **Mn** manganese 25	56 **Fe** iron 26	59 **Co** cobalt 27	59 **Ni** nickel 28	63.5 **Cu** copper 29	65 **Zn** zinc 30	70 **Ga** gallium 31	73 **Ge** germanium 32	75 **As** arsenic 33	79 **Se** selenium 34	80 **Br** bromine 35	84 **Kr** krypton 36
85 **Rb** rubidium 37	88 **Sr** strontium 38	89 **Y** yttrium 39	91 **Zr** zirconium 40	93 **Nb** niobium 41	96 **Mo** molybdenum 42	98 **Tc** technetium 43	101 **Ru** ruthenium 44	103 **Rh** rhodium 45	106 **Pd** palladium 46	108 **Ag** silver 47	112 **Cd** cadmium 48	115 **In** indium 49	119 **Sn** tin 50	122 **Sb** antimony 51	128 **Te** tellurium 52	127 **I** iodine 53	131 **Xe** xenon 54
133 **Cs** caesium 55	137 **Ba** barium 56	139 **La*** lanthanum 57	178 **Hf** hafnium 72	181 **Ta** tantalum 73	184 **W** tungsten 74	186 **Re** rhenium 75	190 **Os** osmium 76	192 **Ir** iridium 77	195 **Pt** platinum 78	197 **Au** gold 79	201 **Hg** mercury 80	204 **Tl** thallium 81	207 **Pb** lead 82	209 **Bi** bismuth 83	[209] **Po** polonium 84	[210] **At** astatine 85	[222] **Rn** radon 86
[223] **Fr** francium 87	[226] **Ra** radium 88	[227] **Ac*** actinium 89	[261] **Rf** rutherfordium 104	[262] **Db** dubnium 105	[266] **Sg** scaborgium 106	[264] **Bh** bohrium 107	[277] **Hs** hassium 108	[268] **Mt** meitnerium 109	[271] **Ds** darmstadtium 110	[272] **Rg** roentgenium 111							

Elements with atomic numbers 112-116 have been reported but not fully authenticated

* The Lanthanides (atomic numbers 58–71) and the Actinides (atomic numbers 90–103) have been omitted.
Cu and **Cl** have not been rounded to the nearest whole number.

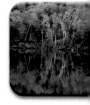

accelerate	increase the velocity of an object.	112
accurate	an accurate measurement is closer to the real value than an inaccurate one. So, if a bar measures exactly 1.0 m a measurement of 0.99 m is more accurate than a measurement of 1.2 m.	100
acid	a chemical that turns litmus paper red – it can often dissolve things that water cannot.	72-75
activation energy	the energy a molecule must have before it can take part in a particular chemical reaction.	88
active transport	in active transport cells use energy to transport substances through cell membranes against a concentration gradient.	16
aerobic respiration	aerobic respiration breaks down glucose using oxygen to make energy available for chemical reactions in cells.	28
agar jelly	a jelly-like substance used to grow micro-organisms.	52
alcohol	a liquid produced when yeast respires sugar in the absence of oxygen.	40
alkali	a substance which makes a solution that turns red litmus paper blue.	72
alkali earth metals	metals like calcium and magnesium that form alkalis when their oxides dissolve in water. They are all in Group II of the periodic table.	62
alkali metals	metals like sodium and potassium that form strong alkalis when their oxides dissolve in water. They are all in Group I of the periodic table.	62-65
alkane	a chemical containing only hydrogen and carbon with the general formula C_nH_{2n+2}, for example methane.	98
alkene	a chemical containing only hydrogen and carbon with the general formula C_nH_{2n}, for example ethene.	98
alternator	an electric generator that produces alternating current.	138
alveolus (pl. alveoli)	the sac-like end of an airway in the lungs. The surface is enlarged to maximise gas exchange.	14
amplitude	the difference between the highest and lowest points on a wave. The larger the amplitude of a sound wave, the louder the sound.	126-129
anaerobic respiration	A series of chemical reactions that transfer energy from glucose into life processes without using oxygen. Carbon dioxide and ethanol or lactic acid are the end-products.	28, 40, 50
anticlockwise moment	circular movement that goes in the opposite direction to the hands on a clock.	108
aqueous	containing water.	72
aqueous system	chemicals dissolved in water.	74
arteries	a blood vessel carrying blood away from the heart under high pressure.	20, 26
arterioles	a small artery. Arterioles connect larger arteries to capillaries.	26
artificial satellite	an artificial object orbiting around a planet or moon.	116
atom	the smallest part of an element. Atoms consist of negatively-charged electrons flying around a positively-charged nucleus.	60
atomic mass	the mass of an atom compared with carbon which has a mass of 12.	60
atomic number	the number of protons in an atom.	62
axis of rotation	the line around which an object spins.	108
bacteria	bacteria are microscopic single-celled living things that have no nucleus. Different bacteria do everything from making us ill to making food taste better!	42
base	an alkali.	72-75
Big Bang	the event believed by many scientists to have been the start of the universe.	148
bioethanol	ethanol produced as a fuel by respiration of sugar from plants.	50
biogas	biogas is a gas made when waste is digested by micro-organisms. The gas is a mixture of methane, hydrogen and nitrogen and burns to release energy.	50
biogenesis	the idea that living organisms develop only from other living organisms and not from non-living matter.	44
black dwarf	the remains of a white dwarf star after it has expended all of its energy and is no longer emitting detectable radiation.	146
black hole	An area of space-time with a gravitational field so intense that its escape velocity is equal to or exceeds the speed of light.	146
blood	the red liquid that carries things like oxygen and food around our body.	20-23
blood flow	the movement of blood along a blood vessel.	26
blood vessels	tubes containing blood, for example arteries or veins.	20
bond	the link between atoms or ions.	88
bond energy	the energy needed to break a bond between atoms or ions.	88

Glossary

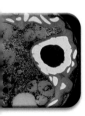

electron arrangement	the number of electrons in shells around an atom. The electron arrangement in an atom or ion controls how it will react chemically.	70
element	a substance that cannot be split into anything simpler by chemical means. All the atoms of an element have the same atomic number although some may have different atomic masses.	60
ellipse	an ellipse looks a bit like a flattened circle.	114
empirical formula	a chemical formula that indicates the relative proportions of the elements in a molecule rather than the actual number of atoms of the elements.	98
endothermic	an endothermic reaction takes in energy when it happens.	88
energy	energy is the ability of a system to do something (work). We detect energy by the effect it has on the things around us, heating them up, moving them, etc.	88, 92
energy profile diagram	a diagram showing the changes in energy levels of reactants during a chemical reaction.	88
equilibrium	when a reversible reaction has reached the point where the forward and reverse reaction rates are equal.	110

essential amino acids	the amino acids needed by human beings in their diet. Essential amino acids cannot be made from other amino acids.	16
ethanol	the chemical name for the alcohol produced by the fermentation of sugar by yeast.	40, 50
excretion	getting rid of wastes made by the body. All living things must do this.	30
exothermic	an exothermic reaction gives out energy when it happens.	64, 88
expiration	breathing out.	14
fermentation	breakdown of food by micro-organisms that does not require oxygen	40, 48-51
fermenter	a container used to grow microbes in a completely controllable environment.	48
filter	to separate the solid particles from a liquid by passing the mixture through a fine mesh or paper.	30

flame test	a test that identifies certain metals by the colour they give to flames.	94
fluoridation	adding fluoride salts to drinking water in very low concentrations to help to prevent tooth decay.	82
focal length	the distance between the centre of a lens and its focal point.	120-125
focus	the point at which light rays meet up to form a clear image.	120
force	a force is a push or pull which is able to change the velocity or shape of a body. Forces only exist between bodies. Every force that acts on a body causes an equal and opposite reaction from the body.	108
free fall	the feeling of 'weightlessness' experienced by an astronaut when he and his spacecraft have exactly the same centripetal acceleration towards Earth.	114
frequency	the number of vibrations per second. Frequency is measured in Hertz.	126-129

friction	friction is a force that acts between two surfaces in contact with each other. It tends to prevent or slow down movement by the two surfaces.	112
fungus	a plant that cannot make its own food by photosynthesis. Mushrooms and yeast are good examples of fungi.	48
gas exchange	the movement of gases across an exchange membrane e.g. in the lungs of mammals. Gaseous exchange usually involves carbon dioxide and oxygen moving in opposite directions.	14

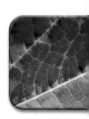

generator	a device for converting energy of movement (kinetic energy) into electrical energy (current flow).	138
geostationary orbit	satellites which remain above the same point on the Earth's surface are in geostationary orbit.	116
glycogen	an energy-storage molecule found in animals.	26
gravity/ gravitational force	the force of attraction between two bodies caused by their mass. The force of gravity produced by a body depends on its mass – the larger the mass the larger the force.	110, 114-117, 146-149
group	a collection of elements with the same number of electrons in the outer shell. Members of a group share common chemical characteristics.	60

guard cells	cells which change shape to open or close the stomata in leaves.	18
haemoglobin	a complex chemical found in red blood cells that can combine with oxygen to help transport it around the body. Haemoglobin is a protein and contains an iron atom.	22
halide ion	the negatively-charged ion in a salt containing a halogen, e.g. sodium chloride.	66, 96
halogens	a group of reactive non-metals with only one electron missing from their outer electron shell, for example chlorine and iodine.	60, 62, 66, 96
hard water	water containing dissolved magnesium and calcium salts, mainly bicarbonates. These make it difficult for soap to form a lather.	84
heart	the muscular pump that moves blood around the body.	20
heart beat rate	the number of heartbeats in a given time, usually given as beats per minute.	26

Glossary

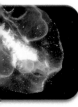

Hertz (Hz)	the unit of frequency. 1 Hertz corresponds to one vibration per second.	126
hydrated	with water added.	72
hydrocarbon	hydrocarbon molecules are molecules that contain only carbon and hydrogen atoms. Many fuels are hydrocarbons, e.g. natural gas (methane) and petrol (a complex mixture).	98
hydroxide	chemicals containing an OH group. Hydroxides are often alkaline.	64, 72-75
hyphae	the cell-like threads of fungi.	48
identify	to find the correct name for something. Ecologists often have to identify the plants or animals living in an area.	100
immune system	the parts of the body that protect against illnesses. The lymph glands are particularly important in the immune system.	32
insoluble	a substance that will not dissolve. Something that is insoluble in water may be soluble in other liquids.	96
inspiration	breathing in.	14
insulated	a substance that will not let energy pass through it easily. You can have insulators for heat, electricity or sound.	92
inverted	turned upside down.	120
ion-exchange column	a column packed with substances that swap ions with water or solutions that pass through it.	84
ionic compounds	compounds consisting of atoms held together by ionic bonds.	64
ionic salts	a salt held together by ionic bonds.	66
kidney	your two kidneys make urine to get rid of waste products from the blood.	30-33
lactic acid	a toxic chemical produced by anaerobic respiration in animals.	28, 42
lactose	a sugar found in milk.	42
Lewis acid	a Lewis acid can accept a pair of electrons and form a coordinate covalent bond.	74
Lewis base	a Lewis base is any molecule or ion that can form a new coordinate covalent bond, by donating a pair of electrons.	74
limescale	limescale is the hard off-white chalky deposit found in kettles, hot water boilers and the inside of poorly maintained hot-water central heating systems.	84
litmus paper	paper containing litmus dyes. It turns red in acid and blue in alkaline solutions.	96
longitudinal wave	in longitudinal waves, the vibration is along the direction in which the wave travels.	126
long-sighted	when only distant objects can be seen clearly. The cornea and lens are not strong enough to focus light from near objects onto the retina.	124
lungs	the lungs swap carbon dioxide in the blood for oxygen in the air.	14
magnetic field	an area where a magnetic force can be felt.	136-145
magnification	to make an object look larger than it is.	122-125
magnifying glass	a convex lens that can make an object look larger than it is.	124
malting	to breakdown starch in barley seeds to make maltose by allowing the seeds to germinate. It is an essential first stage in the production of some alcoholic drinks.	40
maltose	a type of sugar formed when starch is broken down in some plants, for example germinating barley seeds.	40
mass	mass describes the amount of something. It is measured in kilograms.	114
metal ion	a metallic atom that has lost one or more electrons to become positively charged.	94
methane	a colourless, odourless gas that burns easily to give water and carbon dioxide.	50
microbes	another word for micro-organisms.	44
micro-organisms	very small living things. You need a microscope to see them. Most are harmless, some are useful and some cause serious illnesses.	44, 82
Milky Way galaxy	the name for our galaxy.	148
mineral ions	mineral ions in our diet are things like calcium and iron. They are simple chemicals needed for health. Plants also require mineral ions like nitrates and phosphates for healthy growth.	18
moment	the moment of a force acting on one side of a balanced bar is the force multiplied by the distance to the pivot.	108
motor effect	the mutually repulsive force exerted by neighbouring conductors that carry current in opposite directions.	136
mould	another name for some types of fungus, particularly species involved in decay of dead organic matter.	48
muscles	muscles are organs that can contract, they are joined to bones at each end by tendons.	26
mutual induction	the production of an electromotive force in a circuit resulting from a change of current in a neighbouring circuit.	141

mycoprotein	a food, rich in protein, made from processed fungi.	48
natural satellite	a natural object which orbits something else. For example, our moon orbits the Earth.	116
nebulae	diffuse masses of interstellar dust or gas or both, visible as luminous patches or areas of darkness depending on the way the mass absorbs or reflects radiation.	148
nephron	a tubule in the kidney that produces urine.	30
neutral equilibrium	an equilibrium which is neither acid nor alkaline.	110
neutron star	a celestial body consisting of the superdense remains of a massive star that has collapsed.	146
neutralisation	a reaction between an acid and an alkali to produce a neutral solution.	72
nitrate	salts containing the nitrate group (NO_3). Nitrates are particularly important to plants as they help them to grow healthy leaves.	96
Noble gases	the gases in Group VIII of the periodic table. They have full outer electron shells and so do not take part in chemical reactions.	62
nuclear fusion	the joining together of nuclei or subatomic particles to form larger nuclei often with a large release of energy	146
normal	a line drawn at right angles to the surface where a ray of light hits an object.	122
obese	excessively overweight	92
orbit	the path a satellite takes around a larger object. Planets orbit around the Sun.	114-117
organic	a chemical containing carbon. Organic food and farming is a system that avoids the use of modern, synthetic chemicals.	98
oscilloscope	a device that displays a line on a screen showing regular changes (oscillations) in something. An oscilloscope is often used to look at sound waves collected by a microphone.	126, 141
osmoregulation	the control of water levels in an organism.	30
oxide	a compound containing oxygen and one other element, for example carbon dioxide contains only carbon and oxygen.	64
oxygen	a colourless gas with no smell that makes up about 20% of the air.	22, 26
oxygen debt	the amount of oxygen needed to clear the lactic acid produced by anaerobic respiration during vigorous exercise in animals.	28
oxyhaemoglobin	haemoglobin carrying four oxygen atoms. The oxygen is released to body cells in low oxygen regions, e.g. active muscles or the brain.	22
passive	requiring no energy input by an organism.	16
Pasteur	a French scientist who did a lot of work on micro-organisms and helped to form the basis of modern microbiology.	44
penicillin	a medicine that kills some dangerous micro-organisms. It is made from a type of fungus.	48
Penicillium	a type of fungus that has been used to produce antibiotics.	48
period	a horizontal line across the periodic table.	60
pitch	how high or low a note sounds.	126
planet	a large body moving around a star. We live on the planet Earth that is moving around a star we call the Sun.	148
plasma	the liquid portion of the blood.	22
platelets	small, sub-cellular bodies in the blood concerned with clotting.	22
polar orbit	a satellite orbit in which the satellite passes over the North and South poles on each orbit, and eventually passes over all points on the Earth.	116
potential difference	the difference in electrical potential energy between two points, measured in volts.	138
power surge	a sudden rise in the voltage supplied to a circuit. Power surges can occur along the mains and can damage computers and other electronic equipment.	140
precipitate	to fall out of solution.	94-97
primary coil	the input coil in a transformer.	144
principal axis	a line that passes through the centre of curvature of a lens so that light is neither reflected nor refracted	122
prism	a transparent glass or plastic block with straight sides.	122
proton	a positively-charged particle with a mass of one atomic mass unit. It is found in the nucleus of an atom.	62
proton acceptor	a base is a proton acceptor in its typical reactions.	72
proton donor	an acid is a proton donor in its typical reactions.	72-75
protostar	a dense condensation of material that is still in the process of gathering matter to form a star.	148
pulsar	any of several celestial radio sources emitting short intense bursts of radio waves, x-rays, or visible electromagnetic radiation at regular intervals, generally believed to be rotating neutron stars.	146

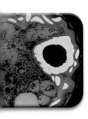

speed of light	the speed at which light travels in a vacuum. It is approximately 300 000 km/second.	122
stability	a measure of the likelihood of change. Stable systems are less likely to change than unstable ones.	110
stable	unlikely to change.	110
stable equilibrium	an equilibrium which changes very slowly or not at all.	110
star	a very large body in the sky that gives out light and heat. Our Sun is a star.	148
starter culture	the micro-organisms added to a sterile culture medium to start fermentation.	42
step-down transformer	a step-down transformer is one which reduces a voltage, i.e. the voltage out is less than the voltage in.	144
step-up transformer	a transformer which increases a voltage.	144
sterile technique	procedures used in microbiological work to prevent contamination of a culture by unwanted microbes.	52
sterilisation	killing all of the organisms in an area, usually used to mean killing micro-organisms.	52
stoma (pl. stomata)	small holes in the surface of leaves which allow gases in and out of leaves.	18
supernova	the explosive death of a star.	146
swan-necked flask	a flask with a long thin S-shaped neck that stops microbes from the air falling into it even when it has no stopper.	44
tension	a force that pulls or stretches.	112
thorax	the chest region.	14
time base	the signal used to drive the spot across the screen in an oscilloscope.	126
tissue type	the combination of compatibility proteins on the surfaces of cells. Transplanted organs must have the same tissue type as the host or rejection will occur.	32
titrations	mixing of liquids in carefully measured amounts to find the amount of one substance needed to react with a measured amount of another.	72
transition elements	metals with an incomplete inner electron shell.	60
transpiration	the release of water vapour from a plant through the leaves.	18
transplantation	to put an organ from one organism into another	32
transuranic elements	elements with a heavier atomic mass than uranium.	60
tubule	a small tube, for example in the kidneys.	30
turning effect	the force that tends to make an object spin. The turning effect of a force depends on the size of the force and how far it is from the turning point (pivot).	108
ultrasound	sounds which have too high a frequency for humans to hear (above 20kHz).	128
unsaturated	an unsaturated solution can dissolve more solute. An unsaturated hydrocarbon can react with more hydrogen because it contains a number of double-carbon bonds.	98
unstable	a condition which is likely to change.	110
unstable equilibrium	an equilibrium which is likely to change, e.g. a coin balancing on its side.	110
upright	the opposite of inverted.	124
urea	a white crystalline substance made by the liver from excess amino acids.	22, 30
urine	a liquid made by your kidneys to get rid of wastes from the blood.	30
vacuum	the absence of matter.	126
veins	blood vessels carrying low-pressure blood back towards the heart.	20
velocity	the speed an object is moving in a particular direction. A change in direction or speed will change the velocity. Velocity is usually measured in metres per second (m/s).	112
vibrate	a regular movement when something moves a very small distance to-and-fro but keeps repeating the movement over and over again.	126
villus (pl. villi)	a small projection on the inner surface of the gut to increase the surface area and so speed up absorption.	16
virtual	something which is not present but appears to be, for example a virtual image is created by the brain in certain optical experiments.	120-125
voltage	the potential difference across a component or circuit.	140
VO_2 max	the largest volume of oxygen contained in a volume of air.	28
water cycle	the cyclical movement of water through the environment as liquid water in rain, streams, river, oceans and vapour in the atmosphere.	82
weight	the force of gravity acting on a body on the Earth. Since weight is a force, it is measured in newtons. People often use the word weight to mean mass but this is not strictly correct.	114

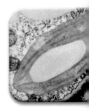

Glossary

whey	the yellowish liquid formed when milk curdles.	42
white blood cells (WBC)	a blood cell which helps to destroy foreign bodies in the body.	22
wilt	a plant wilts when it loses so much water that it cannot hold itself upright.	18
white dwarf	a collapsed star of enormous density.	146
yeast	a unicellular fungus used extensively in the brewing and baking industries.	40, 50